THE ENGLISH BOOK TRADE

THE PROFESSION OF LETTERS

Also by A. S. COLLINS

In THE ENGLISH BOOK TRADE

Authorship in the Days of Johnson [1927]

THE
PROFESSION
OF LETTERS

A STUDY OF THE RELATION
OF AUTHOR TO PATRON, PUBLISHER
AND PUBLIC, 1780-1832

BY

A. S. COLLINS

[1928]

AUGUSTUS M. KELLEY • PUBLISHERS
CLIFTON 1973

First Edition 1928

(London: George Routledge & Sons Ltd., 1928)

Reprinted 1973 by
AUGUSTUS M. KELLEY PUBLISHERS
Clifton   New Jersey   07012

By Arrangement With ROUTLEDGE & KEGAN PAUL LTD.

Library of Congress Cataloging in Publication Data

Collins, Arthur Simons, 1899–
    The profession of letters.

    (The English book trade)
    Reprint of the 1928 ed.
    Originally presented as the author's thesis,
University of London.
    Bibliography: p.
    1. Authorship.   2. Authors and patrons.
3. Authors and publishers--Great Britain.   4. English
literature--19th century--History and criticism.
I. Title.
PN151.C62 1973   808'.02   77-134832
ISBN 0-678-00789-6

12 7885

PRINTED IN THE UNITED STATES OF AMERICA
by SENTRY PRESS, NEW YORK, N. Y. 10013

AUTHOR'S NOTE

I N this book I have sought to continue the history of the profession of letters which in *Authorship in the Days of Johnson* I left at about the year 1780. With every year that one comes nearer to our own day the field becomes a vaster one to survey, and I have limited myself to an attempt at giving a reasonably full outline. Such matters as copyright would have a place only in a fuller study. Moreover, the fact that this study, almost as it stands, is a thesis accepted by the University of London for the degree of Doctor of Philosophy is a reason for its limitation.

The earlier history of the profession of letters in England has been told by Miss Sheavyn thoroughly and in detail in *The Literary Profession in the Elizabethan Age*, and by M. Beljame in his brilliant study (whose period, despite its title, ends at about 1726), *Le Public et les hommes de lettres en Angleterre au 18ᵉ Siècle.*

To M. Beljame's study I owe much for its inspiring qualities, but my greatest debt in respect of both my books is to Professor A. W. Reed, of King's College, London, for his generous and helpful suggestions and advice.

The quotation on pages 12–13 from Mr. Belloc's *The Cruise of the " Nona "* is made by kind permission of Mr. Belloc and Messrs. Constable & Co., Ltd.

A. S. COLLINS.

PREFACE

The profession of letters and the views of Rogers, Coleridge, Byron, Lamb and Mr. Belloc upon it.

THAT literature ever became a profession, or, for the most of those who practise it, a trade, is one of those developments which, when one looks back, seem all the way inevitable, but of which we cannot at times help but feel, that had the world done without them, it had done better. For when we speak of the trade or profession of letters, we mean the pursuit of literature as a means of living, independent of all others, and if we speak of it now as a profession, and now as a trade, it is only to mark off those like Southey who worked for high ideals, from those hacks and compilers whose aim was merely the day's wage.

EVEN on the best, the continual working of the brain and setting of thoughts upon paper for a living has an exhausting and a cramping effect. They have no off-time, so that frequently they write without any impulse save the need of money ; and unless their genius is such that it so transcends that it can command, and is so popular that it need not follow, they must play to the tune the piper calls. And the piper, which is the public rather than their seeming master the publisher, is one of a poor and a capricious taste. For, while the profession grows co-incidently with the public, the bigger public does not mean the better books, but the bigger it is, the less critical it is in its reading, and the more indolent. The second-rate writer, good as he may be, is gripped in the vice of a popular fashion, and can no more change his style than the leopard its spots. And the whole company of writers, from the good to the indifferent and from the indifferent to the bad,

7

crowd the shelves of our libraries until they over-
flow, while as readers we become tired, and as
critics we flag. But all down the years the course
things have taken, seems the course they must have
taken.

THOSE who have been greatest in the practice of
letters have rarely been those to whom letters
was their supporting profession. Instead they
have generally been those in whom the spirit has
worked in the quiet of their leisure, so that all
that they wrote can be remembered, while the
work of the professional has always to be sifted.
Of the poets, of whom can we say that he wrote
for money ? Not of Wordsworth, nor Coleridge,
nor Shelley, nor Keats, nor Byron, nor Rogers,
nor yet Scott. But, in the lower world of prose,
whither shall we ever escape from the novel, and
the essay, and the endless columns of print that
thrust themselves before us, because their authors
write for money ? The small man is always
jostling side by side with the great, and to study
the history of literature as a profession is to find
that Shelley is of less importance than Godwin,
and Wordsworth than Campbell, and Blake than
Holcroft, and all great men than all little men,
in so far as the advancement of their profession
goes.

IN the fifty years that followed the death of
Johnson, only one truly great man lived, " whose
whole estate was in his ink-stand." Others were
clerks, and secretaries, and sheriffs, and bankers,
and Robert Southey was the one general in the
army of letters who had no other resource than the
sums in his pay-book. Most of the great captains
were free lances who marauded among the public

8

in occasional sallies. But the professional private soldier is the backbone of all armies, be they of letters or of states, and he must ever be before the eyes of the historian of his profession, since letters without him would hardly be a profession at all.

SUCH a historian's study is a study not of the peaks, but of the plain, and, if the records of the lower contours are few and incomplete because no-one has thought to preserve them, imagination must call up for us the throng of the writers from whom, in the perspective of time, only the great masters stand out like mountains, and below is mist. For the profession of letters was built up, never so much by genius, as by the industry and popularity of mediocrity. For where the master is mediocre, so must the servant be. And the public is mediocrity's vast embodiment.

DAY in and day out, as the years pass, to write that which shall be worth the writing, surely that were an impossible task, and yet such is the task that is set to the man who trusts to his pen. When his brain is fresh, and when his brain is tired, whether he has something to say, or whether he has nothing, it is the same, and the press must be fed. And sometimes the public will reject that which he has written well, and applaud the empty stuff of his weariness, and again the publisher, it may be, denies him utterance of the noblest that is in him, and asks instead the household drudgery which most finds a public, and fills his own pocket. And yet the pressure of the need of money is not always bad, for it gave us much that, to name only two, Dr. Johnson and Washington Irving had without it probably not written, and the ambition

9

of money added many a Waverley novel. But the pressure of occasion is not the pressure of a living, and the judges who have said that to live by letters is as though a man should make his bed of thorns, are the judges to whom a man should listen. For they are Rogers, and Coleridge, and Byron, and Lamb.

" How sorry I am for Campbell," said Madame de Staël to Rogers when Campbell was the new young poet of *The Pleasures of Hope* ; " his poverty so unsettles his mind that he cannot write." And Rogers replied, " Why doesn't he take a situation as a clerk ? he could then compose during his leisure hours." [1] For Rogers throughout his life held that to make literature the business of life was to make it a drudgery.

AND Coleridge in his *Biographia Literaria* [2] said that he " would address an affectionate exhortation to the youthful *literati*, grounded on (his) own experience . . . *never pursue literature as a trade.*"

AND Byron would by no means have Bernard Barton leave his bank and let his pen alone be his support. " Do not renounce literature," said he [3] in 1812, " but never trust entirely to authorship. If you have a profession, retain it ; it will be like Prior's fellowship, a last and sure resource. Compare Mr. Rogers with other authors of the day ; assuredly he is among the first of living poets, but is it to that he owes his station in society, and his intimacy in the best circles ? No, it is to his prudence and respectability. The world (a bad one, I own) courts him because he has no occasion

---

1 Clayden, *Rogers and his Contemporaries*, ii. 126
2 Chapter xi. (Everyman Library), p. 119.
3 E. V. Lucas, *Bernard Barton and his Friends*, p. 163.

to court it. He is a poet, nor is he less so because
he was something more."
AND who does not know that greater letter in
which Lamb trounced the booksellers and the
public, and blessed his office-stool ? For once
again Barton thought to leave his bank, and this
time it was Lamb who wrote :

" ' THROW yourself on the world without any
rational plan of support, beyond what the chance
employ of booksellers would afford you ! ! ! '
Throw yourself rather . . . from the steep
Tarpeian rock, slap-dash headlong upon iron
spikes. If you had but five consolatory minutes
between the desk and the bed, make much of them,
and live a century in them, rather than turn slave
to the booksellers. They are Turks and Tartars
when they have poor authors at their beck.
Hitherto you have been at arm's length from them.
Come not within their grasp. I have known many
authors for bread, some repining, others envying
the blessed security of a counting-house, all agreeing they would rather have been tailors, weavers
—what not, rather than the things they were. I
have known some starved, some to go mad, one
dear friend literally dying in a workhouse. You
know not what a rapacious, dishonest set these
booksellers are. Ask even Southey, who (a
single case almost) has made a fortune by book
drudgery, what he has found them. Oh, you
know not (may you never know !) the miseries of
subsisting by authorship ! 'Tis a pretty appendage to a situation like yours or mine ; but a
slavery, worse than all slavery, to be a bookseller's
dependant, to drudge your brains for pots of ale

and breasts of mutton, to change your free thoughts
and voluntary numbers for ungracious task work.
. . . Keep to your bank, and the bank will
keep you. Trust not to the public ; you may
hang, starve, drown yourself, for anything that
worthy *personage* cares. I bless every star that
Providence, not seeing good to make me independent, has seen it next good to settle me upon
the stable foundation of Leadenhall. Sit down,
good B.B., in the banking-office. What ! is there
not from six to eleven *p.m.* six days in the week,
and is there not all Sunday ? Fie, what a super-
fluity of man's time, if you could think so !—
enough for relaxation, mirth, converse, poetry,
good thoughts, quiet thoughts. Oh the corroding,
torturing, tormenting thoughts that disturb the
brain of the unlucky wight who must draw upon
it for daily sustenance ! Henceforth I retract
all my fond complaints of mercantile employment ;
look upon them as lovers' quarrels. I was but
half in earnest. Welcome dead timber of a desk,
that makes me live. A little grumbling is a
wholesome medicine for the spleen ; but in my
inner heart do I approve and embrace this our close
but unharassing way of life. I am quite serious." [1]

AND then in our own day there is Mr. Belloc who
has written :

" To those who have had to pursue letters as a
trade . . . it certainly is the hardest and the most
capricious, and, indeed, the most abominable of
trades, for the simple reason that it was never
meant to be a trade.

[1] E. V. Lucas, *Bernard Barton and his Friends*, p. 85.

A MAN is no more meant to live by writing than he is meant to live by conversation, or by dressing, or by walking about and seeing the world. For there is no relation between the function of letters and the economic effect of letters ; there is no relation between the goodness and the badness of the work, or the usefulness of the work, or the magnitude of the work, and the sums paid for the work. It would not be natural that there should be such a relation, and, in fact, there is none.

THIS truth is missed by people who say that good writing has no market. That is not the point. Good writing sometimes has a market, and very bad writing sometimes has a market. Useful writing sometimes has a market, and writing of no use whatsoever, even as recreation, sometimes has a market. Writing important truths sometimes has a market. Writing the most ridiculous errors and false judgments sometimes has a market. The point is that the market has nothing to do with the qualities attached to writing. It never had and it never will. There is no injustice about it, any more than there is an injustice in the survival of beauty or ugliness in human beings, or the early death of the beautiful or the ugly. There is no more injustice about it than there is in a dry year hurting a root crop, and a wet harvest hurting a corn crop. The relationship between the excellence or the usefulness of a piece of literature, and the number of those who will buy it in a particular form, is not a causal relationship, it is a purely capricious one." [1]

AND there is really no more in a general way to

1 H. Belloc, *The Cruise of the " Nona,"* pp. 297–8

13

be said than Mr. Belloc in those words has said,
except, perhaps, what Mr. Gerald Gould suggests,
that " every day, somewhere, good soldiers, sailors,
tinkers, and tailors by the fantastic tricks of fortune
die unrecognised ; why not good poets, and good
novelists ? " To be sure, there is another side,
but it is an exceptional side. Mr. J. H. Morgan
tells us that he said to Lord Morley that " the
prospect of depending upon literature for one's
bread appalled me." But Lord Morley answered :
" It never appalled me ; I don't agree that a man
can write better if he is financially independent ;
I got £700 a year by writing for the *Saturday
Review*, and I had nothing else to depend upon."
So let his exception be the exception that proves
the rule, and let us go back to the profession as it
was in the days of Johnson.

CONTENTS

PREFACE

PROLOGUE

CHAPTER I

BETWEEN JOHNSON AND SCOTT

CHAPTER II

IN THE DAYS OF SCOTT AND CONSTABLE, 1800–1832

15

CONTENTS

EPILOGUE

THE PROSPECT IN 1832

BIBLIOGRAPHY

INDEX   275

THE PROFESSION OF LETTERS
1780—1832

PROLOGUE [1]

Pope founds the profession of letters. Its growth during the life of Johnson.

POPE was the founder in England of the profession of letters. Others before him had done something towards its foundation, but, as M. Beljame says, " S'il eut, grâce à eux, le bonheur de pouvoir être un homme de lettres indépendant, il lui reste ce titre d'honneur personnel d'avoir voulu et d'avoir su l'être, et d'avoir installé la profession littéraire en Angleterre dans la dignité et au rang qu'elle possède aujourd'hui." [2] But for some time he was a founder who had no followers. For it is one thing for a great genius to make himself master of a public and beyond need of patrons, and quite another for a man of even high talent. And while good patrons are still to be found, it requires a certain character in a man to set aside their temptations. And the character and genius of a Pope do not occur twice in a generation.

SINCE all the growth and the health of the profession of letters depend on the public, and the public was in Pope's day very small, it was the public for which men had to wait before they could lay aside the support which patrons offered. But from about 1730 the public did begin markedly to grow larger, and the diminishing and passing into disrepute of patrons between 1730 and 1750 is one of the signs that it was growing. In fact,

1 This section very briefly recapitulates the theme of *Authorship in the Days of Johnson.*
2 Beljame, *Le Public et les hommes de lettres en Angleterre au* 18ᵉ *Siècle,* p. 412.

17

by 1760, as one can see from many writers of the day, the patron had become a creature of tawdry pretensions, and men snapped their fingers in his face, and lashed him with the whip of satire, and put him to ridicule in the fooling of comedy. His day was done, and they need court him no more. Instead, in 1760 there was the public to salute as master. It was as Goldsmith said : " At present, the few poets of England no longer depend on the great for subsistence ; they have now no other patrons but the public, and the public, collectively considered, is a good and generous master." And what was true of the few poets was true of writers in general. " The ridicule, therefore, of living in a garret, might have been wit in the last age, but continues such no longer, because no longer true. A writer of real merit now may easily be rich, if his heart be set only on a fortune ; and for those who have no merit, it is but fit that such should remain in merited obscurity." [1]

THE profession of letters in its early years, which were the thirties and forties, while Johnson was hard at it to earn his daily bread by the journey work of journalism for Cave and *The Gentleman's Magazine*, suffered from the number of scribblers who aspired to what Johnson aspired, but who were of those of whom Johnson said, that " they have seldom any claim to the trade of writing, but that they have tried some other without success." The profession, in fact, began by being badly overcrowded, so that Johnson said that " the present age, if we consider chiefly the state of our own country, may be styled with great

[1] Goldsmith, *Selected Essays*, ed. J. H. Lobban (1915), p. 65.

18

propriety the Age of Authors," and that " there is no reason for believing that the dogmatical legions of the present race were ever equalled in number by any former period . . . so widely is spread the itch of literary praise." [1]   Therefore, between an overcrowded profession and a small public, it was no wonder that Johnson had the hard times he did have, and needed all his sturdy courage to follow the profession which Pope had founded.   In the days when Johnson had to go without his supper and could not write by night because he had no candle, Thomson did wisely to take the patronage of even Frederick, Prince of Wales, for Johnson's early years coincided with the gap between the patrons and the public. When Johnson began in London, Thomson had gained all his patrons, and Thomson's patrons were the last of the patrons of the old school. Thereafter a good patron is rarely to be met, but easily before 1756, when Johnson labelled him in the *Dictionary*, a patron was " commonly a wretch who supports with insolence and is paid with flattery."

BUT the hardships of the thirties and forties were soon over.   For the thirties had seen the rise of the magazines, and the forties had given birth to the novel and the circulating library, and by the middle of the century there was an evident quickening of intellectual life throughout the country. " One of the improvements of life," said a writer in 1753, " in which the present age has excelled all that have gone before, is the quick circulation of intelligence, the faithful and easy communication of events past and future, by the multitudes of

[1] *The Adventurer*, No. 115.

newspapers which have been contrived to amuse or inform us." [1]   And a writer of 1755 had " to congratulate the great world on that diffusion of science and literature which for some years has been spreading itself abroad upon the face of it." [2] He discerned something of a levelling revolution in the appearance of the magazines, and the libraries, and in the prophecy of universal knowledge.   And when to the magazines we see added the reviews, the *Monthly* in 1749 and the *Critical* in 1756, poor though they may be, we see further signs that literature and knowledge are spreading.

ANOTHER sign that people were reading more was the Indian summer of the periodical essay in the decade 1750 to 1760, with *The Rambler*, and *The Adventurer*, and *The Connoisseur*, and *The World*, and *The Idler*, and, at the end, Goldsmith's Chinese Letters in *The Public Advertiser*.   Johnson, reckoning from the stamp-tax figures, estimated the average sale of *The Spectator* at nearly seventeen hundred,[3] but of *The World*, which had rivals and no clear field to itself, the usual number printed was two thousand five hundred.

GOLDSMITH, after he had been working for publishers for only three or four years, was commissioned to write his essays for about £100 a year, so much shorter was his struggle to earn his way than Johnson's twenty years earlier. And, if we will look from 1712 to 1776, we may see the way the public had increased, by comparing the sale of Swift's *Conduct of the Allies*

1 *The Adventurer*, No. 35.   2 *The World*, No. 55.
3 *Lives of the Poets*, ed. G. B. Hill (Addison), ii. 98.

with that of Dr. Price's pamphlet on the American war. Of the former, said Johnson, " it is boasted that between November and January eleven thousand were sold ; a great number at that time, when we were not yet a nation of readers." [1] But of the latter the sale in a few months was sixty thousand.[2] And the comparison is a fair one, for both had behind them all the force of party passion and public interest. The phrasing of Johnson is significant, too, for it shows that in 1780 he did think that England was " a nation of readers."

THAT literature began in the middle of the eighteenth century to be looked upon as a profession, is shown by the coming into frequent use at that time of the phrase " an author by profession," which does not seem to occur earlier. But in 1758 there is Ralph's *Case of Authors by Profession or Trade*, a pamphlet written in a fit of spleen against the booksellers, and in 1762 Guthrie, the political hack-writer, pleading to Lord Bute for the continuance of his pension, makes it the strength of his plea that he is " an Author by Profession." [3] And an author by profession was naturally no specialist. It was only those who were independent that could study a chosen field. Hume, because he had a small income, could keep to his history and philosophy, and Robertson, because he was a clergyman, had leisure to start, and because, after his success, he had " a revenue exceeding what had ever been enjoyed before by any Presbyterian clergyman in Scotland," [4] had the means to continue his

1 *Lives of the Poets*, ed. G. B. Hill (Swift), iii. 19. 2 Clayden, *Early Life of Rogers*, p. 34.
3 I. D'Israeli, *Miscellanies of Literature* (1840), p. 52.
4 Stewart, *Life of Robertson* (1801), p. 50.

substantial works. But the man who wrote to live, wrote to order, and as he wrote upon each and every theme, wrote in a style that was popular and not scholarly. Smollett's *History* succeeded Hume's at the bidding of the booksellers, and was spread throughout the country in popular numbers. In fact the professional writer became the literary man of all work who only specialized by an effort when he could. The day had come when, Boswell tells us, " as one of the little occasional advantages which [Johnson] did not disdain to take by his pen, as a man whose profession was literature, he this year [1756] accepted of a guinea from Mr. Robert Dodsley, for writing the introduction to *The London Chronicle*, an evening news-paper." [1]

AFTER 1760 there was a plentiful demand for a writer to supply. People were beginning to read everywhere, even in a small way in the little towns and villages of the West. Lackington, the poor shoemaker, in Wellington and Taunton, and other parts of the west country, read eagerly Wesley's tracts and sermons, and was led on to read more, first theology, next poetry and general literature. Then in the sixties, when he was a young man at Bristol, he and his friend and fellow-workman, Mr. John Jones, " worked very hard . . . in order to get money to purchase books, and for some months every shilling [they] could spare was laid out at old bookshops, stalls, etc., in so much that in a short time [they] had what [they] called a very good library." [2] And though their library chiefly consisted of evangelical theology, it

1 Boswell, *Life of Johnson*, i. 317.
2 Lackington, *Memoirs*, 1803, p. 85. (All subsequent references are to this edition.)

22

included *The Pilgrim's Progress*, Gay's *Fables*, Pomfret's *Poems*, *Paradise Lost*, Hobbes's *Homer* and Walker's *Epictetus*. And assuredly Lackington was not the only young man of twenty-two who was beginning about the year 1768 to read as widely as he could. Booksellers were ready with their commissions for popular books for this growing body of readers, and so for a man like Goldsmith there was good money to be earned by his *Life of Voltaire*, and his histories of Greece and Rome, and Animated Nature. His payments soon ran into hundreds, and it is on record that " Dr. Goldsmith cleared in one year £1,800 by his pen." [1]

IN fact, in the last twenty years of Johnson's life the profession of letters was no bad profession, as far as payments went, and quite average work was most generously rewarded. Topical satire quickly filled the pockets of Churchill as he dashed off his careless but stinging verses. About 1764 the learned Mrs. Carter says, " I have heard lately that Churchill, within two years, has got £3,500 by his ribald scribbling." Whereas Johnson had thought in 1738 to leave literature for teaching, Churchill's friend Lloyd, in 1763, rather than teach, would write for the booksellers even in prison. And he who wrote wholeheartedly for the booksellers, made a good living. Such a man was Dr. John Hill. Hogarth has humorously portrayed a brawny porter almost sinking to the ground under a huge load of his works, and he was a mainstay of the publishers who were pushing the weekly ' number ' trade [2] with works

---

1 Lackington, *Memoirs*, p. 226.
2 i.e. the sale of works in periodical parts or ' numbers. '

of popular knowledge. He wrote, moreover, such remunerative volumes as *Mrs. Glasse's Cookery*, and altogether is said to have made fifteen guineas a week, and in one year as much as £1,500.

PERIODICAL journalism as well had become very profitable. For example, Arthur Young, the political economist, is said to have earned as much as £1,167 by writing for the press in the year 1770. Regular newspaper work, too, was established by then and improving in status. We see an illustration of that again in Young, who was acting as Parliamentary Reporter to *The Morning Post* for five guineas a week in 1773. And, further, journalism provided an opportunity for would-be writers to gain a footing in the profession of letters. Holcroft, for instance, began in 1765, when he was only nineteen, to write in *The Whitehall Evening Post* for five shillings a column and in 1775 he was paid a guinea and a half for reporting. In addition, writers were in demand to contribute to the encyclopædias, for in 1771 the *Encyclopædia Britannica* was published in its first edition of three volumes, and in 1778 *Chambers's Cyclopædia* began to appear weekly until it was complete in 418 numbers.

THE signs are many that the profession of letters was making good headway. We may judge from the successive editions of new books that were called for, in 1773 even the poems of Mrs. Barbauld passing through four editions in their first year. In 1776 the first volume of Gibbon's *Decline and Fall* sold its first impression of a thousand copies in a few days, and a second and a third were hardly equal to the demand. Blair's sermons sold so well that although the publisher had already given for them so much as £600, he added another £100. But examples are too numerous to quote. And again we may judge of the progress of the profession from the prices men had, such as the £500 which Strahan paid for the first edition only of the *Wealth of Nations*, the author to have half profits on all subsequent editions, and the £4,500 which Robertson had for *Charles V.*, and the £1,000 which Mickle gained by his *Lusiad*. The usual price given for the copyright of a play had been £100 in 1750, but in 1771 it was £150. Perhaps the clearest sign of all was that, when the claim of the dominating group of London booksellers to perpetual copyright, which they thought they had established in 1769, was finally done away with by the House of Lords in 1774, the prices those booksellers paid for copyright did not fall. They could continue the good prices they had been paying, because the demand of the public was steadily rising, and their feelings found enough relief in rhetoric.

ENGLISH life was changing. The hardships of life were going for other classes besides authors. When Johnson was a boy, the shopkeeper had a fire in his parlour only on Sunday, but when Johnson was threescore years and ten, the bare simplicity of life in the lower middle class was giving way to greater comfort. The amenities of life were increasingly spreading downwards, and the middle class was stepping forward to play a more important part in the affairs of the nation. Johnson noted in the English merchant a new kind of gentleman. Booksellers like Cadell and Strahan made fortunes, and kept their coaches, and Strahan was a member of Parliament. The press gave expression to interests wider than those of the aristocratic cliques that had been sharing in a system of government which they had made a system of spoils. And through the newspapers public opinion was born, and the seed sown of the Reform Bill. The newspaper public, too, passed into the reading public, and as the higher circles of society became more self-contained, authors became less fashionable, and passed from the select *milieu* of the small society to the wide *milieu* of the new middle class. Honoured by the highest though Johnson was, we see something of the new order in the words of Lady Lucan, " Nobody dines with us to-day ; therefore, child, we'll go and get Dr. Johnson." [1]   And not the least change in English life was that, with improvements in the roads, life in the middle class became less static. The humorous figure of Matthew Bramble was not alone in its pursuit of health. Volumes of *Tours* became popular, and before Johnson's *Journey to the Western Isles*, there was Pennant's lively account in 1771 of his tour in Scotland two years before. " It was very widely read and may be said to have turned the tide of holiday travel northwards." [2]   And the success of that led to three more volumes upon his second tour published about the same time as the *Journey*, while in 1772 William Gilpin had begun to discover the picturesque in the counties of England and Wales. The provinces were brought nearer to London. Books circulated more freely.

---

[1] G. H. Powell, *Table Talk of Samuel Rogers*, p. 6.
[2] Clayden, *The Early Life of Rogers*, p. 19.

26

Sixpenny volumes of the poets came into many a humble home. Women began to read and to write, and to rise above the dull monotony of the domestic round. The England of to-day was in many ways coming into being.

CHAPTER I

BETWEEN JOHNSON AND SCOTT

(i) The reading public and its books in 1780 in London and the provinces. (ii) The effect of improved communications, better roads and the mail-coach on the public. (iii) The effect of the industrial revolution. The growth of the towns, and the spread of radicalism and free-thinking. The chapel, the revolutionary club, and the pamphlet. (iv) Education : its awakening and its popularity. It breeds readers. (v) The reading of children and others, 1780–1800. Circulating libraries, popular reprints, knowledge for the people, second-hand books and remainders. Literary Societies. (vi) The effect on reading of the French Revolution. (vii) Estimate of the increase in reading ; 1780–1800. (viii) The condition and prospects of the drama, of poetry, of the novel, and of the periodical press. (ix) Publishers ; progress in ' the trade.' (x) Patronage : the policy of Pitt ; the Literary Fund. (xi) The profession in 1800.

(i)

FROM about the year 1780 all these changes began to develop speedily, and the twenty years until the end of the century, or, perhaps more exactly, until 1802 and the appearance of the *Edinburgh Review*, were years of steady preparation from which the profession of authorship emerged to enjoy the bright prospects which opened for men of high talent in the days of Scott and Byron. And the early eighties saw a quite distinct break in the old world of authorship. In 1779 Garrick died, and the same year saw the passing, too, of Armstrong, Kenrick and Warburton, familiar figures of Johnson's time. Hume and Smollett and Sterne and Goldsmith had been dead some years. Beattie's Minstrel sang no more, and three new poets, Hayley and Crabbe and Cowper, came as rivals into the deserted field. The idea of perpetual copyright was soon forgotten, and the new publishers, to whom its abolition had given life, were making cheap books for the people a real thing. In 1779 Lackington published his first catalogue of 12,000 second-hand books, and soon he invaded the remainder market. Then in 1784 the old lion himself was gone, and the younger generation was alone in its heritage.

THE growth of the reading public and of popular literature is probably the most important aspect of the literary profession in these two decades. It is the period when literature began to penetrate almost throughout society, and to pass from the capital to the provinces. And as literature is itself an educative force it is part of the story of the growth of education, which, again, is affected by the Industrial Revolution.

IN the nineties Burke estimated the reading public to be some 80,000 readers, and most of them were in London, which, so Lackington said in 1803, " as in all other articles of commerce, is likewise the grand emporium of Great Britain for books." [1]   Bath was the great meeting-place of society outside the capital, and a good deal of reading was done there. Miss Lydia Languish, and many another, sent her maid to every circulating library there for her favourite authors.[2] And, indeed, everywhere, as *The Annual Register* of 1761 notes, " the reading female hires her novels from some Country Circulating Library, which consists of about a hundred volumes," and " the several great cities, and we might add many poor country towns, seem to be inspired with an ambition of becoming little Londons of the part of the Kingdom wherein they are situated." [3]   But apart from Bath it was an ambition that fell far short of being realized. Bath was really fashionable, had a good coach

---

1 Lackington, *Memoirs*, p. 286.   2 Sheridan, *The Rivals*, I. ii.
3 See *Annual Register*, 1761, pp. 205–8.

service, and was visited by the chief London actors ; its dramatic audiences were second only to London's, and new plays were tried on them. Bath, too, in the rule of polite manners from the reign of Beau Nash had been an example to the gentlemen of the neighbouring shires. But other provincial towns had in 1780 little more claim to literature than the possession of a small literary clique. There was at Exeter the small group centring round Jackson, and at Lichfield the circle round its Swan, Anna Seward, together with Hayley and Cary.

THE general position of the provinces in regard to books is told by Lackington : " In September, seventeen hundred and eighty-seven," he says, " I set off for Edinburgh, and in all the principal towns through which I passed, was led from a motive of curiosity, as well as with a view towards obtaining some valuable purchases, to examine the booksellers' shops for scarce and valuable books ; but although I went by the way of York, Newcastle-upon-Tyne, etc., and returned through Glasgow, Carlisle, Leeds, Lancaster, Preston, Manchester, and other considerable places, I was much surprized, as well as disappointed, at meeting with very few of the works of the most esteemed authors ; and those few consisted in general of ordinary editions, besides an assemblage of common trifling books, bound in sheep, and that too in a very bad manner. It is true, at York and Leeds there were a few (and but very few) good books ; but in all the other towns between London and Edinburgh nothing but trash was to be found : in the latter city indeed, a few capital articles are kept, but in no other part of Scotland.

" In seventeen hundred and ninety, I repeated my journey, and was much mortified to be under a necessity of confirming my former observations. This remarkable deficiency in the article of books, is however not peculiar to the northern parts of England ; as I have repeatedly travelled into the western parts, and found abundant cause for dissatisfaction on the same account." [1]

Lackington also tells us that even when a country customer required a book it was not easy for him to get it, for " thousands of books are yearly written for from the country, that are never sent ; " [2] while, in the early years, " many in the country found it difficult to remit small sums that were under bankers' notes, (which difficulty is now done away, as all post-masters receive small sums of money, and give drafts for the same on the post-office in London)." [3] And the charge against the booksellers that they were reluctant to send the books is made also by Cowper.[4]

What the life of the small towns and villages was like in the seventies and eighties we can gather from the memoirs of Holcroft and Lackington, and from the life and poems of Crabbe. The two former were born in 1745 and 1746 and the latter in 1754, and the life of the small towns and villages is the background of their boyhood and youth. Rude literature there was ready for them in the ballads pasted round the walls of the public-house and of the peasant's cottage, along with prints of the Lady Godiva, of the prize ox, and of the pugilist. " Books were not then," says Holcroft, " as they fortunately are now, great or

---

[1] Lackington, *Memoirs*, p. 286.   [2] *Ibid.*, p. 229.   [3] *Ibid.*, p. 217
[4] Southey, *Life and Works of Cowper* (1835), xv. 58.

small, on this subject or on that, to be found in almost every house : a book, except of prayers or of daily religious use, was scarcely to be seen but among the opulent, or in the possession of the studious ; and by the opulent they were often disregarded with a degree of neglect which would now be almost disgraceful. . . . [But] even the walls of cottages and little alehouses would do something ; for many of them had old English ballads, such as Death and the Lady, and Margaret's Ghost, with lamentable tragedies, or King Charles's golden rules, occasionally pasted on them. These were at that time the learning, and often, no doubt, the delight of the vulgar." [1] From one of these as a boy he learnt by heart the ballad of Chevy Chase, and his father rewarded him with a halfpenny for his industry. And, in addition, there were the cheap little chap-books for children. He had his *Seven Champions of Christendom*, and the *History of Parismus and Parismenes*, and through the years of his restless and precocious youth as cobbler, and hawker, and stable-boy he managed to pick up enough education to try his hand, when he was only nineteen, as a teacher and a journalist. Like Lackington, he knew Bunyan, and he tells us " the *Whole Duty of Man* was my favourite study, and still more Horneck's *Crucified Jesus*." [2] Another cobbler lent him *The Spectator* and *Gulliver's Travels*, and altogether he found plenty to stir his ambition to be himself a writer.

IT was a wandering life that Holcroft led ; born in London, a boy in the stables at Newmarket,

1 Hazlitt, *Memoirs of Thomas Holcroft* (World's Classics), p. 55.
2 *Ibid.*, p. 57.

selling coal on the midland roads, teaching in Liverpool. Lackington, too, going round the west, now in Wellington, now in Taunton, in Bristol, in Bridgwater, in Exeter, scraped together in like manner his acquaintance with books. The old dames praised his repetition of the New Testament, but print was not common in Wellington in 1760, and he did not see much of it at a time except for the bundles of almanacs which, round Christmas, he used to cry for sale along with the pies and puddings of his master the baker. But when Methodism made him its enthusiast, he found in the tracts, that were plentiful, stimulating reading, and he became so fond of books that when he was cobbling in London in 1774 and was told of a vacant shop, he immediately jumped at the idea of taking it as a bookseller. He tells us : " for several months past I had observed a great increase in a certain old book shop. . . . I loved books, and . . . if I could but be a bookseller, I should then have plenty of books to read, which was the greatest motive I could conceive to induce me to make the attempt." And " notwithstanding the obscurity of the street, and the mean appearance of my shop, yet I soon found customers for what few books I had ; and I as soon laid out the money in other old trash which was daily brought for sale." [1] Lackington admits that it mostly was trash, but his memoirs show us that in the seventies people were eager for something to read, poor though it might be, and not only in London where he opened his shop, but in the provinces where he himself had picked up his knowledge.

[1] *Memoirs*, pp. 121-4.

CRABBE, as the son of the saltmaster of Aldborough, had a better chance of education than the son of the versatile huckster or of the drunken cobbler, but, apart from his schools at Bungay and Stowmarket where he gained his first acquaintance with the classics, the literary education he gained for himself was of much the same quality as theirs. " My father," says his son, " was, indeed, in a great measure self-educated. . . .   He was a great favourite with the old dames of the place. . . . He admired the rude prints on their walls, rummaged their shelves for books or ballads, and read aloud to those whose eyes had failed them, by the winter evening's fireside."   Once he had been taught by an old dame to read, " he was unwearied in his reading ; and he devoured without restraint whatever came into his hands, but especially works of fiction—those little stories and ballads about ghosts, witches and fairies which were then almost exclusively the literature of youth, and which, whatever else might be thought of them, served, no doubt, to strike out the first sparks of imagination in the mind of many a youthful poet." [1]   They were the same tales as in his *Parish Register* of 1807 the poet still numbers in the chosen stock of cottage-reading, the tales of the Wandering Jew, Tom Thumb, Hickathrift the Strong, and Jack the Giant-Killer, many doubtless from the shop of Mr. Newbery of St. Paul's Churchyard, the great eighteenth-century publisher of children's books.

THESE popular old tales, " unbound and heap'd " in the corners of the cottages, came from the pedlar as he passed through with his pack, for not

---

[1] Crabbe, *Life and Works*, 1860, p. 5.

many small towns and no villages until late in the eighteenth century as a rule had shops, but the merchants of all kinds of wares were accustomed to send their goods by pedlars who carried them on their own backs or on the back of a single pack-horse.[1] The roads were too bad throughout the country for any regular transport of wholesale goods except between the larger towns. The isolation of the countryside was up till about 1780 pretty complete, and it is no wonder that not many books but chap-books and the humble contents of the pedlar's bag circulated beyond the districts near to well-populated towns on the main roads. News circulated more freely than formerly, but the newspaper was still slow in passing from the squire's to the vicar's, and from the vicar's to the village, and its snippets of news and notes were not much to read.

NOT till the end of the century did life begin to stir much in the backwaters of the countryside. It is said that before the French Revolution the income of the assistant clergy was settled by the bishops at some figure which could not exceed £50, and that the ordinary wife for the poorer country parson was a servant or an innkeeper's daughter. In spite of the general progress in London and the towns, that is a picture little better than Macaulay's of the condition of England in 1685, a century earlier. But generally the advance throughout the country was considerable. " By the end of the peaceful century the rough and ignorant Osbaldistones and Squire Westerns had disappeared. The small provincial gentry of the West, as drawn by Miss Austen . . . are nice

[1] J. L. and B. Hammond, *The Rise of Modern Industry*, p. 69.

in their gentility almost to a fault, and are all either well-read or accustomed to pay a conventional homage to the Muses." [1] To pass from *Joseph Andrews* to *Sense and Sensibility* is to pass from a provincial life that was rude and rough and on the whole illiterate to one which is essentially cultured. We as much expect to see a book on the table in one of Jane Austen's interiors as we should be surprised to see any in one of Fielding's, unless it were the Æschylus in the pocket of Parson Adams. It is another world we are in when a young lady says to her sister of an acquaintance : " I have seen a great deal of him, have studied his sentiments, and heard his opinion on subjects of literature and taste ; and, upon the whole, I venture to pronounce that his mind is well informed, his enjoyment of books exceedingly great, his imagination lively, his observation just and correct, and his taste delicate and pure." [2] The squirearchy were less constantly resident, and as they moved more about, other interests began to take their place with that of the chase, and to check the boorish excess of the board and the bowl. The library, if only for show, was a recognized part of the country houses, its shelves were filled with the best authors, ancient and modern, and no more were the few old volumes of heraldry and hunting all that was needed in the way of book furniture. In 1797 one might find a copy of *The Seasons* even in the parlour of a Somerset inn.

[1] G. M. Trevelyan, *British History in the Nineteenth Century*, 1782–1901, p. 20.
[2] *Sense and Sensibility*, chap. iv.

(ii)

BUT between 1780 and 1800 town and country were quickly drawing closer to-gether. Men were at length setting to upon the improvement of the roads. As late as the middle of the century through the greater part of the country travelling, even in summer, was poor, and in winter was as bad as could be ; broken axles, and squelching mud, and dangerous ruts made it quite hazardous enough without the threat of a lingering highwayman. In fact, Trevelyan says that in North Herefordshire as late as 1788 " from the autumn until the end of April all intercourse between the females of neighbouring families was suspended, unless they would consent to ride on pillions, a mode of travelling then in general use." But private enterprise, with the sanction of the Government, began to develop the roads by means of the turn-pike system, and in the fifties turnpike trusts were becoming common. Yet it was a haphazard development, and needed the agitation of Arthur Young in the eighties to introduce some kind of regular control. Pitt then set up in 1793 the Board of Agriculture of which Young was secre-tary, and the work of linking up went on steadily with the help of the great road engineers who came in the half-century from 1770, Metcalfe and Telford and Macadam.

THE year 1784 saw a very important advance in the appearance of the first Mail Coach. It was the idea of one Palmer, lessee of the theatre at Bath, and he proposed that the Post Office should step in and play its part in arranging coach services and helping in the construction of roads. The first mail coach of 1784 ran from London to Bristol, and the progress was such that in 1792 sixteen mail coaches left the General Post Office in London each day, and to see them start was one of the sights of the town.[1] Of the service to Manchester we are told by a writer of 1816, that " in 1770 there was only one stage coach to London and one to Liverpool, which went or came into Manchester, and these set out only twice a week. There are now seventy distinct coaches which run from hence, of which fifty-four set out every day, and sixteen others three times in the week, to their different places of destination." In 1816 there were six a day from Manchester to London completing the journey in from twenty-four to thirty hours. To the older generation it must have seemed that the world was, indeed, becoming a smaller place in this swift rush of travel, when a man could make the journey from London to Leeds in 1815 in twenty-four hours, where a century ago it had been the journey of a week but to York. The provinces were very close neighbours after all, and it is one sign of the new age that men of letters like Coleridge and Southey found it no hindrance to their profession to pass much of their time not in London but in the Lake district or in Somerset. For between all the chief towns there was a service of stage coaches as regular as that of the railways to-day.[2]

[1] De Quincey, in *The English Mail-Coach* (Going down with Victory), gives an account of the night mails. " From eight p.m. to fifteen or twenty minutes later imagine the mails assembled on parade in Lombard Street ; where, at that time [i.e. before Waterloo], and not in St. Martin's-le-Grand, was seated the General Post-office. In what exact strength we mustered I do not remember ; but, from the length of each separate *attelage*, we filled the street, though a long one, and though we were drawn up in double file. On *any* night the spectacle was beautiful." *Works*, 1897, xiii. 293.
[2] For the development of transport see J. L. and B. Hammond, *The Rise of Modern Industry*.

So important were these coaches, indeed, that we must count them as among the influences which educated the mind of the nation, for speed is a mental as well as a physical conquest. In the words of De Quincey, " through velocity at that time unprecedented—they first revealed the glory of motion." They were something of a message of change and progress even to the yokel who saw them flashing by in their " royal simplicity of form and colour," " the mighty shield of the imperial arms " emblazoned on the dark ground of chocolate colour, their horns sounding as they went down with the news of the Peninsular victories. To the dreamer of stupendous visions " the mailcoach, as the national organ for publishing these mighty events, thus diffusively influential, became itself a spiritualized and glorified object to an impassioned heart." He saw in its passage through the country an " awful *political* mission," and, as he sat on his seat outside, felt " the conscious presence of a central intellect, that, in the midst of vast distances—of storms, of darkness, of danger—overruled all obstacles into one steady co-operation to a national result." But a man did not need to be an opium-eater to share to some extent in these feelings. It was an education to see a coach on its way with mails to Ireland along the new road to Holyhead which Telford had constructed. A man's horizon was broadened, and he began to see the country more as a whole. He felt linked more closely to his fellows, and national opinion became a more substantial power as the village and the town were seen not so much as units in themselves, but as units of a larger unity. The passing of the coaches gave him, too, a sense of something regular and systematic and secure. He knew that there were people in authority in London who were organizing and controlling these coaches for the service of the whole country. ALTOGETHER the existence of these coaches made for a more intelligent public, and, as the general public is the basis of the reading public, in course of time for many more readers. And what the coaches did in the way of circulating news and newspapers it would be hard to exaggerate, while, although the cost of posting letters [1] rose, the higher rates were compensated for by the quicker and surer delivery, and the transaction of business and the communication of ideas had found a valuable and much more efficient medium.

(iii)

ONCE the country had ceased to be static, the drift to the towns set in, and, as that drift was in large part the product of the industrial revolution which was taking place in England, the study of the origins of the reading public leads to an examination of the trend of industrial development. The inventions which came in the eighteenth century one after another led before long to a complete revolution in the means of production. The machine took the place of the hand. The work which had formerly been a source of added income in the cottage, when the women plied their hand looms, was henceforth too slow, and could not compete with the growing factories. A new class of capitalists arose, and

---

1 Halévy, *Histoire du Peuple Anglais au XIXe Siècle*, I, p. 287. " Une lettre envoyée de Londres à Chester, qui coûtait 4*d*. au début du XVIIIe siècle, coûte 6*d*. à partir de 1784, 8*d*. à partir de 1786, 10*d*. depuis 1812."

drew largely upon the smaller landowners and tenants. They sold their ancestral farms or borrowed £100 or so, and invested in the modern machinery. So they headed the exodus from the countryside, and the call of their factories, and the pressure of poverty as the cottage industries were strangled, together with the pressure of " improving " landlords in the enclosure of commons and the break up of the old village community, sent many of the land-workers after them into the cities. And the cities grew, and the chimneys multiplied, because from about 1780 it seemed that the only thing in the world that mattered was industrial expansion. Between 1781 and 1801 the population increased by about twenty-one per cent. and it began to grow denser and denser round the coal-fields of the North.

THE immediate effect was an all-round impoverishment of life. It meant the passing away of that old rural society which had nourished boys like Crabbe and Lackington. There was no more time for the ballads and legendary tales. The newly transplanted urban population, sweating in the mills, men, women and children alike, was denied in the squalor and drudgery of its manufacturing life even the solace of the little chap-books of the pedlar's pack. Uprooted as they were, for them the rich traditions of the old English countryside withered away and were forgotten, and there was practically nothing to replace them. For the thousands of children who were each year born into the succession of slaves for the cotton and woollen mills, for the mines, and the furnaces, and the iron foundries, education did not exist. They were denied even the little schools of the old village dames where for two-pence a week a boy might learn his alphabet, and so set foot on the ladder of a self-education. In fact they were taken from a society which, whether it had books or not, could at least educate, to one which, without exaggeration, gave little but existence and misery.

IN the villages, as the towns drew away the inhabitants, the old customs went as well. By the end of the century the mediæval system of apprenticeship was being given up and could not be reinforced, and so a long-tested means of practical education came to an end. The last descendants of the wandering minstrels, the story-tellers who went from village to village, died out. The village pageants and spectacles passed away until even the maypole was no more. It was as though the smoky clouds of the manufacturing cities must cast their drab over the countryside too.

BUT there was a reaction. The very vileness of the life in the herded towns and the very misery and discontent became creative forces. They drove men into thinking about the nature of society and the rights of man, and they compelled men to turn from the soul-deadening drudgery of every day to the chapels and the debating clubs where a man might again feel himself a man who mattered to his Maker or to his fellows. For the harsh discipline of the factories and the ugly wretchedness of the houses that were often no better than hovels, led men naturally to a sphere where they might find some self-expression, and to dreams and theories which might feed hope in their starved spirits. When many men are gathered together, and particularly when they are banded together beneath oppression, the leaven of ideas is a quick worker, and when the French Revolution let loose for the masses the ideas which had been gaining ground among philosophers throughout the century, the masses quickly took them up, and in the nineties and onwards the manufacturing towns of northern England quickened with thought. They were the homes of thousands of citizens and patriots who read the wild pamphlets of Thomas Paine. Those gloomy tenements were the forcing houses of intellectual discontent, and from them shot up a new class of uneducated readers. Their minds were grappling with unaccustomed ideas before ever they had been trained to think. But in the revolutionary clubs they tried to thrash out their ideas of a new order of society, and to scheme for its fulfilment, and that was a process of self-education.[1]

In fact the industrialization of society meant a new order of mental life. Industrial towns have always been radical and progressive in their ideas, just as agricultural towns remain conservative and averse to any innovation in the things of the mind even more than to any change in the things of daily life. And if a man is to be a radical of any worth, he must be a reader of some sort. And if, as well as being a radical, he is a man of religious instinct, he is most likely to be a Nonconformist, and to find in the chapel the opportunities for the exercise of talents for which there is no scope in his ordinary work. The chapel came to play a prominent part in the towns, and it was in the towns that

1 For a picture of the clubs and chapels in 1814 see Mark Rutherford, *The Revolution in Tanner's Lane.*

Methodism at the end of the century was continuing most steadily to advance. The sermon, the prayer-meeting and the Bible-class gave colour and courage to the lives of men and women. They were the school of the working class, and " it was in the Little Bethel that many of the working-class leaders were trained." [1] And as regards reading there must have been many who began with Wesley's evangelical tracts but passed on to worldly literature, while the hymns and the Psalms were in their way too an introduction to poetry.

WHERE religion was absent, atheism sprang up in the unfed minds, and the towns acquired a reputation for free-thinking. It was in London that Crabbe laid the scene of his learned boy's downfall,[2] but it might almost as well have been any of the industrial towns. There the rustic lad, fresh from a pious home, found strange new books and reasonings. Men would tell him of the Bible that

> " The book has wisdom in it, if you look
> Wisely upon it as another book."

So, without judgment to refute, but with presumption to accept, the new-fledged man would soon be another mouthpiece of current wisdom. Before long he had on his lips the matter and the smart phrases of the last pamphlet he had read. In the towns in 1800 men were talking freely of " no God, no devil, and the rights of man."

(iv)

OF education in these two decades it is safe to say that it was almost at a standstill. Over the grammar schools, the public schools and the

[1] Trevelyan, *British History in the Nineteenth Century*, p. 160.
[2] *Tales*, 1812, Tale xxi.

Universities, there still lay the dead hand of an outworn classical tradition. The grammar schools were for the greater number confined to the old curriculum by the statutes of their founders, and had to wait till such time as Parliament would grant them the dispensation to teach English. And that was not till 1824. The public schools, as well as being bound by old traditions, were poor enough places of education with their harsh discipline, rough living and low morals. In their occasional mutinies they were like bear-gardens. And for their morals there is the testimony of Coleridge, that " to those who remember the state of our public schools and Universities some twenty years past, it will appear no ordinary praise in any man to have passed from innocence into virtue, not only free from all vicious habit, but unstained by one act of intemperance, or the degradations akin to intemperance." [1]   Christ's Hospital is, perhaps, as good an example as we may find, but as we see it in the accounts which Coleridge, Lamb and Leigh Hunt give of it, it is far from admirable. The strength of its teaching lay in literature, and Coleridge tells us that the English lesson on Shakespeare or Milton " required the most time and trouble to *bring up*, so as to escape [the master's] censure." But the brutality of the discipline and the lamentable gaps in the curriculum are clear in the pages of Lamb and Leigh Hunt, in the former's whimsical ignorance of modern geography, in the tales of unfeeling punishment, and in the latter's complete incompetence in face of a sheet of figures. In his survey in *The Wealth of Nations* Adam Smith denounced the

---

[1] *Biographia Literaria*, p. 35.

45

whole system as one in which the security of endowments had thoroughly corrupted all diligence.

OF the Universities the account is no better. Adam Smith says that " in the University of Oxford the greater part of the public professors have, for these many years, given up altogether even the pretence of teaching."[1]   The custom had become usual of sending young men fresh from school not to the University, but to tour the Continent, and Smith held that " nothing but the discredit into which the Universities [were] allowing themselves to fall, could ever have brought into repute so very absurd a practice as that of travelling at this early period of life."[2] In his opinion the spirit of Oxford and Cambridge was the spirit of monopolists, " narrow, lazy, and oppressive."   And it was the judgment of Cardinal Newman that Oxford "gave no education at all " prior to 1800.   A man can hardly speak so broadly as that without exaggerating,[3] but the truth about the Universities of that day is, that they were " comfortable monastic establishments for clerical sinecurists with a tinge of letters ; while young men of family, between Eton and the Grand Tour, and a number of more ordinary individuals designed for the Church, spent their time there very pleasantly, some with a great deal of drinking

[1] *The Wealth of Nations* (1776), ii. 343.   [2] *Ibid.,* ii. 358.
[3] In estimating the condition of the Universities (and, indeed, of the schools too) it is well to have in mind the judgment of Professor Ker. See W. P. Ker, *Collected Essays* (Warton). " Warton was an idle fellow, the editor of the *Oxford Sausage,* a lover of ale and tobacco and low company in taverns. . . . Oxford in the eighteenth century is a favourite shocking example, and Thomas Warton in his neglect of his pupils did little, seemingly, to contradict the prevalent opinion about the inefficiency of Oxford teaching at that time. But we were reminded lately by Mr. Dicey, speaking of Blackstone (a friend of Warton's), that the dispraise of Oxford may be overdone ; ' the apathy or somnolence of Oxford in the eighteenth century has been a subject of exaggeration.' Among the idlers there were some adventurers who used their leisure in a right academic way. The names of Blackstone and Warton are enough to make the censurers reconsider and modify their estimate of those quiet generations of University life."

46

and cheerful noise, and some with a little reading of books." [1] How heavy the dead hand of antiquity still lay on them, the ashes of Crabbe's English Essay on Botany might testify. Though he had made so much progress with it as to approach Dodsley about its being published, he put it aside because of the remonstrances of the vice-master of Trinity College, Cambridge, " who, though little tinged with academical peculiarities, could not stomach the notion of degrading such a science by treating of it in a modern language." [2] That was as late as the nineties. In the phrase of Adam Smith the universities were still the " homes of exploded philosophies."

In the higher places of education there was more or less fitful slumber until the end of the century. The awakening began with Butler when he went as headmaster to Shrewsbury in 1798. But, because in the light of later progress the educational facilities of that time seem small, it is not to be thought that in these decades, when the world of everyday literature was becoming so much more active, education was making no progress at all. The English merchant, the new kind of gentleman whom Johnson had noted, was hardly to be satisfied with the lads whom the endowed schools offered for the desks in his office. The private schools stepped in where the older schools failed, and replaced the classical by a more commercial curriculum. They were such Academies as that of Mr. Blanchard at Nottingham to which Kirke White went as a boy of six to learn the rudiments of writing, arithmetic and French.

1 Trevelyan, *British History in the Nineteenth Century*, p. 27.
2 *Life and Works*, p. 38.

And naturally they had the contempt and distrust of those engaged in the regular educational system, and they were depreciated as " schools for the shop, the warehouse, the counting-house, and the manufactory." But their existence and the fact that even in 1832 a large proportion of the sons of farmers and tradesmen received from them their education show that they did supply a better, or at least a more acceptable, training than could be had elsewhere. As the success of Donaldson with his cheap books was due to public weariness of the monopoly of ' the trade,' so the success of these English or Commercial schools arose from the dissatisfaction of people with the way in which their requirements were met by these other monopolists. And, on another side, the close preserve of the Universities was in a way invaded by the establishment in 1784 of Hackney College for Nonconformists.

BUT to study the growth of the reading public is to look farther afield than only to regular schooling, for regular schooling is not necessary for a man to read or to reason. It is not one tithe of the schooling that a boy has, for he is out of school many more hours than he is in, and the books of the master are dull compilations compared with the books of the home. In the latter he reads absorbed, in the hayloft or in bed, or crouching over the evening fire, the glow of the coals on his face and the glow of the adventurous tale in his mind. The key of the alphabet is enough to open the door to the world of books, and the little school of the old village dame may do as much for the pockets of the publisher as the great school of an old foundation. For, after all,

48

the reading public is very wide. If it begins with the highest, yet its majority is the poor, and we must not make the mistake of identifying it with the relatively small literary public. The one was, in this period, educated in the little cottages where parents sent their children for twopence a week, the other almost entirely in the better endowed schools, while the latter had, too, its superior dames' schools where such a boy as Crabb Robinson, the diarist, went for five shillings a quarter. The charity schools begun by the Society for the Promotion of Christian Knowledge in 1696 had spread quite extensively. " In Scotland," wrote Adam Smith, " the establishment of parish schools has taught almost the whole common people to read, and a very great proportion of them to write and account. In England the establishment of charity schools has had an effect of the same kind, though not so universally, because the establishment is not so universal." [1]

In fact education began to improve at the bottom, before it began to improve at the top. In 1780 Robert Raikes of Gloucester, proprietor of *The Gloucester Journal*, was moved by seeing the ignorance, immorality and wretchedness of the children employed in the factories. He engaged four women teachers, and, with a supply of Bibles and Testaments, set up in that year the first of the modern Sunday schools to teach children to read their Bibles, and to learn and understand their catechism. A report of his efforts in his *Journal* of November 3, 1783 was copied into the London papers, and a notice soon after in *The Gentleman's Magazine* gave the scheme still greater

---

[1] *The Wealth of Nations*, ii. 370.

attention, until on September 7, 1785 Raikes, together with other philanthropists, set on foot the Society for Promoting Sunday Schools. Their success was immediate, and in the next two years there were one hundred and forty-seven new schools set up, and the system became general. Lackington reports that " the Sunday Schools are spreading very fast in most parts of England, which will accelerate the diffusion of knowledge among the lower classes of the community, and in a very few years exceedingly increase the sale of books." [1] Indeed they were probably one of the strong forces that began to lead the poorer classes to believe in and seek the advantages of reading and writing.

IN 1801, according to Sarah Trimmer, " every town and most villages have their schoolmasters who keep evening schools for those who cannot attend in the day-time . . . besides, the desire for these acquirements is so general amongst the poor that parents will for the most part contrive that their children shall attain them." [2] So general did the power and habit of reading become that in the nineties people like Hannah More, lest the reason of the poor should be perverted by the pamphlets of the revolutionaries, wrote tracts for them, and they sold by thousands and by tens of thousands. In 1799 the Religious Tract Society was founded to supply the Sunday schools with literature. Then, as the century went out, popular elementary education received a very great impulse from the new methods of teaching of Bell and Lancaster.

---

1 *Memoirs*, p. 251.
2 J. W. Adamson, *History of Education*, p. 231.

(v)

AFTER briefly surveying the linking up of town and country and the passing of the old static life, the appearance of the industrial towns and the quickening of thought in them, and the condition of the schools and the spread of knowledge, we come back again to what people actually were reading in the last twenty years of the century, and how far the booksellers met and encouraged the demand for cheap, popular books. And since, in a progressive historical study, it is the next rather than the last generation that counts, it is as well to see first what books there were in the eighties for a child to read.

WE have seen from the memoirs of Holcroft and poems of Crabbe, the ballads and chap-books that there were for a boy to delight in. And for children who were better off, there were tales in plenty. Egerton Brydges says that about 1766, when he was a child learning to read, his " mother had a trunk full of romances and fairy tales." [1] Newbery, the publisher for whom Goldsmith worked, issued a series of books for children, some of which Goldsmith wrote. Nor was the fame of Little Goody Two Shoes and her fellows the fame of a day, but it lived for generations of children. In fact, the second half of the eighteenth century became increasingly rich in literature for children, and to scan a bibliography [2] of it is to realize that the children of that time had every chance to become readers and to maintain the England of 1800 as much a nation of readers as it had seemed to Johnson in 1780, and to make it yet more so.

[1] S. E. Brydges, *Autobiography*, i. 111.
[2] See *Cambridge History of English Literature*, vol. xi, ch. xvi.

51

Apart from the books written especially for children, there would be for the child in many a home a copy of *The Pilgrim's Progress*. Cowper hesitated to name it " lest so despised a name should move a sneer " among the readers of his poetry, for it was in those days perhaps the most popular book of any with children and the poor. And the quality of the books that were written for children improved. According to Leigh Hunt, who was a boy in the early nineties, " books for children during the latter part of the eighteenth century had been in a bad way, with sordid and merely plodding morals—ethics that were necessary perhaps for a certain stage in the progress of commerce. . . . Every good boy was to ride in his coach and be a lord mayor ; and every bad boy was to be hung, or eaten by lions. The gingerbread was gilt, and the books were gilt like the gingerbread. But the first counteraction came, as it ought, in the shape of a new book for children. The pool of mercenary and time-serving ethics was first blown over by the fresh country breeze of Mr. Day's *Sandford and Merton*—a production that I well remember, and shall ever be grateful to." [1]   But the gilt gingerbread books were doubtless the joy of many a child, and he was only still the luckier when Thomas Day made a change.

AND the children of the end of the century were lucky because in their day there was a change in school books too. " It is worth remarking," wrote Lackington in 1803, " that the introducing histories, romances, stories, poems, etc., into schools, has been a very great means of diffusing a taste for reading among all ranks of people.   While

[1] *Autobiography* (1860), pp. 49-50.

in schools the children only read the Bible (which was the case in many schools [1] a few years ago) children did not then make so early a progress in reading as they have since they have been pleased and entertained, as well as instructed ; and this relish for books, in many, will last as long as life." [2] Nor should we forget the magazines for children that also became more numerous. The first had been Dodsley's *Preceptor* of 1748, and little collections of tales and knowledge came one after another, sometimes in very short-lived succession, after 1770. Reading-matter for children became a field for journalists, and particularly for women journalists. And educators became all the better educators because they began to study the classics less and children more. Rousseau was rich in followers, and in England no followers were greater than the Edgeworths, father and daughter. Maria Edgeworth's *Parent's Assistant* of 1796 was another advance in reading books for children.

BUT, to pass to better things, a boy like Walter Scott had quite a large library at his command. What the poorer boy had, he had too. The ballads he used to learn and copy out, and before he was ten years old he had made a collection of several little volumes. At the same early age he was making a collection of Penny Chap-books little humorous stories in prose, which for years remained popular with the lower classes in Scotland. In addition, he would spend hours as a young boy not yet old enough for the High School in reading aloud to his mother Pope's translation of Homer. Then, "in the intervals of my

[1] Adam Black, the Edinburgh bookseller, born in 1784, records in his memoirs that before going to the High School " our ordinary school book was the Bible."
[2] *Memoirs*, p. 253.

53

school hours," he says, "I . . . always perused with avidity such books of history or poetry or voyages and travels as chance presented to me— not forgetting the usual, or rather ten times the usual, quantity of fairy tales, Eastern stories, romances, etc." [1] Also he found odd volumes of Shakespeare in his mother's dressing-room, and would sit of a night in his shirt reading them by the light of the fire. The learned Dr. Blacklock lent him Ossian and Spenser. In the circulating library he " waded into the stream like a blind man into a ford." When he was thirteen he found the *Reliques* of Percy, and was so enthralled by them that, as he sat in the garden, " the summer day sped onward so fast, that notwithstanding the sharp appetite of thirteen, [he] forgot the hour of dinner, and was sought for with anxiety, and was found entranced in [his] intellectual banquet." [2] And about the same age he became acquainted with the works of the great eighteenth-century novelists, and continued to devour anything and everything that was adventurous and romantic. In brief, he is the best example we can have of what reading there was for an eager boy in a cultured home in the early eighties of the eighteenth century.

AND not only in a cultured professional home, but in an everyday home, a growing boy would have had in those days a quite ample chance of making himself familiar with some of the best of the English classics. Donaldson's cheap editions had sold very widely years before the House of Lords' decision made them legal. In 1771, when

---

[1] Lockhart, *Life of Scott* (Everyman Library), p. 27. (All subsequent references, unless otherwise indicated, are to this edition.)
[2] *Ibid.*, p. 30.

54

Donaldson was prosecuted over *The Seasons*, the ' owners ' complained that he had sold about 11,000 copies. And there is every reason to suppose that these cheap editions were read in many a home throughout the country, together with the reasonably priced editions which, to be fair to the ' monopolist owners,' we must admit ' the trade ' did keep on the market. When Crabbe was a boy, his father " used occasionally to read aloud to his family, in the evenings, passages from Milton, Young, or other of our graver classics." [1] And a Prussian visitor to England in 1782 noted, that " the English national authors are in all hands. My landlady, who is a taylor's widow, reads her Milton ; and tells me that her late husband first fell in love with her because she read Milton with such proper emphasis." [2] We know, too, that Crabbe as a boy found stimulus to poetical imitation because his father took in a periodical work called *Martin's Philosophical Magazine*, which contained at the end a sheet of occasional poetry. In Johnson's words, we begin to see England as " a nation of readers."

ONE of the first of the more immediate causes of this growth of the habit of reading was the circulating library. It had appeared at the same time as the great novel in the early forties, and before the fifties were out it was very popular and widespread. Women, in particular, made good use of it, and fiction above all was in great demand, and the combination was naturally a tempting one for the satirists. In the comedies of Foote and

---

[1] Crabbe, *Life and Works*, p. 4.
[2] Trevelyan, *British History in the Nineteenth Century*, p. 29, note.

Sheridan the novel-reading girl is already on the stage. Nor is there any doubt that the influence of the library was considerable on the increase of reading. Lackington said : " I have been informed, that when circulating libraries were first opened, the booksellers were much alarmed, and their rapid increase added to their fears, had led them to think that the sale of the books would be much diminished by such libraries. But experience has proved that the sale of books, so far from being diminished by them, has been greatly promoted, as from those repositories many thousand families have been cheaply supplied with books, by which the taste of reading has become much more general, and thousands of books are purchased every year, by such as have borrowed them at those libraries, and after reading, approving of them, become purchasers." [1] And there is no need to dispute his judgment of their effect both on reading and on sales. They flourished in town and country alike. A Dr. Thomas Campbell noted in his diary of his visit to London in 1775 : " Strolled into the Chapter Coffee-house, Ave Mary Lane, which I had heard was remarkable for a large collection of books, and a reading society. I subscribed a shilling for the right of a year's reading, and found all the new publications I sought " ; [2] while Cowper tells in a letter of 1781 that he subscribes to " some well furnished circulating library." Also, they appealed to the young as well as to the old. The young ladies in Bath we have noticed before, and Walter Scott " wading " into their stream of books

1 *Memoirs*, p. 255.
2 *Diary of a Visit to England in 1775*, ed. S. Raymond, 1854; March 21, 1775.

56

in Edinburgh. In addition there is Leigh Hunt's testimony of his boyhood in the nineties : " I had subscribed while at school to the famous circulating library in Leadenhall Street, and I have continued to be . . . a glutton for novels ever since." [1]

BUT even more important was the cheap reprint. From about 1780, Nichols the printer says, the prices of new books began to rise. An era of expensive new books set in. The old publishers shut off the new public from the general run of new publications by their costly format, and most readers were compelled by their pockets to confine themselves to the older writers. But of them the newly enfranchised booksellers issued a plentiful and a cheap supply, and, perhaps after all, it is as well that economic conditions should make men read the old, which is good and tested, rather than the new, of which much is sure to be mediocre. At least the little popular pocket volumes of the English classics which date from the eighties had a very stimulating influence on many a boy reader. THEY began very soon after the rejection of perpetual copyright made them legally possible. First there was the edition of the Poets which made ' the trade ' look to their laurels, and retaliate with Johnson's edition. That was Bell's. Then Bell, in partnership with Martin, " sent forth his British Theatre to drive out of the market the old octavo editions of Shakespeare's plays, or the cumbrous collections of the works of dramatic authors, from Dryden and Farquhar to Thomson and Colman." And Bell, though his *Poets* according to Leigh Hunt were the best, was not

1 *Autobiography*, p. 140.

57

alone. In the nineties appeared Cooke's *British Poets*, of which Hunt wrote : " How I loved those little sixpenny numbers containing whole poets ! I doted on their size ; I doted on their type, on their ornaments, on their wrappers containing lists of other poets, and on the engravings from Kirk. I bought them over and over again ; and used to get up select sets, which disappeared like buttered crumpets ; for I could resist neither giving them away, nor possessing them." [1]   They were familiar to him as a boy, and his " favourites, out of school hours, were Spenser, Collins, Gray, and the Arabian Nights."

NOT only the poets, but the novelists too, were reprinted. Hazlitt, in his essay *On Reading Old Books*, tells how as a boy he came under the spell of Cooke's edition. Harrison had begun in 1779 his *Novelists' Magazine*, in octavo with double columns, stitched in small weekly numbers for sixpence, with engraved embellishments by Stothard and others. It is said that 12,000 copies of each number were sold weekly,[2] and it ran into twenty-three good-sized volumes before it was completed. Its success encouraged him to issue his *New Novelists' Magazine*, a collection of short tales. And Harrison was also in the forefront of popular ' number ' publishers with his *British Classics* and *Sacred Classics*, while he developed the periodical with his three-volume *British Magazine* which came out from 1782 to 1784 with highly finished plates by Heath from Stothard's designs and was hailed with intense curiosity. In addition he published the *Wit's Magazine*, the

---

1 Leigh Hunt, *Autobiography*, p. 76.
2 For Harrison, Cooke, Bell and Hogg, see Britton and Rees, *Reminiscences of Literary London*.

Pocket Magazine, and the *Lady's Pocket Magazine*, to the last of which the Dibdins contributed.

IN fact, between them, Harrison,[1] Bell and Cooke have some claim to be named the greatest educational force of the last decade of the century. Their little, convenient, attractive volumes found their way into the homes of the new middle class everywhere, and the taste for reading was born where it had never had a chance to be born before. Perhaps there were not many lads with the seriousness and precocity of Kirke White to write to their elder brothers : " I also now read the *British Classics*, the common edition of which I now take in ; it comes every fortnight . . . it is Cooke's edition ; "[2] but there was many another lad in 1800 who was reading them with as much enjoyment and as much profit. And readers in 1800 were all the more numerous and all the readier for new writers, because of this twenty years' succession of sixpenny numbers.

As well as reprinting the English classics the ' number ' publishers quickly brought forward in the same way educational works, making them accessible by their cheapness and attractive by their engravings. In his early days Cooke issued periodically Southwell's *Commentary of the Bible*, which by its large sale earned him a profit of thousands of pounds. Hogg, too, made a handsome fortune by a similar *Bible* with annotations. IN Crabbe's pictures the cottages are not complete without them.

> " Bibles, with cuts and comments, thus go down,
> E'en light Voltaire is *number'd* through the town,"[3]

[1] With Harrison we see the appearance of one form of modern advertising. As a draw for his *Musical Magazine*, a selection for the piano, he gave out that " the purchaser of the entire work would be entitled to receive a square pianoforte."
[2] *The Life and Remains of Henry Kirke White*, p. 169. [3] *The Library*, lines 191-2.

and not only through the town, but through the country too. The Wesleyan revival had created the demand for Bibles, and the ' number ' method brought them within reach of the pockets of the poor, while the growing population of the cities was ready to sharpen its dissatisfied mind on the cynicism of Voltaire.

POPULAR knowledge continued [1] with such works as Harrison's *General Geography*, which consisted of forty numbers of closely printed quarto. Hogg produced a slipshod Encyclopædia. Cooke, when the copyright expired, re-issued the history of Hume and Smollett in weekly numbers. The first *Encyclopædia Britannica*, which had been projected by Mr. Colin M'Farquhar, a printer in Edinburgh, was completed in 1771 in three volumes, and turned out a very profitable undertaking. Its first edition was of about three thousand copies. The second, which was also first issued in numbers, was completed in 1785 in ten volumes. It was a large impression and was still more successful. And the demand was so keen that in 1787 the third edition was begun, and, running into eighteen volumes, was not finished until 1796, while its popularity so grew that from an initial impression of five thousand it came to end with a sale of ten thousand. Since 1778, too, it had had the competition of *Chambers's Cyclopædia*, which continued weekly with a current sale for years of five thousand copies under the editorship of Alexander Rees until its 418 numbers were gathered into four large volumes with numerous prints. Nor was the public demand even then satisfied, but a revised edition

[1] It had begun in the 'numbers' of Dr. John Hill.

was called for in 1802 and ran until completed in 1818.

IN general, what Isaac D'Israeli called the household stuff of literature, which he said was paid for with " princely magnificence," went on increasing in bulk and scope. Knowledge was written down to the people, and the people responded with an eager demand. For, as we have seen from Hannah More's letter, by 1800 the poorer classes were realizing that knowledge was a valuable asset, and those who would go to evening classes to acquire it, would be ready buyers of all they could afford of this new output of the publishers.

NEXT in importance to the publisher of cheap ' numbers ' for serving the new public comes the cheap second-hand and remainder bookseller. He entered on a much larger scale of business after Lackington had appeared to show the way, for Lackington began a new system by selling for cash only and refusing credit, whereby he was enabled to trade more economically and therefore more extensively, and Lackington it was who first sold remainders off cheaply in spite of the opposition of the booksellers. His rapid success indicates the growing demand. He had set up shop in 1774 in quite a small way ; in 1779 he issued his first catalogue of 12,000 books ; by 1803 he writes : " I publish two catalogues for the public every year, and of each of these public catalogues I print between four and five thousand copies ; most of these copies are lent about from one to another ; so that supposing only four persons see each copy, above thirty thousand persons look over my catalogues annually." [1] So by keeping to his

1 *Memoirs*, p. 281.

motto of " small profits, bound by industry, and clasped by economy," he soon earned himself a fortune. Already in 1791 his profits for the year were £4,000, and in 1792 £5,000. By 1803 he says, " I now sell more than one hundred thousand volumes annually."

THE effect on the reading public is fairly described in the claim Lackington himself makes : " Many who purchase part of these [100,000 volumes] do so solely on account of their cheapness ; many thousands of these books would have been destroyed . . . but for my selling them on those moderate terms : now when thousands of these articles are sold, they become known by being handed about in various circles of acquaintances, many of whom wishing to be possessed of the same books, without enquiring the price of their friends, step into the first bookseller's shop, and give their orders for articles, which they never would have heard of, had not I, by selling them cheap, been the original cause of their being dispersed abroad; thus, by means of the plan pursued in my shop, whole editions of books are sold off, and new editions printed of the works of authors, who, were it not for that circumstance, would have been scarcely noticed at all." People would say to him, he writes, " you not only sell such books cheap, as are but little known, but you even sell a great deal under price the very first-rate articles, however well they may be known, or however highly they may be thought of by the literary world. I acknowledge the charge, and again repeat that as I do not give any credit, I certainly ought to do so, and I may add, that in some measure I am obliged to do it ; for who would come out of their way to Finsbury-square to pay me the same price in ready money, as they might purchase for at the first shop they came to and have credit also?

" AND although first-rate authors are very well known, yet I am confident that by selling them cheaper than others, many are purchased of me that never would have been bought at the full price ; now every book that is sold tends to spread the fame of the author, rapidly extends the sale, and as I have before remarked, sends more customers to other shops as well as to my own."[1]

IN particular, Lackington makes a strong and just claim for the increase in reading which was due to his innovation in the matter of remainder sales. The custom in his first years as a bookseller was to destroy a half or three-quarters of them and sell the rest at or near the published price. But he " resolved not to destroy any books that were worth saving, but to sell them off at half or a quarter of the publication prices." He held that the poorer classes had received by his action a benefit they could not otherwise have had. " Thousands . . ." he wrote, " have been effectually prevented from purchasing (though anxious so to do) whose circumstances in life would not permit them to pay the full price, and thus were totally excluded from the advantage of improving their understandings ; and enjoying a rational entertainment. And you may be assured, that it affords me the most pleasing satisfaction, independent of the emoluments which have accrued to me from this plan, when I reflect what prodigious numbers in inferior or *reduced* situations

[1] *Memoirs*, pp. 280–1.

of life, have been essentially benefited, in consequence of being thus enabled to indulge their natural propensity for the acquisition of knowledge, on easy terms : nay, I could almost be vain enough to assert, that I have thereby been highly instrumental in diffusing that general desire for READING now so prevalent among the inferior orders of society." [1]

AND, meanwhile, the thorough, if heavy reading of former days gave place to something more superficial, but more pleasing. For popular appeal rather than scholarly exhaustiveness began to be the aim of all literature. Publishers, as the big average public grew, paid to it more, and to the small literary public less attention. Crabbe notes the change in his *Library*.[2] The popularity commenced of abstracts, and abridgements, " from men of study, and from men of straw." " Pamphlets and plays, and politics and rhymes " were the books chosen by the reader of the new generation, not the solid, learned folios of his father. Indeed, writers seemed to be encouraged by the taste of the times to pour all kinds of trifles from the press. A man who visited Edinburgh in 1776 was glad to be there, because he found himself away from " those weekly, daily and almost hourly pamphlets which everywhere meet one's eye in London, under the names of Nuptial Elegies, Sentimental Scruples, Juvenile Poems, Amorous Epistles, and a thousand others of the same ingenious and tender natures." [3]

1 *Memoirs*, p. 224.
2 " Our patient fathers trifling themes laid by,
And roll'd, o'er laboured works, th' attentive eye ; . . .
Our nicer palates lighter labours seek,
Cloy'd with a folio number, once a week."
3 *Letters from Edinburgh*, 1776, B. M. 10370, aa. 25 (Letter 22).

FURTHER the taste for smaller and slighter books showed itself in the popularity of anthologies and collections. Volumes of select passages from favourite authors sold well. A *Beauties of Sterne* published in 1783 was in its tenth edition in 1787. And it was a taste of the times that had the approval of Johnson. " No man, Johnson used to say, reads long together with a folio on his table. Books, said he, that you may carry to the fire, and hold readily in your hand, are the most useful after all. Such books form the great mass of general and easy reading. He was a great friend to books like the French *Esprits d'un Tel* ; for example, *Beauties of Watts*, etc., at which, said he, a man will often look and be tempted to go on, when he would have been frightened at books of a larger size, and of a more erudite appearance." [1]

SOON this general and easy reading received an important addition when Isaac D'Israeli published his *Curiosities of Literature* in 1791. It was " an experiment whether a taste for literature could not be infused into the multitude," and its success showed clearly that a large body of readers were ready for it. In fact it ran quickly through five editions, and its author felt called on to revise and enlarge it. Many imitators testified to its success, too, with their *Varieties*, and *Delights*, and *Delicacies*, and *Relics of Literature*.

THE new love of what Johnson so aptly called " general and easy reading " (which is really the character of most reading once a big reading public has appeared) is seen also in the fashion of literary anecdote which prevailed at the end of the

¹ Johnsonian Miscellanies, ed. G. B. Hill, ii. 2.

century. Boswell's collection was the greatest, but it was one of a considerable company. And the whole tendency is natural, for when a man begins to read many books he is soon apt to read none so long nor so deeply, and the reader of 1800 was such a man. Even a country clergyman, as we may see from the diary of the Rev. James Woodforde, was no longer a man of only a few books.

FINALLY the development of the reading public is indicated in the way in which women were becoming prominent both as readers and writers, and in the formation of book clubs and of the debating societies of the nineties. And perhaps the more striking is the prominent place of the women. Their education had been very neglected, and their domestic sphere limited in the days when Addison had felt it necessary to use his *Spectator* to give them more intellectual diversions, and interests beyond those of the kitchen and the boudoir. We have the impression that then women were rarely readers, or at any rate rarely readers of anything better than the romances of Mrs. Manley and Mrs. Haywood. Also in the country it was not to be expected that the tastes of the wife would have much chance to be any better than a little more refined than those of her husband the squire. But in the writing itch that seized people in the thirties women seem to have had their share of interest. In 1737, when Pope wrote that

" Those who cannot write, and those who can,
All rhyme, and scrawl, and scribble to a man," [1]

" man " might still be true for the writer, but

[1] Pope, *Epistle to Augustus*, lines 187–8.

66

woman as much as man was the reader. In that day

" Our Wives read Milton, and our Daughters Plays,
To Theatres, and to Rehearsals throng," [1]

and the way of the " sober Englishman " in his home is changed. Then his women began to write. In 1753 Johnson, in a paper in the *Adventurer*, declares that " the revolution of years has now produced a generation of Amazons of the pen, who, with the spirit of their predecessors, have set masculine tyranny at defiance," [2] and in after years the satirical moralist mockingly wrote " and here a female atheist talks you dead."

WOMEN certainly began to write and talk with assurance and knowledge, and to the circulating libraries much of the credit was due. As Lackington affirmed, " circulating libraries have also greatly contributed towards the amusement and cultivation of the sex ; by far the greatest part of ladies have now a taste for books." And again he stated : " Ladies now in general read, not only novels, although many of that class are excellent productions, and tend to polish both the heart and the head : but they also read the best books in the English language, and many read the best authors in various languages ; and there are some thousands of ladies, who frequent my shop, and that know as well what books to choose, and are as well acquainted with works of taste and genius, as any gentleman in the kingdom, notwithstanding they sneer against novel readers, etc." [3] Indeed, the reading of women is the butt or the commonplace of the novelists and playwrights, and, when

---

1 Pope, *Epistle to Augustus*, lines 172–3.   2 *The Adventurer*, No. 115.
3 *Memoirs*, p. 259.

girls are difficult, the die-hard guardian stands up like Sir Anthony Absolute and says, " Ma'am, this is the natural consequence of teaching girls to read." But the die-hard could not stop this general education of women, and in 1778 Johnson could say, " All our ladies read now, which is a great extension." [1]

INDEED, in Johnson's day there were many ladies to whom literature owed not a little for their writings, and their example, and their literary gatherings. The group of blue-stockings was a distinct feature of the world of letters of the seventies. The salon of Mrs. Montagu was a circle of wits round a woman of taste and wit, whose *Essay on the Writings and Genius of Shakespeare* had won her considerable fame as an author. Her rooms were filled nightly, and the talk was good, and the fashion and respect of the arts radiated from her house. There was her friend, Mrs. Chapone, whose *Letters on the Improvement of the Mind* were in high esteem. " Lay Mrs. Chapone in sight," says Lydia Languish in the flutter of her aunt's arrival, " and leave Fordyce's sermons open on the table." There was Mrs. Macaulay with her popular history, a best-seller of its day. There was learned Mrs. Carter of whom Johnson said, " My old friend, Mrs. Carter, could make a pudding as well as translate Epictetus from the Greek, work a handkerchief as well as compose a poem." There were Mrs. Lennox, and Mrs. Delany, and Mrs. Barbauld, and in Lichfield there was Anna Seward, Lichfield's Swan, a rival to Johnson in his very birthplace and writing of him most dis-

[1] Boswell, *Life of Johnson*, iii. 333.

respectfully as a nasty, buzzing hornet, while the magazines were crowded with poems in her honour. And in the next generation there were Helen Williams the novelist, Charlotte Smith the popular poet, Fanny Burney, Hannah More, Miss Edgeworth, the Misses Porter, and many more. In 1795 Miss Edgeworth in her *Letters to Literary Ladies* put forward a defence of the education of women. And we can see a growing tendency to teach girls in the country towns in the fact that to the school at Stowmarket where Crabbe was a boy some girls used to go of an evening to learn writing. In fact Mathias, in his satires, was much disgusted with the lengths to which women were going and the way in which they were leaving the sphere of the home. " Our unsexed female writers," he says in 1797, " now instruct, or confuse us and themselves in the labyrinth of politics, or turn us wild with Gallic frenzy." [1]

IN addition to the appearance of women as readers and writers, the rise of book-clubs and debating clubs shows the increase of the public. The book-club was a kind of private circulating library, and is described thus by Lackington : " A number of book-clubs are also formed in every part of England, where each member subscribes a certain sum quarterly to purchase books : in some of the clubs the books, after they have been read by all the subscribers, are sold among them to the highest bidders, and the money produced by such sale, is expended in fresh purchases, by which prudent and judicious mode, each member has it in his power to become possessed of the work of any particular author he may judge

---

[1] *The Pursuits of Literature*, Dialogue IV (1797), Advertisement, p. ii.

deserving a superior degree of attention ; and the members at large enjoy the advantage of a continual succession of different publications, instead of being restricted to a repeated perusal of the same authors ; which must have been the case with many, if so rational a plan had not been adopted." [1]

MANY towns began to have, too, their literary societies. They were not very literary, at least many of them were probably like that which Crabbe sets down in *The Borough*,[2] where the wine passes so quickly and the dishes are so many, that there " is no time for intercourse of mind " and " all the genial flame goes off in smoke," and where the members, when no feasting is on hand, will stifle a discussion or toss aside a book at the first chance of a game of cards. Yet Crabbe's pictures generally make the most of the dark side. There were probably some books lying about for him who wished them, and a literary society does some honour to literature by its name, if not by its life. The men in the country would imagine its delights, and believe that literature was respected in the town. As Crabbe says,

> " To [them] our Book-club has peculiar charm
> For which [they] sicken in [their] quiet farm." [3]

And certainly there were societies whose members did have a real love of letters. We read that Kirke White at fifteen years old " was admitted a member of a literary society in Nottingham, and distinguished himself one evening at their meeting, by lecturing extempore a full hour on

1 *Memoirs*, p. 250.   2 Letter X. *Life and Works*, p. 210.
3 Crabbe, *The Borough*, Letter X, lines 7–8.

70

genius : upon which the members unanimously elected him their professor." [1]   In fact the popular literary society of to-day dates from about the beginning of the nineteenth century.

AND as well as the book-club and the literary society there had arisen in succession to the coffee-house the Conversation-club. Perhaps the best around 1800 was the " King of Clubs " where Sydney Smith and Mackintosh were the most brilliant talkers.   In these clubs, as in the coffee-houses, men would assemble, particularly in the evenings, to discuss the latest book or play, to express their opinions of the last move in politics, to survey the state of the nation, and to exchange the news of the day. So they both created and sent abroad a certain kind of public opinion, and in the matter of books and plays helped to build up the average of criticism and to elevate or depress the sales. In the higher social scale they influenced current thought in the same way as the revolutionary clubs began to affect the lower classes.

THE latter clubs became very numerous and popular, especially in London, in the last five years of the century and for the first years of the next.   The most important were the Corresponding Society founded by Thomas Hardy, which was the first political and educational club of working men, and the Friends of the People Society. In addition there were almost innumerable debating societies. Some were supported by private subscriptions and managed by committees, and were frequented by crowded companies who were admitted by ticket, and also

---

[1] Kirke White, *Life and Remains*, p. 7.

71

there were many public societies formed and governed by speculating and hackneyed orators who derived pay and profit from admission fees paid at the doors. In fact following the revolution all was talk. Mathias deplored that " mere talkers now, not writers are preferred." And these talk-shops were one of the crazes of those years of wild and undisciplined vision.

(vi)

THE years of the French Revolution certainly were years of vision to masses of the people of England. The new ideas might not be new to philosophers, but they were new to the ordinary man. It was a real dawn to thousands of workers in the towns, and though it failed to prelude any immediate political change, it was a strengthening and a dazzling light. Men questioned where before they had hardly so much as thought. The people began to grow conscious of themselves as the People, and the idea of democracy was sown as an ineradicable seed. In fact, for probably the first time in the history of the English people the lower classes were permeated with the leaven of ideas, and began to question their place in and the very nature of the social order. Everyone assumed himself as capable as another of discussing and judging the rights and limits of government, the sphere of politics, and the nature of liberty. For it was the early youth of the working-class move-ment, and with the usual cocksure ardour of youth they exercised their newly-awakened intellects on each and every problem that occurred to them. These were years when many a mind, which fifty years before would have accepted existing conditions as unquestioningly as any, launched itself quite young on the ocean of thought. Men could hardly think fast enough, but plunged straightway into the deep waters of political thought. For many of these new thinkers were young and clever (" our excessively clever people," writes R. P. Gillies,[1] looking back), and, scorning the accepted boundaries, they led the way out to the uncharted seas. For them whatever was, was wrong, and, above all, religious faith was a pitiful delusion. And Crabbe, in his tale of the learned boy, shows how a lad of weak character soon foundered in the welter of these ideas in the towns, because, by 1800, it would have been hard for a man to have been unmoved by them, they were in the very air.

THE effect of the Revolution was felt most widely at the beginning. Its ideas took root in England almost before the upper classes were aware of what was going on. In the words of Mathias : " the visionary prospect from the shore of France opened on the eyes of our modern Reformers. England looked upon these Reformers, and the government neglected them. Societies, in the very face of an insulted legislature, boldly multiplied, and magnified, and consolidated each other. All grew up in silence. There was no publick apprehension among the well-affected, no distrust. We laughed at metaphysical distinctions, and idle terms of scholastick art, and at revolutionary dinners, and republican toasts. It was an hour of general and of unaccountable indifference."[2] But the indifference was only at the top ; else-

1 See R. P. Gillies, *Memoirs of a Literary Veteran* (1851), i. 137–141.
2 T. J. Mathias, *The Pursuits of Literature*, Advertisement to Part III (1812), p. 156.

where the ideas were very welcome, and the enthusiasm thoroughly genuine. Thousands, as well as Wordsworth, found it " bliss in that dawn to be alive."

IT was not till the extremities in France roused horror and fear, that the generous enthusiasm of liberal minds was checked. Then men were alarmed lest those in England who shared the same ideals should give them expression in the same atrocities. The sudden marked increase in the reading of the working class, and its character and its effects, were ominous signs. Of 1794 Gillies writes that " at that date the works of Voltaire and Tom Paine were reckoned class-books for infidel argumentators. The sneers, irony and sarcasm of the one, and the complicated sophistries of the other were reckoned most dangerous ; indeed, *were* dangerous reading ; from which the inference is almost unavoidable that the previous education of the readers had not been very exemplary. They were, indeed, but poorly fortified by sound knowledge or logical discipline, if their minds could be swayed and their previous creed upset by such productions. Many were so swayed, however."

IN the early nineties *The Rights of Man*[1] and *The Age of Reason* were for a while selling in thousands. Both Burke and Paine were eagerly read and discussed by men to whom political speculation was a new, indeed the first, intellectual adventure. Helen Williams, fresh back from France where she had been a Girondist, became a political writer with her *Letters written in France* of 1790, and brought her ideas into her novels,

---

[1] Timperley, *Dictionary*, p. 772, says 150,000 were sold in 1791.

74

like *Perourou, the bellows mender*, and found a good public. There came in fact " a swarm of free-thinking and democratical pamphlets," such as Thelwall's *Politics for the People : or Hogswash*, and the Government became frightened. In 1793 Richard Phillips, the bookseller, then in Leicester, was imprisoned for eighteen months for selling *The Rights of Man*, and in 1794, in one of those periodical outbursts of political frenzy that seize the English nation, came the trials for high treason of Hardy, Horne Tooke, Thelwall and Holcroft. The reaction set in with a partisan fury that shocked such a youth as the poet Campbell, who witnessed with the passionate disgust of a lad of seventeen the prejudice of the trials in Edinburgh. There, according to Lord Cockburn,[1] the judges were terrified, absolutely strained for convictions, and passed fierce sentences of transportation. In Scotland Henry Dundas, as representative of the Government, was absolute dictator, and feeling ran so high that " even in private society, a Whig was viewed somewhat as a Papist was in the days of Titus Oates."

BUT no amount of reaction among the elders and the Tories could stop the new intellectual ferment. In his account of Scotland (and the conditions were not very dissimilar in England) Cockburn states of the last years of the century : " Grown-up people talked at this time of nothing but the French Revolution and its supposed consequences ; younger men of good education were immersed in chemistry and political economy." Favourite authors were Lavoisier and Adam Smith, and of the latter Cockburn says, " the young, by which

1 See Cockburn, *Memorials of his Time*, chap. i.

I mean the liberal young of Edinburgh, lived upon him. With Hume, Robertson, Millar, Montesquieu, Ferguson, and De Lolme he supplied them with most of their mental food. But the food of the liberal young was by no means relished by the stomachs of their seniors. It all tended towards awakening the intellect and exciting speculation, which were the very things that most of the minds that had been formed a little earlier thought dangerous." [1] But the severity of the reactionaries had, according to Cockburn, other effects than those intended. "The trials," he says, "sunk deep not merely into the popular mind, but into the minds of all men who thought. It was by these proceedings, more than by any other wrong, that the spirit of discontent justified itself throughout the rest of that age." [2]

THE important thing was that the French Revolution had awakened the intellect and excited speculation in England. Education might, and did, become suspect as savouring of Jacobinism. Coleridge considered one of the factors which made against the success of his *Watchman*, the avowal of his conviction "that national education and a concurring spread of the Gospel were the indispensable condition of any true political amelioration." The country clergy might do their best to suppress it along with Methodism. In fact Whitbread's Bill of 1807 to introduce compulsory education in parish schools, was stripped of its compulsion by the Commons, and rejected without a division by the Lords, because the Archbishop of Canterbury complained that it did not leave enough power to the clergy. But

1 Cockburn, *Memorials of his Time*, pp. 41–2.   2 *Ibid.*, p. 94.

no man could put back the clock, and stop the thinking and the reading which had become so general. The pamphlet and the periodical went on with their propaganda. Coleridge had for the mottoes of his *Watchman* ' Knowledge is Power,' and ' that all might know the truth, and the truth might set us free,' and he was only one of many moved by the same motives. Their papers were as so many small stones thrown into the waters of popular thinking, and the circles went criss-crossing out and out.

THE consequence was a nation of readers greater than Johnson had lived to see, so that Mathias declared in 1797, " We no longer live in an age of ignorance. . . . Our peasantry now read the *Rights of Man* on mountains, and moors, and by the wayside." [1] And when Godwin came along, enthusiasm for the new ideas swept off more thousands. About 1800 " he blazed as a sun in the firmament of reputation ; no one was more talked of, more looked up to, more sought after, and wherever liberty, truth, justice, was the theme, his name was not far off. No work in our time [Hazlitt's] gave such a blow to the philosophical mind of the country as the celebrated *Enquiry Concerning Political Justice*. Tom Paine was considered for the time as a Tom Fool to him, Paley an old woman, Edmund Burke a flashy sophist. Truth, moral truth, it was supposed, had here taken up its abode, and these were the oracles of thought. ' Throw aside your books of chemistry,' said Wordsworth to a young man, a student in the Temple, ' and read Godwin on Necessity.' "[2]

---

[1] T. J. Mathias, *Pursuits of Literature*, Advertisement to Part IV (1797), p. ii.
[2] Hazlitt, *Spirit of the Age* (1904), p. 24.

In fact his effect on young men was exhilarating. Crabb Robinson tells us in his diary, the mere reading of his famous and notorious book made the heart of generous youth beat even more generously, and flushed the mind with sure and certain hopes. IT was the same with young men of all classes. The best the upholders of the old order could do, was to accept the new habit of reading, and to reply as widely and as popularly as they were able. It did not matter that the revolutionary books in their original form might be beyond popular reach. As Mathias bewailed, " It is not enough to say, a book is bulky and voluminous, and therefore can have no effect on the mass of the people, because that opinion is not true. Such a book can not only be abridged and dispersed abroad ; but a man like Thomas Payne, with a rude, wicked and daring manner of thinking, and with vulgar but impressive language, may blend the substance of the opinions with his own, and in a short popular tract make them familiar and intelligible to every apprehension. Thus are men *fooled* out of their understanding, *fooled* out of their security, and *fooled* out of their happiness." [1] So the Anti-Jacobins began their own short popular tracts. And it was Hannah More who, at the suggestion of friends, took on the task of writing pamphlets for the lower classes to counteract the revolutionary ideas. Her initial effort, a tract *Village Politics*, was so remarkably successful in its sale that she and others were encouraged to project a series of tales, songs and dialogues with a moral, simply written and adapted to people of poor education.

1 T. J. Mathias, *The Pursuits of Literature*, Advertisement to Part III (1796), p. i.

THUS began the series of *Cheap Repository Tracts* [1] which circulated very widely for the three years, 1792 to 1795, three instructive little tales appearing monthly. In the first year two million tracts were sold, and their popularity was well maintained, but, as they were sold at a nominal price, the projectors were finally left with a loss. Very many of them were of such general elementary Christian instruction that their importance as an indication of an increase in reading is not to be estimated too highly. Thousands, too, were sent abroad to help missionary work. [2] But in their way they are another sign of the growing tendency to think and to read.

ANOTHER phase of these years which has its bearing on the growth of the reading public, was the way in which some of the class barriers were passing away. That meant a freer interchange of ideas. The class to which literature had formerly been almost confined was no longer a class apart. Culture ceased to be the privilege of so small a circle. The love of letters and the talk of books were shared with an ever-increasing number of newcomers. Even the close preserves of the Universities were invaded by the new people and the new ideas, and the change is noted thus by Mathias : " I know not into what form our University may at last be changed. . . . It may be *supported* by the violation of every principle of academick dignity, and by an unworthy familiarity

---

1 See A. M. B. Meakin, *Hannah More*, pp. 314–20. A typical title of a tract by Hannah More is *Turn the Carpet : or, the two weavers : a new song in a dialogue between Dick and John.* Its " object is to vindicate the justice of God in the apparently unequal distribution of good in this world by pointing to another."

2 See a letter of the Bishop of London, Jan. 16, 1797. " The sublime and immortal publication of the *Cheap Repository Tracts* I hear of from every quarter of the Globe. To the West Indies I have sent ship-loads of them. They are read with avidity at Sierra Leone, and I hope our pious Scotch missionaries will introduce them into Asia." Meakin, *Hannah More*, p. 320.

of learned gownsmen with mechanicks and shop-
folks. It may become an appendage to the
Corporation of the Town of Cambridge. Are *we*
not elbowed on the floor of our own Senate House
by an impudent, unqualified intrusion of borough-
mongering mercers, and rustling men-milliners ?
. . . Let the University of Cambridge, however,
be converted into anything, but a seminary for
French principles and *tutorial* democracy." [1] The
trend is evident from his fears ; while the same
change in Edinburgh is related by Lord Cockburn,
who tells that around 1800 Edinburgh underwent
a rapid transformation due to the increase in the
population and the rise of the New Town, with
the result that " the aristocracy of a few pre-
dominating individuals and families came to an
end."

MUCH more might be said of the other forces of
that time which stimulated the reading public.
There was the birth of new thought in theology,
shown in the appearance of the new translation of
the *Bible* by Dr. Geddes, with a preface denying
the plenary inspiration of the Old Testament.
And, above all, there was the swelling revolt
against the old barriers of literary taste, and the
inflowing tide of the Romantics.

INDEED, between 1794 and 1805 there was a
complete revolution in literary taste, which could
not help but draw on more and more readers by the
greater interest and charm of the new school. It
was heralded largely in Germany, and by 1793 the
German version was beginning to become known
in England. Among the first to spread it was
William Taylor of Norwich with his translations

1 Mathias, *The Pursuits of Literature* (1812), p. 276, note 38.

and his critical notices in the reviews. Coleridge and Scott contributed their share, and from Crabb Robinson's diary we gather that the vogue was in a few years a widespread one. And its general effect was to broaden literary taste and to lessen its insularity, and so to educate the reading public. Romantic literature seems by its very nature to beget readers. It has much more of the siren note. It is also more essentially popular. The spirit and appeal of Elizabethan literature had on the whole a popular quality which was absent in the literature of the succeeding generations until it came again in the writing of men like Scott and Byron. The poetic tales of both and the novels of Scott could stir the heart of the least literate of men. And that spirit of much of the Romantic Revival must have accounted for a great deal more reading.

(vii)

ALTOGETHER it is beyond dispute that the reading public increased considerably in the last twenty years of the century. And the record of the number of books sold indicates that the demand in those days was quite large. The first impression of Hannah More's *Percy* in 1778 was 4,000, and it was bought up almost at once. The whole of the first impression of Boswell's *Journal of a Tour to the Hebrides* was sold in a few weeks, and it passed through three editions within a year. When Cowper's *John Gilpin* caught the popular fancy and he rivalled in fame Mrs. Bellamy, and the Learned Pig, it sold everywhere, and one London printseller (for, as a ballad, it was published with a print) disposed of six thousand copies.

81

Cowper, writing in 1791 to New York, said : " I send you . . . *The Importance of the Manners of the Great*, and *An Estimate of the Religion of the Fashionable World*. [They] are said to be written by a lady, Miss Hannah More, and are universally read by people of that rank to which she addresses them." [1] In fact, the former tract went through five editions in a very short time. And in another letter also of Cowper's there is a suggestive passage. Writing to Lady Hesketh of his *Homer* when the quarto edition was out of print, he declared, " the bulk of readers are those who purchase octavos : the rich only can afford quartos, and they read nothing. My proper business therefore is to consult the inclinations of the former, who have long clamoured for an edition that they can afford to purchase." [2] In that " clamoured " and the previous " universally " we may read something to our purpose. Then it is said that the poems of Peter Pindar were read very extensively at the end of the century, and the fact that Walker, the publisher, gave Wolcot £250 a year for their copyrights is sufficient proof that the sale really was extensive. Again, Lackington's statement that " sometimes I have purchased six thousand copies of one book, and at one time I actually had no less than TEN THOUSAND COPIES of Watts's Psalms, and the same number of his Hymns, in my possession," [3] is further corroboration.

A VERY instructive example is *The Pleasures of Memory*. Its first edition in 1792 was only 250, but it passed through four editions, probably of 250 each, in the year, and each year up to 1800

---

1 Letter, 15/6/91, to Dr. James Cogswell (Southey, *Life*, vii. 32).
2 Letter, 30/6/93 (*Ibid.*, vii. 213).   3 *Memoirs*, p. 230.

another edition was called for of 1,000 copies, and in two years two editions, so that by 1800 there had been 8,000 copies printed. It is a steady demand for a poem of a limited appeal. And in 1799 it met a rival in *The Pleasures of Hope*, whose popularity began with a second edition of 2,000 in its first year. Of the latter " it was said that the lover presented it to his mistress, the husband to his wife, the mother to her daughter, the brother to his sister ; and that it was recited in public lectures, and given as a prize volume in schools." [1] But *The Pleasures of Memory* kept equal with it, with fresh editions of 1,500 each in 1801 and 1802, and of 2,000 each in 1803 and 1806. It is a fair indication of the growth of the reading public.[2]

THIS general tendency for the last years of the century is affirmed by Lackington, and, as he was actively in trade as a bookseller at the time, he should be a sound judge. " I cannot help observing," say his *Memoirs*, " that the sale of books in general has increased prodigiously within the last twenty years. According to the best estimate I have been able to make, I suppose that more than four times the number of books are sold now than were sold twenty years since. The poorer sort of farmers, and even the poor country people in general, who before that period spent their winter evenings in relating stories of witches, ghosts, hobgoblins, etc., now shorten the winter nights by hearing their sons and daughters read tales, romances, etc., and on entering their houses, you may see *Tom Jones*, *Roderick Random*,

[1] Beattie, *Life of Campbell*, i. 265.
[2] For sales of *The Pleasures of Memory* see Clayden, *Early Life of Rogers*, pp. 216-7.

and other entertaining books, stuck up in their bacon-racks, etc. If John goes to town with a load of hay, he is charged to be sure not to forget to bring home *Peregrine Pickle's Adventures* ; and when Dolly is sent to market to sell her eggs, she is commissioned to purchase *The History of Pamela Andrews*. In short all ranks and degrees now READ. But the most rapid increase of the sale of books has been since the termination of the late war with America." [1]

YET general as reading was becoming, we must not imagine it too general, but should remember that there were many people of good middle-class position like Coleridge's tallow-chandler who cried out in alarm at the thought of a periodical of thirty-two pages, large octavo, closely printed : " Thirty-two pages ? Bless me ! why except what I does in a family way on the Sabbath, that's more than I ever reads, Sir, all the year round. I am as great a one, as any man in Brummagem, Sir ! for liberty and truth and all them sort of things, but as to this —no offence, I hope, Sir—I must beg to be excused." [2] But Lackington's estimate of a fourfold increase remains. And that increase was only the beginning.

(viii)

THAT the profession of letters improved in its conditions along with the growth of the public seems a probable deduction, but direct evidence is not very plentiful. The drama certainly continued to be the most profitable field for an author. Its greater profits, the copyright for publication being well paid in addition to the author's third-

---

[1] *Memoirs*, p. 250.   [2] *Biographia Literaria*, p. 90.

nights, had accounted for many an earlier author writing for the stage without particular dramatic talent, like Thomson, and even Johnson. The usual price given for the copyright had risen from £50 in Queen Anne's reign to £100 in the middle of the century, and to £150 by 1770. Then it suddenly increased very much more, at least for an exceptional play such as *The Road to Ruin*, for which Holcroft received in 1791 from £300 to £400, while the profits from the theatre were £900. Hannah More's *Percy* in 1778, in addition to her £150 for the copyright, made some £400 for her during its run of twenty-one nights. And when *Evelina* came out a few months after *Percy* and Fanny Burney had only a few pounds for it, her friends urged her to try next something for the stage.

INDEED, if we may judge from the industrious achievements of Holcroft, the drama had great attractions for an author who needed money. In 1783 Colman advanced him £100 in anticipation of the success of *The Noble Peasant*, and in 1784, when, by his great feat of memory, he had succeeded in pirating in Paris *Le Mariage de Figaro* and had translated and adapted it as the *Follies of a Day*, his profits were £600 from the theatre as well as a considerable sum for the copyright. For years he maintained himself comfortably by his dramatic output. And Richard Cumberland and George Colman the younger made good sums, while Murphy, though in his last years he was poor, had always boasted of the money he had made by his plays.

IN fact, despite the increase in reading, reading had not begun to compete with play-going, and, according to Leigh Hunt, the theatre at the end of the century was more popular than in the succeeding years. " I speak," he says in his *Autobiography*, " of my own feelings, and at a particular time of life : but forty or fifty years ago people of all times of life were much greater play-goers than they are now. They dined earlier, they had not so many newspapers, clubs, and pianofortes ; the French Revolution only tended at first to endear the nation to its own habits ; it had not yet opened a thousand new channels of thought and interest ; nor had railroads conspired to carry people, bodily as well as mentally, into as many analogous directions. Everything was more concentrated, and the various classes of society felt a greater concern in the same amusements. Nobility, gentry, citizens, princes—all were frequenters of theatres, and even more or less acquainted personally with the performers. Nobility intermarried with them ; gentry, and citizens too, wrote for them ; princes conversed and lived with them. Sheridan and other members of Parliament were managers as well as dramatists. . . . The Kembles, indeed, as Garrick had been, were received everywhere among the truly best circles : that is to say, where intelligence was combined with high breeding." [1]

So the theatre retained much of its pride of place as a source of income for writers into the early years of the next century, although novel-writing was already a close rival. Nor should we omit the opportunities offered to a man whose profession was literature by the popular entertainments at Vauxhall. In the nineties it was still in its prime.

[1] *Autobiography*, pp. 134-5.

"Vauxhall Gardens," Boswell says, "must ever be an estate to its proprietor, as it is peculiarly adapted to the taste of the English nation ; there being a mixture of curious shew—gay exhibition—music, vocal and instrumental, not too refined for the general ear—for all which only a shilling is paid."[1] There, too, a literary man of all work could find employment for his pen. Holcroft in 1777, before he had won success in the theatre, was writing popular songs for Vauxhall, and the sailor songs of Charles Dibdin, selling in their thousands, had their place there as well.

BUT poetry lost ground while the stage and the novel gained it. For it was a sad day for poetic inspiration. The Augustan vintage, more or less diluted, was still the general favourite, and it was for the most part very mediocre stuff. From 1778 to 1785 the poet of the day, unless Miss Seward could be said to share his honours, was William Hayley. His frigid epistles on Painting, and History, were good enough to win approval in the dearth of poetic talent in those years. And then he strutted as a moralist on prosaic stilts of verse through the dreary *Triumphs of Temper* of 1781. The way in which he spoke of his own purpose would be enough to put off a modern reader. "His observation," he said, "of the various effects of spleen on the female character induced him to believe that he might render an important service to social life, if his poetry could induce his young and fair readers to cultivate the gentler qualities of the heart and maintain a constant flow of good humour."[2] But such prosing in verse was acceptable in his own day. One mother at least

[1] *Life of Johnson*, iii. 308.   [2] Hayley, *Memoirs*, p. 207.

87

wrote to thank him for the " absolute and delightful reformation in character of her eldest
daughter." The popularity of the poem lived
on for twenty years, with a steady demand for it as
a school-prize or as a present.

MEANWHILE Crabbe had his first success, gained
general praise and an established reputation, and
passed into silence for twenty years, during which
the public had only popular *Elegant Extracts*
to remind them of him. Then came Cowper's
Task (for his first volumes had fallen flat), and it
gained a " success as immediate as it was complete
—except *The Rosciad* there had probably been no
instance of a poem obtaining so rapidly a great
reputation." [1]   But even then it had as a rival in
public esteem Charlotte Smith's Sonnets, and they
kept what Cowper thought their " well deserved
popularity " for several years.   In fact, it needed
the French Revolution to lift the poetry of Cowper
nearer its proper level, and then it became the
admired poetic stand-by of Evangelicals against
the insidiousness of Jacobinism.

THE poets, or rather the versifiers, who made the
most noise in the late eighties and early nineties
were Merry and his Della Cruscans.   They were
the poetic revolutionaries, flaunting their un-
creative unrest in the eyes of the latter-day
Augustans.   To-day they seem unutterably feeble,
Merry with his ten-guinea patent of creation as a
Count of the Holy Roman Empire hanging in his
parlour, and all the rest of the " namby-pamby
school of modern English Cruscans."   But, in the
poetic quiet and convention of their time, the
select poetry of *The Gentleman's Magazine* still

1 Southey, *Life of Cowper* (1835), ii. 174.

being hardly distinguishable from any of the
middle of the century, their crackers spluttered
and banged in many an ear. Bell, the publisher,
" thought the Della Cruscans fine people, because
they were known in the circles." But they soon
went out " with a smoke and a stink " when
Gifford turned his clear, cold satire upon them.
Their sole credit was that they gave birth to *The
Maeviad* and the *Baviad*, those last clear drops
from the cask of Popeian satiric vintage. Their
efforts for a change were of no effect. And the
century went out with the old school still in favour
as far as the general reader went. Satire lived to
the last in *The Pursuits of Literature* and *The
Anti-Jacobin*, and Rogers, with his growing name,
was hardly less an Augustan than Akenside,
perhaps with just a touch of something more
mellow and roseate than the earlier poets had
possessed. So unbroken was the Peace of the
Augustans, despite the stacks of unpublishable
vision that Blake was accumulating in his room,
that in 1799, when Campbell published *The
Pleasures of Hope*, he appeared like a meteor, and
" the world was taken by surprise at the vigour
of thought and richness of fancy."
IT had been one of the honourable marks of the
Augustan period that poetry had had the place
of honour with critics and public alike, but as
that age declined, the love of poetry seems to have
declined too with the wider public. Perhaps
the comparative dearth of good poetry contributed to the lapse of poetry from favour. But
the new readers were, as a whole, less interested
in it than in prose. Not that they did not continue to honour the English poets, but it was the

established English classics which they chiefly read and honoured. The fact that the popular editions, except Bell's, omitted Chaucer and Spenser, is a sign that the public was not very ripe for the new movement. And as in our own day we find working-class students a little inclined to be suspicious of the values of literature, so then it is noticeable that instructive, informative prose was beginning with the new readers to come before poetry, and that poetry was less read and poets more poorly rewarded.

AMONG professional men it was not so. The father of James and Horace Smith, himself an occasional writer for the reviews, encouraged his sons to write verse, and introduced one boy to Dr. Johnson. But among the new merchant class the feeling of Isaac D'Israeli's father was commoner, who was " seriously alarmed " when he found his son a budding poet. " The loss of one of his argosies, uninsured, could not have filled him with more blank dismay. His idea of a poet was formed from one of the prints of Hogarth hanging in his room, where an unfortunate wight in a garret was inditing an ode to riches, while dunned for his milkscore." [1] So " the unhappy poet was consigned like a bale of goods " to a commercial correspondent at Amsterdam. The rising private schools, too, the commercial Academies, would probably foster a love of poetry less than the grammar schools, however inefficient, had done with their classical curriculum. And, again, the growing volume of journalism might leave readers less time and inclination to turn to the poets.

[1] I. D'Israeli, *Works* (1858), i. p. xii.

AT any rate the general esteem of poetry, though
not that of the older literary public, seems to
have dwindled. Commercially poetry declined.
Hayley thought the prices Dodsley gave him
" very liberal," but social position probably was
with him, as with most, a reason for it. Hayley
had private means and was the friend of Pitt
and Gibbon. But Crabbe could hardly get a
hearing. Dodsley told Burke that he could not
himself risk accepting the *Village* because in
the matter of poetry " there was no judging of the
probability of success. The taste of the town was
exceedingly capricious and uncertain." [1]   And
though Crabbe gained in his first years a high place
as a poet, he gained little money by his reputation
until 1819 when Scott and Byron had altered the
whole standard of prices for copyright.

COWPER did not set out to make money, and gave
his bookseller the rights of the first two volumes.
But when he began to bargain over *Homer*, he
did not find the bookseller, in spite of the success
of *The Task*, inclined to make much of an offer.
" His first proposal," complained the poet,
" which was to pay me with my own money,[2] or,
in other words, to get my copy for nothing, not
only dissatisfied but hurt me ; implying, as I
thought, the meanest opinion possible of my
labour ; for that for which an intelligent man will
give nothing, can be worth nothing. . . . His
second offer, which is to pay all expenses and
give me one thousand pounds next midsummer,
leaving the copyright still in my hands, is more
liberal. With this offer I have closed." [3]   And

[1] Crabbe, *Life and Works*, p. 27.
[2] i.e. the money he had received as subscriptions.
[3] Southey, *Life of Cowper* (1835), iii. 10.

that offer seems a very good one, but the fact that Johnson, of whose liberality Cowper and others always spoke very highly,[1] should have made that first proposal suggests some very serious hesitation about the market value of poetry.

CAMPBELL sold the copyright of *The Pleasures of Hope* for £60, and although after his success he realized it was worth " an annuity of £200 for life," he was not surprised at what he had originally got because " poetry is generally considered by the ' trade ' as a commodity by which money is more likely to be lost than gained." Indeed, it is not unfair to quote as typical examples *Gebir* and the *Lyrical Ballads*. The former, though much praised, was little read, and De Quincey claimed that " he and Southey were the sole purchasers " ; and the latter, for whose copyright Cottle had given Wordsworth and Coleridge thirty guineas each and of which he had printed five hundred copies, sold so slowly that Cottle was glad to dispose of most of them at a loss to a London bookseller and gave back to the poets their valueless rights.

IN fact the only man who really made money by poetry in the last decades of the eighteenth century was Wolcot, and not even he with his first *Odes to the Royal Academicians*, for on them he lost £40. It was only the coarse, wanton satire of the *Lousiad* and of *Ode upon Ode*, ridiculing with their rollicking buffoonery the king's private life, that made his fame. In them " the novelty and boldness of his style and his reckless intrepidity carried the million with him," so that his copy-

---

[1] e.g. Letter of Cowper, July 1791. " I verily believe that, though a bookseller, he has in him the soul of a gentleman."

92

rights were worth the annuity of £250 which Walker paid him up to the end of his life. But his success is scarcely a true exception, for there is no ware so marketable on its first production as strong topical satire. Churchill had found that so twenty years earlier. And Wolcot soon had to give in when the King's madness made his theme unpopular, and Gifford and *The Anti-Jacobin* lashed with scorpions " the profligate reviler of his sovereign, and the impious blasphemer of his God."

IT was the novel that, with the progress of the circulating library, was coming most into favour. From the middle of the eighteenth century, when they were but just founded, until to-day the charge has always been made that such libraries are frequented for the greatest part by mere novel-readers. Coleridge spoke scathingly of the " devotees of circulating libraries," and said that their reading was on a level with " conning word by word all the advertisements of a daily newspaper in a public house on a rainy day." But that was no bad thing if we only consider the man who wanted to earn his living by literature and to whom fell the chance of supplying this growing demand. He could not well have too many " gluttons for novels." And gluttons for novels need not be a bad kind of public to write for. Leigh Hunt labelled himself one. And his son says of Crabbe in the nineties " that even from the most trite of those fictions, he would sometimes catch a train of ideas that was turned to an excellent use ; so that he seldom passed a day without reading part of some such work and was never very select in the choice of them." He would walk along the green lanes around Glemham of a summer evening, with his wife, and children, reading some novel aloud to them ; indeed, he wrote three himself, but consigned them to his periodic bonfires. And, if we would see from one example the grip which the circulating libraries had on many readers and the proportion of novels read, we can look at a list of the books which Miss Mitford took from one in a month about 1804 and which she presumably read or glanced at, when she was a girl just back from school. The list includes : [1]

St. Margaret's Cave.
St. Claire of the Isles.
Scourge of Conscience.
Emma Corbett.
Poetical Miscellany.
Vol. 4 of *The Canterbury Tales.*
Midnight Weddings.
De Clifford.
Vincenza.
A Sailor's Friendship and a Sailor's Love.
The Castles of Athlin and Dumbayn.
Polycratia.
The Citizen's Quarter.
Robert and Adela.
Travels in Africa.
The Novice of St. Dominick.
Clarentina.
Leonora.
Count de Valmont.
Letters of a Hindu Rajah.
Amazement.
The Three Spaniards.

1 G. E. Mitton, *Jane Austen*, pp. 168–9.

Nor are indications wanting that she was by no means a rare devotee. We find Jane Austen also writing in a letter : " Our family who are great novel readers, and not ashamed of being so." And very few were ashamed except the readers of *The Christian Observer* and its editor Mr. Zachary Macaulay, who, " morning or evening, disapproved of novel reading."

TOWARDS the end of the century there were some very good novels written. The principles of the new school of political philosophy found expression in the novels of ideas produced by Bage and Holcroft and Godwin. They wove their theories into their plots, but, although they hung up their stories while their characters talked their ideas, they generally had the grace of pleasing to atone for the fervour of doctrine. They were wild and visionary where their characters were phantoms of the human perfectibility to come, but they were vivid and lively where they kept to the delineation of ordinary life. And even where, as Hazlitt said of *Anna St. Ives*, Holcroft dealt with a philosophical hero and heroine who were " the organs through which the voice of truth and reason is to breathe and whose every action is to be inspired by the pure love of justice," there is a naïve charm which must have had a strong appeal in those heady years. Bage presented the new Utopianism in *Hermsprong, or Man as he is Not*. Holcroft, somewhat as Mr. H. G. Wells does, expressed the new political idealism in *The Adventures of Hugh Trevor*. And Godwin wedded the doctrine of *Political Justice* to the novel of suspense to bear *Caleb Williams* and *St. Leon*. And in that world of melodrama, which Godwin

95

thus entered, there was a very considerable enchantress in the person of Mrs. Radcliffe, " a poetess," in the eyes of Mathias, whose satire left few unlashed, " whom Ariosto would with rapture have acknowledged." [1]

BUT the great majority of the novels of that age were poor stuff. Crabbe speaks of " the flowing pages of sublime distress " to which he " early gave his sixpences and tears " :

> " I've watch'd a wintry night on castle-walls,
> I've stalk'd by moonlight through deserted halls,
> And when the weary world was sunk to rest,
> I've had such sights—as may not be express'd."

Gifford wrote that " there is a certain class of novelists in whose drama nothing is real : their scenes are fancy, and their actors mere essences. The hero and heroine are generally paragons of courage, beauty and virtue ; they reside in such castles as were never built, in the midst of such forests as never grew, infested by such hordes of robbers and murderers as were never collected together." [2] For as Mathias said, " [Walpole's] Otranto Ghosts have propagated their species with unequalled fecundity. The spawn is in every book shop." Mathias, in fact, is thoroughly scornful of the novel in general.

> " Say must I tempt some *Novel's* lulling theme,
> Bid the bright eye o'er *Celestina* stream ? "

And to *Celestina* he appends the note : [3] " Put for almost any modern novel. Mrs. Charlotte Smith, Mrs. Inchbald, Mrs. Mary Robinson,

1 Mathias, *The Pursuits of Literature* (1812), p. 72, note 26.
2 Crabbe, *Life and Works*, p. 240, note.
3 Mathias, *The Pursuits of Literature* (1812), p. 72, note 26.

Mrs. etc., though all of them are very ingenious ladies, yet they are too frequently *whining* or *frisking* in novels, till our girls' heads turn wild with impossible adventures, and are now and then tainted with democracy, and sometimes with infidelity and with loose principles." Mathias " cannot condescend among all the modern farrago of novels, which are too often, as they have been named, receipts to make whores." And so he dismisses " all such works as abound in what is called in modern jargon, the sublime instinct of sentiment." But one novel he could not pass over in his general condemnation. *The Monk* was too " full of open and unqualified blasphemy." But neither could his satire destroy it ; it was too popular.

So the writing of novels took its place prominently in the profession of letters. Godwin made good bargains for *Caleb Williams* and *St. Leon.* He arranged his contracts before a line was written, and lived on the produce of them at the same time as he was composing them. Fanny Burney published her mediocre *Camilla* by subscription and gained about £3,000. Novels had become one of the first branches of literature to which an author in need of money looked. When Crabbe was fighting poverty in London in 1780 he confided to his diary : " I don't know whether I shall not write a Novel; those things used to sell, and perhaps will now." [1] And certainly they would for some price, though perhaps a small one. Egerton Brydges began in 1792 with an anonymous novel, *Mary de Clifford*, of which he said, " it found its way without name, advertisements or the smallest interference on my part ; and after a few

[1] *Life and Works*, p. 18.

months the publisher soliciting to buy the copyright of me I sold it for a mere trifle, happy to release myself from the expense of printing and paper."

THERE is a good indication of the tendency in Hayley's *Memoirs* where it is stated of his religious novel *The Young Widow* of 1788 that, though it was not popular, it was " of considerable service to the writer in supplying him with a sum of money. . . . For this he was partly indebted to the zealous friendship of Dr. Warner who sold the novel for him to a respectable bookseller for £200,"[1] which was a very respectable price considering that Swift got only as much for *Gulliver's Travels*. For the time was fully come when most professional men of letters turned at some period of their career to the novel, as in 1792 did Charles Dibdin, who broke away from his sailor songs and dramatic pieces to write *Hannah Hewitt* and *The Younger Brother*.

THE hacks too had plenty of work in supplying Lane's Minerva Press which sent out a large number and variety of popular novels, which were the mainstay of the circulating libraries and for which the writers were usually paid from £10 to £20. And the level of the hack novel it did not require much talent to reach. According to Gillies : " a three volume novel of the year 1794 might well have been scribbled in a week, for it had come to be an understood convention that each volume of a truly fashionable romance should contain just as much of printing as might conveniently be perused during one sitting, under the manipulations of a fashionable friseur ! "[2]

---

[1] W. Hayley, *Memoirs*, p, 377.   [2] R. P. Gillies, *Memoirs*, i. 5–6.

BUT the most obvious field to enter for a man who set out to live by his pen was the ever-widening field of journalism. Small though it is compared with the press of to-day, the newspaper world of 1780 seemed to its own day already a big thing. " Now," said Johnson in 1778, " they have a trick of putting everything into the newspapers." In 1787 Bishop Horne wrote : " Amongst the improvements of modern times there is none on which I find more reason to congratulate my countrymen than the increase of knowledge by the multiplication of newspapers. At present the provision made for us is ample. There are morning papers for breakfast, there are evening papers for supper—I beg pardon, I mean dinner ; and, lest during the interval wind should get into the stomach, there is a paper published by way of luncheon about noon." [1] And that ample provision tended constantly to become ampler. The better papers achieved a continuity of existence instead of a short life and a change of title. *The Morning Post* had been founded in 1772 and *The Times* in 1785. Soon the Sunday newspaper appeared. *The Oglio* was running in 1784, and *The Observer* was founded in 1791. Then as the mail coaches sped farther, and quicker, and more frequently along the roads, so did the circulation of the newspaper expand, and the number of newspapers in Great Britain and Ireland, from being seventy-nine in 1784, rose by 1834 to be nearly four hundred. But, up to 1800 at least, their quality was poor. Crabbe wrote in his preface to *The Newspaper* in 1785 that " until I see that paper wherein no great character

Crabbe, *Life and Works*, p. 126, note 13.

is wantonly abused, nor groundless insinuation wilfully disseminated, I shall not make any distinction in my remarks upon them," although he felt bound to add that " it must, however, be confessed that these things have their use; and are, besides, vehicles of much amusement." [1]

FOR the time, however, the newspapers were not very closely connected with literature. It was not until the next century that men of first-class literary talent, like Coleridge and Hazlitt, gave the Press the service of their pens. Meanwhile it was supplied for the most part by hacks and volunteers. The prospects for the hack opened, as we have noted earlier, with work like the five shilling a column political notes which Holcroft wrote for *The Whitehall Evening Post*, and the guinea and a half a week reporting. In 1782 we find Holcroft making of the latter a means of maintenance for a journey to France. On those terms he engaged to send over paragraphs on events of the day, on public amusements, on fashions and so on, for *The Morning Herald*, and he had a similar contract with Rivington to supply him with notices of new works and with translations. It was very useful odd work which gave him opportunities for producing something better as well ; and soon he rose to be a popular dramatist and novelist. But there is hardly another name so great as Holcroft's associated with newspaper journalism of that day. It was, in Professor Saintsbury's phrase, an " office-boy " period, in which most of the writing was done by literary drudges, men like the George Dyer whom we meet in the pages of Crabb Robinson's

---

1 Crabbe, *Works*, p. 125.

diary, who " made indexes, corrected the press, and occasionally gave lessons in Latin or Greek."

YET, however poor the work and the workers, there was a growing power in the Press, and it began spreading down to the lower classes, becoming more and more the reading matter of the less educated. It encouraged them to read and stimulated their interests. And as its public grew, it needed better writers, and many young men thinking to live by literature set out to serve their apprenticeship to it. For in addition to the newspapers there were the reviews and magazines. THESE latter, too, were multiplying. They were quite well circulated by 1780, when such an ordinary man as Crabbe's father, in a provincial town like Aldborough, took in Martin's *Philosophical Magazine* and Wheble's *Lady's Magazine*, in which latter the son became a profuse versifier to Mira and other sentimental damsels of his imagination. In the following years one new magazine succeeded another. In 1783 Murray started *The English Review*, in 1788 Johnson began *The Analytical Review*, in 1793 came Rivington's *British Critic*, and in 1796 appeared the *Monthly Magazine* of Phillips under the editorship of Aikin. From the earlier period survived the *Monthly Review* and the *Critical Review*, and new and old, there were others, particularly new.

AGAIN they were poor stuff in themselves, so feeble that the *Edinburgh Review*, when it came, seemed something wholly different, but they performed their service of helping to prepare a public, and not less important, of helping to prepare a generation of writers. They made journalism a good first rung on the ladder of the profession of letters, so that a man could support himself on it while he summoned the strength and the means to climb higher, and journalism was something on which a man could always fall back for support between other and bigger undertakings. Cowper seems to have made small but useful sums by contributing to the *Analytical Review.*

WOLFE TONE, studying law in London in 1784, helped to make both ends meet by reviewing for the *European Magazine*, and it brought him some £50 in two years. About the same time Thelwall was trying to get a footing in literature by editing the *Biographical and Imperial Magazine* for £50 a year, making perhaps another £50 by contributions to other magazines. But Thelwall dropped out of literature for a time, and when he was considering its prospects as a second string to other schemes ten years later, he had the advice of Coleridge, then a newcomer to the profession, and Coleridge's letter gives a good idea of the general position. " For your comfort," he wrote to Thelwall,[1] " for your progressiveness in literary excellence, in the name of everything that is happy, and in the name of everything that is miserable, I would have you do anything honest rather than lean with the whole weight of your necessities on the Press. Get bread and cheese, clothing and housing independently of it ; and you may then safely trust to it for beef and strong beer. . . . £50 you might, I doubt not, gain by reviewing and furnishing miscellanies for the different magazines ; you might safely speculate on £20 a year or more from your compositions published separately—

Coleridge *Letters*, ed. E. H. Coleridge, i. 214.

$£50 + £20 = £70$; and by severe economy, a little garden labour, and a pigsty this would do. And if the education scheme did not succeed, and I could get *engaged* by any one of the Reviews, and the new *Monthly Magazine* I would try it, and begin to farm by little and slow degrees. You perceive that by the Press I mean merely *writing without a certainty*. The other is as secure as anything else to you."

COMING from Coleridge, that is a fair admission that the journalistic side of the profession of letters, though not able of itself to support the free-lance, was able to support quite considerably the regular worker. Indeed, for a time Coleridge threw himself wholeheartedly into it. In December 1799 we find him writing to Southey [1] : " I am employed from I rise to I set (that is from nine in the morning to twelve at night) a pure scribbler. My mornings to booksellers' compilations, after dinner to Stuart, who pays *all* my expenses here, let them be what they will ; the earnings of the morning go to make up an hundred and fifty pounds for my year's expenditure. . . . For Stuart I write often his leading paragraphs on Secession, Peace, Essay on the French Constitution, Advice, etc., etc., to Friends of Freedom, Critiques on Sir W. Anderson's Nose, Odes to Georgiana Duchess of D., Christmas Carols, etc., etc."

THAT was the miscellaneous work to which a writer in his first years must put his hand. It was the same as in Goldsmith's day, but with the difference that the field was much wider. Goldsmith had indignantly rebutted the emissary

---

[1] Coleridge, *Letters*, i. 319.

of a patron and told him he could earn enough by his pen. And in these later days failure to support himself by writing must even more have been a man's own fault. Poor journalists there were, but to such always applies the comment which Leigh Hunt passed on one Badini, editor of the *Weekly Messenger*, who " looked the epitome of squalid authorship." " I had never before," he says, " seen a *poor author* such as are described in books, and the spectacle of the reality startled me. Like most authors, however, who are at once very poor and very clever, his poverty was his own fault." Badini's enemy was the alehouse, and Hunt adds, " I have since met other authors of the same squalid description ; but they were destitute of ability, and had no more right to profess literature as a trade than alchemy. It is from these that the common notions about the poverty of the tribe are taken." [1]   And he would have us believe that, in the days of his youth at the beginning of the century as much as in the days of his commentary in 1850, any man who had a right to profess literature, had the power to profess it to profit. CERTAINLY Hunt himself found little difficulty in making a start. " I had been told," he says, " but could not easily conceive that the editor of a new evening paper would be happy to fill up his pages with any decent writing," [2] yet about 1805 it was so, and Hunt began as an essayist in the *Traveller*. And this reminds us that there is one other aspect of the magazines that deserves notice, which is the value they were to the unfledged young writer. Kirke White, as a boy of fifteen, contributed prose and verse to the *Monthly Magazine*, the *Monthly*

[1] Leigh Hunt, *Autobiography*, p. 151. [2] *Ibid.*, p. 137.

104

Visitor and the *Monthly Mirror*, and there were no doubt many who similarly gained experience and confidence. Crabbe had been encouraged by a prize in a magazine to go on practising verse. In fact it was as Southey said : " Magazines are of great service to those who are learning to write ; they are fishing boats which the Buccaneers of Literature do not condescend to sink, burn and destroy : young poets may safely try their strength in them ; and that they should try their strength before the public, without danger of any shame from failure, is highly desirable." [1]

(ix)

IN the publishing world, also, this period was one of steady progress. Business advanced slowly. The first John Murray in his quarter of a century of publishing from 1768 to 1793, with all his industry did not double his capital. He began to push the Indian, and West Indian and Irish markets, but as a publisher he was above all cautious. It was an age of consolidation in ' the trade,' after the considerable advance made by men like Strahan, and Cadell and Dodsley. The publishers kept what they had made and expanded their dealings with prudent foresight. As yet there were no signs of that brilliant *flair* which Constable was to show. Change was coming, but it was coming almost imperceptibly. For years the fiction of perpetual copyright had a certain reality in the continued sale of shares in such old books as *Tom Jones*. The earlier spirit of co-operation still held men together, although a new spirit of competition was inevitably making its

1 *Works of Henry Kirke White*, ed. Southey (1852), p. 10.

way into publishing, and in the early years of the nineteenth century shares in the *Rambler* and similar works were still changing hands.

BUT innovation there was in smaller things such as Carnan's successful invasion of the claim of the Stationers' Company to the sole rights of publishing almanacs,[1] and Bell's substitution of the " s " for the old f-like character, and in a bigger thing in the invasion we have noted earlier of Lackington into the remainder market. The old popularity of subscription as a method of publication was passing, too. Johnson the bookseller was against the scheme of subscription for Cowper's *Homer*, but Cowper insisted. He found, however, that though his list was a good one " he would have liked it as well had it been more numerous," and a friend who tried his influence for him at Oxford received for answer that they subscribed to nothing there. Perhaps the objections to subscription were being realized which Dr. Johnson had pointed out : " He that asks subscriptions soon finds that he has enemies. All who do not encourage him, defame him. He that wants money will rather be thought angry than poor ; and he that wants to save his money conceals his avarice by his malice."

BUT while these changes took place, one side of the publishing trade retained an old and excellent custom. Publishers and authors still gathered together at the festive table of the former,[2] and

1 See W. West, *Recollections of an Old Bookseller.*
2 An example of this happy custom in the earlier days is given in the following anecdote. " Hume told Cadell the bookseller that he had a great desire to be introduced to as many of the persons who had written against him as could be collected ; and requested Cadell to bring him and them together. Accordingly Dr. Douglas, Dr. Adams, etc., were invited by Cadell to dine at his house in order to meet Hume. They came ; and Dr. Price, who was one of the party, assured me that they were all delighted with David." Rogers, *Table Talk*, p. 67.

in the booksellers' shops authors met as formerly to talk. In Debrett's bookshop in the late nineties there would be Holcroft discussing the perfectibility of human nature, and the laws of morality, and the nonsense of saying that death is inevitable. It meant greater intimacy in the world of letters, both between one author and another, and between an author and his publisher. On the one hand the brotherhood of men of letters had a genial meeting-place wherein to share its ideas, and on the other a kindly and appreciative spirit of co-operation was fostered between the author and his publisher.

THE general spirit of the ' trade ' was a liberal one. That is evident in nearly all mention that writers made of their booksellers. Hayley admitted that Dodsley always gave him " very liberal prices," although he added that " he had a most ungracious mode of grumbling at his bargains without reason for complaint." But grumbling from one or other party was quite usual, and did not affect the average of their mutual esteem. Even Cowper had his moods of doubt and would write of Johnson to a fellow-grumbler, " I am not much better pleased with that dealer in authors than yourself," but such moods soon passed and his more usual tone is that in which he wrote of the winding up of the *Homer* accounts, that " I am now satisfied with my bookseller, as I have substantial cause to be, and account myself in good hands," [1] and later, when the question arose of a second edition that " his behaviour has been so liberal that I can refuse him nothing."

IN fact, those who spoke harshly of booksellers

1 Southey, *Life and Works of Cowper*, vii. 196.

were frequently those who had most cause to speak well, like Wolcot with his saying that "booksellers drank their wine in the manner of the heroes in the hall of Odin, out of authors' skulls." Reliable testimony is that of Lackington : " I promised in my last," he wrote, " to give you a few remarks on purchasing manuscripts; and as I seldom make such purchases, being out of my line, and but rarely publish any new books, I think you may fairly credit me for impartiality. Nothing is more common than to hear authors complaining against publishers, for want of liberality in purchasing their manuscripts. But I cannot help thinking that most of these complaints are groundless ; and that were all things considered, publishers (at least many of them) would be allowed to possess more liberality than any other set of tradesmen, I mean so far as relates to the purchase of manuscripts and copyright." [1]

THE price of £1,500 which Phillips gave Holcroft in 1804 for his *Travels into France* is one which might be quoted as a good example of generosity, while the experience of Campbell over *The Pleasures of Hope* is another. It is true that the copyright was sold out and out for £60, but Campbell justly remarked, " let me not forget that for two or three years the publishers gave me £50 on every new edition." And he added, " when his resources were so scanty and precarious, the immediate possession of a very moderate sum might very easily seem preferable to the uncertain expectation of a very great one. Nor is the publisher to be censured for his want of

[1] *Memoirs*, p. 225.

liberality : the author was an obscure young man ; and few booksellers are disposed to incur the risk of publishing the works of a Poet so untried and unknown." [1] Three years later a London publisher offered £200 a year for life ; and certainly that was a very liberal offer.

THE only illiberality for which Lackington found occasion to blame booksellers was their attitude towards an author who did not sell them the copyright or agree for a share of the profits, but who wished to use them merely as agents to publish his books. " In general," he wrote, " where authors keep their own copyright they do not succeed, and many books have been consigned to oblivion, through the inattention and mismanagement of publishers, as most of them are envious of the success of such works as do not turn to their own account ; very many just complaints are made on his head, so that I am fully of opinion, that for authors to succeed well, they should sell their copyright, or be previously well acquainted with the character of their publishers. Many works might be mentioned that never sold well, whilst the author retained the copyright, which had a rapid sale after it was sold to the trade : and no wonder, for if the publisher wishes to purchase the copyright, he sometimes will take care to prevent the sale of the work, in order to make the author out of conceit with the book, and be willing to part with the copyright for a mere trifle ; but this is only true of some publishers ; I am sorry that any such should be found, but I am sure as to the fact." [2]

BUT that was an illiberality on their part which an

---

1 Beattie, *Life of Campbell*, i. 236.   2 *Memoirs*, p. 229.

author had little, if any, need to court. He need seldom sell his copyright altogether, but could secure good terms for the rights to the first or other editions. If he contracted for a share of the profits on an edition he also had a good bargain, for as high a division as two-thirds of the profits would sometimes be his. That was the proportion for which Gibbon agreed for the first edition of the opening volume of the *Decline and Fall*. And if he could not secure two-thirds, he would very generally obtain half-profits, the terms on which Adam Smith published the later editions of *The Wealth of Nations*. But to make the publisher in some degree a proprietor of his book, and not to try to be his own publisher and to leave the publisher only as agent to collect his profits, that was the prudent course. And a professional man of letters would naturally take it, for he would realize that the bookseller stood to him in the profession of letters (using that term widely) in something of the same way as the solicitor stands to the barrister in the profession of the law. And for another reason there is what Coleridge said as the result of his experience with his *Friend*: "The most prudent mode is to sell the copyright, at least of one or more editions, for the most that the trade will offer. By few only can a large remuneration be expected; but fifty pounds and ease of mind are of more real advantage to a literary man than the chance of five hundred with the certainty of insult and degrading anxieties": words which, he added, were not written with any "desire of detracting from the character of booksellers or publishers."[1]

1 *Biographia Literaria,* p. 87.

THE chief complaint the public could find with the booksellers, or rather with the main publishers who brought out new books, was that in these years they were raising the prices of new works beyond what the general reader could afford to pay. The bigger firms, after they had lost their prerogative in lapsed copyrights, left very largely the sale of cheap books to the new men whose claims had defeated theirs, and concentrated themselves on the production of new publications. And they went on the principle, a bad one for the middle-class people who wanted to keep up with contemporary literature, that the sale of a few books at a high price was as good as the sale of many cheaply. Cowper's *Homer* may serve as an example of the practice and of the complaint it called forth, and Cowper leaned to the side of the publisher. " That the price should be thought too high," he wrote, " I must rather wonder. The immense labour of the work considered, and the price of Pope's first edition also considered, which was seven guineas, it does not appear to me extravagant. I question if there is a poet in the three kingdoms, or in any kingdom, who would sell such a commodity for less. Two or three guineas may now be as important as seven were fifty years ago, and I suppose that they are ; but if everything else is grown cheaper, why should the produce of the brain in particular grow cheap ? We may comfort ourselves, too, with reflecting that twenty subscribers at two guineas are just as good as forty at one." [1]

THE pocket of publisher and author alone considered, that fact might be comfort, but not

[1] Southey, *Life*, v. 283.

if we put first, or even equal (which is their least due), the needs and pockets of the public. And the pity was that the high prices which kept the audience, apart from the extension which the facility of the circulating libraries could afford, so selectly limited, went just to beautify the external format. For, from about 1780, according to Nichols, publishing entered on " an age of luxurious printing and high prices." [1] The day began of costly artistic editions such as that of Milton which Boydell and Nicol projected in 1792, to have a life by Hayley and designs by Westall. It was one of the evils of the age against which Mathias wrote in *The Pursuits of Literature.* " The paper ? " asks he. " Yes ; ten shillings every quire."

> " In one glaz'd glare, tracts, sermons, pamphlets vie,
> And hot-press'd nonsense claims a dignity."

And he adds the note : " I allude to and condemn the needlessly expensive manner of publishing most pamphlets and books at this time. If the present rage of general printing on fine, creamy, wire-wove, hot-press'd paper is not stopped, the injury done to the eye from reading and the shameful expense of the books will in no very long time annihilate the desire of reading and the possibility of purchasing. *No new work whatsoever should be published in this manner*, or Literature will destroy itself." [2] It is a pity that satire should so often thus overcharge itself with exaggeration, but the purpose of Mathias was a sound purpose. Yet the publishers of the years

1 Nichols, *Literary Anecdotes*, iii. 464.
2 Mathias, *The Pursuits of Literature* (1812), p. 199, note 56.

round 1800 maintained their principle of twenty copies at two guineas, and continued as a general rule to bring out books of any pretensions in quarto at a price not less than two guineas a volume.

IT was the new men in ' the trade ' who went out to meet the public. Theirs was the enterprise, and the old-established firms kept their dignity and caution. Some of them had unhappily a tendency to speculate in trash. Of them the prince was Lane with his Minerva Press. He poured out his novels one after another like a swarm of gaudy insects fluttering out their brief life in a dazzling burst of fashionable sunshine. The readers who were pleased by the sparkle of their tinsel must have been child-like in their tastes, but for some years they sold wonderfully well, and as Lane paid his authors little for them, he grew a rich man on the proceeds. Rogers could " perfectly remember the splendid carriage in which he used to ride, and his footmen with their cockades and gold-headed canes."

THE enterprise of other men like Bell, Cooke and Harrison (with their popular reprints in ' numbers ') we have already sufficiently noticed.[1] In addition, the provinces began to develop more, although not very considerably, their presses. Before 1800 there was no daily paper published outside London, but some progress there was in provincial newspapers and bookshops. And the most progressive bookseller in the provinces was Richard Phillips, later the eccentric vegetarian caricatured in *Lavengro*. In 1790 he established

1 See above, pp. 57–59.

himself as a stationer at Leicester selling books, and what was then not an uncommon side-line, patent medicines. Soon he added music and a circulating library. And next, in 1792, having set up a press, he, together with Dr. Priestley, founded and edited the *Leicester Herald*, and used it zealously to uphold the rights of man. Indeed, his fervour in that cause led to his prosecution and imprisonment for selling Paine's book. Then came a fire which destroyed his shop, and so in 1795 he removed to London, set up the *Monthly Magazine*, and became a prolific publisher, and employer of hacks.

PHILLIPS was a man with a shrewd eye to profits, as the anecdote of his hearing Coleridge talk suggests, when he said how he " wished he had him up in a garret." " Dirty little Jacobin," as some called him, he looked to the people for his sales, and made the supply of cheap manuals and elementary class books the chief part of his business. And by them he won a fair fortune, and rose to the aldermanic bench and a knighthood. Nor is he undeserving of the honour of posterity, for he helped to educate and build up the reading public. He set out to give popular instruction to the people, when hardly a man made a step in that direction, but popular elementary education was still suspect of Jacobinism and of upsetting the social order. In fact he was the legitimate forerunner of the Chambers brothers and Charles Knight, whose literature for the people had the advantage of coming on the wave of the " New Broom " movement. Phillips was a herald of the March of Mind.

(x)

PATRONAGE was one of the most important aspects of which a study of the profession of letters in the half-century preceding 1780 had to take account. But its importance became less and less, until in the eighties it was of quite minor importance. A man who took to his pen for a living in 1780 gave patronage scarcely a thought. It had outgrown its use, which had been an honourable use when a writer could not well maintain himself without a patron. When he could not get a public to support him, because the reading public was too small, it was no shame to be dependent on a patron. By being so a writer could do better work than he could have done by struggling alone. But by the late fifties the support which the public could give was quite adequate. By then, too, the support which a patron was willing to give was very often thoroughly contemptible.

AROUND 1760 Johnson, and Goldsmith, and Churchill, and Foote, in a kind of chorus representative of their profession, spoke in one voice against the despicable ways of the would-be patron, and their voice was full of assurance. They did not need a patron any longer, because their patron was the public which had so quickly and steadily grown up, and which, as we have seen, continued just as steadily to increase. They were scornful in their confidence of good earnings. " Patron ! " says one of Foote's characters with shot-out lips, " the word has lost its use." [1] And, in fact, when patronage went out it went as something discarded in derision. For, though it would be nonsense

[1] Foote, *The Patron*, 1757.

to say that even by 1780 the conditions of author-ship were ideal, the conditions were certainly too good to justify patronage. Therefore patronage went unlamented, and henceforth it was just something occasional, the rare reward of a few writers who by no means always had merit as writers to recommend them. It becomes the story of a grant now and then from the Govern-ment through the pressure of influential friends, and of warm hearts here and there moved to help a talented young man.

So in 1780 when a man determined that litera-ture should be his profession, he had in his mind the bookseller with his demand for good work and for hack work too, and journalism and the public. If he was wise, he only thought of a patron as a figure of his grandfather's world. And the class which had formerly been patrons thought no more of patronage than he did. Crabbe [1] was distinctly old-fashioned in the way in which the hope of a patron seems to have been firmly at the back of his mind. He refused to understand that a man who wanted to live by his pen, must write what the public or the publisher wanted him to write as well as what he wanted himself to write. Because he did not keep his eyes open for the odd jobs of his profession, he watched his few guineas go and no more come, until in the fever of despair battling with his last hope he walked up and down Westminster Bridge all night after he had delivered his letter to Burke. Lord North, then Premier, and Lord Shelburne had both ignored his requests. Lord Thurlow sent him " for answer a cold, polite note, regretting that

1 See *Life and Works*.

his avocations did not leave him leisure to read verses.'' And Crabbe, thinking of the old days, answered him back in respectful but manly verse that the encouragement of literature had been formerly considered a duty belonging to the high position he occupied. But the Lord Chancellor took no notice whatever of this reminder. Though he might seek precedents in the past for the purpose of the law, he lived his life by the rules of the present, and in the present there was no rule of patronage. And so he was silent. It was his generosity that put in the poet's hand, one day after Burke had helped him make his name, a note for £100 in a sealed envelope, and that bade him say, " The first poem you sent me, Sir, I ought to have read—and I heartily forgive the second." [1] And, even without this later generosity of his, it is not hard to excuse him. For although Crabbe did indeed deserve patronage, it was because he was exceptional, and a busy man need not be ashamed of sparing the trouble to find out whether the poet who besought him was exceptional or not. It really required an exceptional man like Burke to do so.

ALSO when we consider what patronage secured for Crabbe after he had become the protégé of Burke, we find nothing to lessen, but all to confirm the impression that patronage had not much left to offer : Holy Orders were the only avenue of preferment, and they required some little negotiation to obtain for one whose education had been irregular, and but for Crabbe's for the most part self-gained knowledge of the classics it would probably not have been possible even

[1] Crabbe, *Life and Works*, p. 29.

with Burke's help. But Burke was able to get him ordained, and in the meantime served him with all the zeal of a friend. He introduced him gradually to his literary friends, and his wife and her niece were unwearied in their personal efforts to promote the sale of *The Library*. But even helped like this, and living as an honoured guest in the happy retirement of Beaconsfield, Crabbe was not quite comfortable, for he was not making money, and as Burke had too much delicacy to press it, he had from time to time the awkwardness of an empty pocket. Then followed the chaplaincy to the Duke of Rutland, and, though the Duke and Duchess were both very kind to him, he could not but feel the etiquette of the Castle irksome. He was glad to go to his curacy at Stathern, where he profited from his early experience to add the care of bodies to the cure of souls, and there he would spend happy hours interesting himself in botany and in geology. So Crabbe came to settle down as a country clergyman, comfortably preferred, but soon, by the Duke's early death in 1787, become ' of the old race ' as regards Rutland patronage and unable to expect more. And by entering the profession of the Church he had ceased to belong to the profession of letters. It was no longer a question of his living by his pen. He had the liberty to write, and to trim what he had written, and then to write again, which, no doubt, was a good thing, but when patronage led to that, it was the negation of literature as a profession. Such patronage must be a rare gift, and rarer, too, because not every man could fit into the Church so well as did Crabbe. If Crabbe had not had that aptitude, it would have been a harder thing still for Burke to have opened up for him another patronal avenue, for the gate of patronage was getting very narrow.

POLITICIANS no longer had gifts to bestow. What places they had were the necessary due of their political servants. The King's attempt to dominate had failed, and Johnson exposed the new position when he said that " the House of Commons is no longer under the power of the Crown, and therefore must be bribed." But under Pitt that bribery system of patronage, too, began to give way. Burke had brought in a sweeping scheme of economic reform, and that had abolished the greater proportion of the old superfluous sinecures and had also strictly limited the Pension List and the Secret Service Fund. Pitt's years of chill control and a close hand on the Exchequer confirmed the change, and by 1800 there was little to be given even to politicians. It was only with peerages that Pitt was lavish, and to them and not to offices the new politicians began to look. As for writers, they had long taken a back place. Gibbon had had a great position in a Government office with a good salary and negligible duties, but it had not been for his literature but for a pamphlet and his " sincere and silent " vote, and it went all too soon, to the commiserating distress of Hayley.

HAYLEY, indeed, was so moved by the threat to Gibbon's salary that he wrote in 1782 : " I shall hope, however, that if his revenue is diminished by the annihilation of the Board of Trade, some equivalent will be found to support the dignity of the Roman eagle. . . . If his appointment should be taken from him, without anything to counter-balance the loss, I apprehend he will retire into France, which would be not only an affliction to his friends, but a disgrace to our country. Indeed, I think our nation should form some kind of establishment to insure ease and independence to her most eminent men of letters." [1] But Hayley's apprehensions were fulfilled. Eminence in literature had to be its own reward. And in the next year we find Gibbon writing to Robertson, that if " the means of patronage had not been so strangely reduced by our modern reformers, I am persuaded [Lord Loughborough's] constant and liberal kindness would more than satisfy the moderate desires of a philosopher." But the strange reduction had taken place and not even moderate desires were to be satisfied.

IN particular the personality of Pitt was inimical to patronage of literature. Its charms counted little more with him than the charms of women. A pamphlet by one Montagu, a member of Parliament, reproached him for his " improvident and systematic contempt and neglect of all ability and literary talents," while Mathias says that he views alike

> " The fount of Pindus or Bœotia's bog,
> With nothing of Mæcenas, but his frog."

Where he patronized it was indiscriminately, a mere " wholesale rule " under which

> " Left to themselves all find their level price,
> Potatoes, verses, turnips, Greek, and rice,"

so that Mathias justly said : [2]   " I must own that

---

1 Hayley, *Memoirs*, p. 269.   2 Mathias, *The Pursuits of Literature* (1812), p. 121.

unless the province of encouraging Letters, which should belong to the great, is administered with wisdom and discretion, it is more desirable that there were no encouragement at all." And again, commenting on the instance of Burns, also in the time of Pitt, Mathias thought that " greater liberality might have been *prudently* exerted to obtain an adequate employment, and a safe as well as honourable support for A MAN destined to bear up the full fame and dignity of ' THE POET OF SCOTLAND ' instead of the strange and unaccountable occupation [of exciseman] which they *conferred* on him." [1]

PERHAPS Pitt did have some of that feeling which Coleridge attributed to him and to politicians generally. " All men in power," Coleridge held, " are jealous of the pre-eminence of men of letters ; they feel, as towards them, conscious of inferior power. . . . So entirely was Mr. Pitt aware of this, that he would never allow of any intercourse with literary men of eminence ; fearing, doubtless, that the charm which spell-bound his political adherents would, at least for the time, fail of its effect." [2]

AT any rate, the record of patronage to Pitt's credit is very small. There is William Combe, whose connexion with him earned a pension of £200 ; and there is Pye, who had the laureateship in 1790 probably because as member for Berkshire he had had his uses, certainly not for his poetry, of which it is description enough to quote Southey's saying : " I have been rhyming as doggedly and dully as if my name had been Henry James Pye."

1 Mathias, *The Pursuits of Literature* (1812), p. 357, note 173.
2 S. T. Coleridge, *Table Talk*, ed. T. Ashe (1884), p. 313.

There is, again, Dibdin, who for some time had a pension of £200 from the Government " for the loyalty of his songs," which sold so well in the troubled days of muttered revolution. And there should be mentioned Peter Pindar, whom the Government once thought to bribe from his attacks and from his bid for the Prince's favour by a pension of £300, an arrangement which, however, broke down on the details and was given up because Wolcot himself gave up too. All which examples, when we are considering the relation of patronage to the profession of letters, come to very little indeed.

BUT all the same, we must remember as well certain pensions which seem linked more closely with the King himself than with his First Minister. For from his accession George III had shown a very pleasing and honourable patronage of literature and of art. We think at once of the pensions and the audiences he gave to Johnson and Beattie. In addition there was the £100 a year which he bestowed on Henry the historian in 1781 on the recommendation of the Earl of Mansfield, and in 1794 the £300 which came to Cowper after the efforts of Hayley and other friends, while the poverty of the last days of the once successful and prosperous Murphy the dramatist was relieved by a pension in 1803.

HOWEVER, the King's example, even in his early years when he most sought to patronize, was an isolated example. In those years, too, the King could look round for himself. But the time came when he wanted prompting, and there was not anyone to prompt him. For patronage was not in the mind of the age any more. Johnson in 1775 had reflected thus at St. Andrews : " The dissolution of St. Leonard's College was doubtless necessary ; but of that necessity there is reason to complain. It is surely not without just reproach, that a nation, of which the commerce is hourly extending, and the wealth increasing, denies any participation of its prosperity to its literary societies ; and while its merchants or its nobles are raising palaces, suffers its universities to moulder into dust." [1] And the nation and the Government went on forgetting men of letters as having any particular claim upon them.

IT remains to consider the patronage shown here and there by kind hearts to deserving men whom they chanced to know. For naturally there were generous men and women in the world then as there may be now, whom we cannot forget but whose existence does not at all indicate a general habit of patronage among their contemporaries. Burke's kindness we may be sure was at the service of not a few beside Crabbe. At Beaconsfield he would now and then patronize a band of strolling players and help to replenish their wardrobe. And there was a Mrs. Mathew, " whose door and purse were constantly open and ready to cherish persons of genius who stood in need of assistance in their learned and arduous pursuits, worldly concerns or inconveniences." [2] It was she who asked her husband to join Flaxman in paying the expenses of printing Blake's *Poetical Sketches*. And Blake found other patrons—Butts, who once took fifty copies of his drawings at a guinea each, and Hayley, with whom he stayed at Felpham and to whose

[1] *Journey to the Western Isles*, ed. R. W. Chapman (1924), p. 7.
[2] J. T. Smith, *Nollekens and his Times*, ii. 367.

kindness Southey paid tribute with "there is nothing bad about the man except his poetry." While for a noble but inconspicuous patron there is the example of Cookesley the country surgeon, "one of Nature's gentlemen," who brought Gifford out of the rough and tumble of his youthful life by buying up the remainder of his apprenticeship to a shoe-maker, raising subscriptions for his education, and with the help of his friends obtaining for him the post of Bible reader at Exeter College, Oxford.[1] That was in 1779, and the offers of help to send him to the University which Kirke White, too, had, in 1805, show that there were quite a few generous folk in the provincial towns, for according to Southey "there were many friends of literature who were ready to have afforded him any support he had needed, if he had not been provided for" by the scholarships he won.

In Ireland something of the old spirit survived. Lady Moira was a prominent patroness there in the last years of the century and the early years of the next.[2] But in England, apart from these scattered examples, the only general tendency to patronize is seen in the foundation in 1792 of the Literary Fund. It had been projected first in 1773, but it did not at that time get beyond talk. Like so much philanthropy it required some shocking example to spur its projectors into doing something, and it was the sad death in a sponging house of Sydenham, who had devoted his life to a laborious version of Plato, that appears to have brought about the actual foundation. Then, once it

<hr/>

[1] See *Memoir of Gifford* (a collection of the most instructive lives, etc., vol. xi., 1827), pp. 18-21.
[2] See W. J. Fitzpatrick, *Lady Morgan : her career, literary and personal.*

was founded, the Literary Fund, no doubt, did help many who deserved its help. But in the story of patronage what a miserable dwindling it is from the magnificence of Montagu to the dreary efforts of organized relief.

(xi)

EXCEPT that after a few years he was one of the very lucky ones who gained a government pension, the experience of Campbell[1] is a fair example of the conditions of the profession of letters at the turn of the century. In 1797 he was in Edinburgh with an impulse to the law but with insufficient money to pay a premium, and his idea was to obtain employment in a lawyer's office and from there to make his essay into literature by writing for the periodicals. He had been early devoted to poetry and he had nearly ready two translations from Euripides and Æschylus for which he was ignorantly confident he could find a publisher. But he could not, because with the general reader eclipsing the learned public, publishers were looking out for more popular work. So he began with the drudgery of a copying clerk, and kept his eyes open for the chance to write.

THAT chance came when an introduction to Dr. Anderson, the well-known man of letters who " acted as editor-general to all incipient poets," led to a further introduction to the publisher Mundell. Then Campbell made a beginning. His first gain was £20 for abridging Bryan Edwards's *West Indies*, and in the winter of 1797–8 he was contributing to a geographical work. But

---

[1] See Beattie, *Life of Campbell*.

it did not pay very well, for Edinburgh publishers
had still to wake up, and he added coaching
to his labours. Then, he says, he had " a complete livelihood as long as [he] was industrious,"
and he worked on at *The Pleasures of Hope*. For
that he had the not unreasonable price, considering the risk of publishing new poetry, of £60,
and its success in the general dearth of good poems
was such that it gave him a wide circle of
acquaintance in Edinburgh. It went quickly
into a second edition of two thousand, for which
the publisher gave him another £50, and on the
strength of it he made a pilgrimage to Germany
to gain a first-hand acquaintance with the literature that was in those years coming into favour.

THEN in 1801 he settled in London. But his
fame did not introduce him into fashionable
society, as it would have done a generation or so
back. It opened to him only the literary circles,
where he met such people as Mrs. Inchbald, and
Mrs. Barbauld, Dr. Burney, Mrs. Siddons and the
Kembles, and in higher society he met as friends
only Rogers and Lord Holland. And " no profession, no lectureship, no ' appointment ' was
forthcoming." He had really to live by the pen by
which, before he had tried it, his ambition had
urged him to live. And so he set to upon literary
journey-work, and he writes in 1802 : " I have been
engaged in supplying an Edinburgh bookseller
with anonymous and consequently inglorious
articles in prose—a labour, in fact, little superior
to compilation and more connected with profit
than reputation." [1] This work was *Annals of
Great Britain* in three volumes, paid by £100 a

[1] Beattie, *Life of Campbell*, i. 405–6.

volume, and after it he wrote a continuation of Smollett's history for a sum he considered " not sufficient to put my name to it." But he earned his living, and could, no doubt, have gone on earning it without the pension that came to him in 1805 through the influence of Lord Minto and Lord Holland. In fact, by 1803 he was writing : " I have but a few rivals in my own way in the literary world, and find my station in literature such as will with a very little money in my pocket (just enough to get over the necessity of asking for employment) enable me to command my own terms with the booksellers." [1]

To receive a pension certainly was very welcome, but as surely it was unnecessary. Campbell had proved that the profession of letters was able to support him, albeit with some drudgery inevitable, and if he had not thrown up that profession as his mainstay, he might have accomplished more in literature than he did, for it was his favourite saying " that necessity, not inspiration, was the great prompter of his Muse." And if it had not been for the good fortune that had singled him out, he would have had to rely on literature. Nor, in some moods, is it easy to see why he should not. If he wished to make literature his profession, it was there to be followed. If it entailed drudgery so did any other. But if he wanted literature to be the love of his leisure, he should have taken the advice of Rogers and been a clerk. It is almost possible to hear a scornful Johnson saying, " Sir, there was a good public, and liberal booksellers, and you should not have let yourself be seduced by a pension."

Beattie, *Life of Campbell*, i. 447.

CHAPTER II

IN THE DAYS OF SCOTT AND CONSTABLE,[1] 1800–1832

(i)

IN the world of letters the new century opened quietly. Cowper's pitiful death was but a passing long expected and the popularity of his poems went on just as steadily increasing among the ranks of the evangelical. The flashing daggers of the satirists were sheathed. Crabbe maintained his rustic silence. There was seemingly nothing to break the dull level of mediocrity, and all was languid, journalism, the drama, poetry and the novel, each alike. Those who sat in the seats of honour were Hayley, Godwin, Holcroft, Mrs. Radcliffe, and writers of a similar inferior calibre. Young men, indeed, were astir, Coleridge and Wordsworth, and Southey and Landor. The public, however, were not yet aware of them.

YET there were two young men of whom in 1800 no one was expecting anything unusual, but who were between them to change the face of things with almost the quickness and wonder of magicians. The one, Walter Scott, in the

---

1 The following works are constant authorities for the whole of this chapter : S. Smiles, *A Publisher and his Friends* ; Mrs. Oliphant, *William Blackwood and his Sons* ; Clayden, *Early Life of Rogers* ; Clayden, *Rogers and his Contemporaries* ; T. Constable, *Archibald Constable and his Literary Correspondents*.

leisure of preparing for a career in the Parliament House of Edinburgh, was busy with the old ballads that had charmed him from boyhood. He collected them with the twin zeal of a poet and an antiquary, and his zest for literature found other expression in his translating the ballads of the newly fashionable German literature. The other, Archibald Constable, three years younger, had served his apprenticeship to Mr. Hill of Edinburgh, the bookseller to whose shop it had been the habit of Burns, and was still the fashion of the professors and clergy to resort. He had, also, had some experience in London, especially with Longmans, and since 1795 he had kept his own business in Edinburgh. But so far he had published only a pamphlet or so. When he had ventured to acquire his first copyright he had paid £100 for a volume of *Discourses* by Dr. Erskine, and he was so conscious of the risk he ran that he shared it with Mr. Creech, the aristocrat of the bookselling trade in the northern capital, because, for one thing, he felt that Creech's name would add respectability to the title page : for Creech was well known by his breakfasts to the literati. Constable's business in old Scottish books was then almost as important as his publishing, perhaps more so, because in the flush of an antiquarian revival his good knowledge of early books made him much sought after, and highly respected. He, like Scott, was laying the foundations, and the next twenty years saw both raising on them many fine buildings. For Constable had in his way hardly less imagination than Scott had in his. They were two magi who created great castles in the air, and brought them down to earth with all their magnificence intact. Between them, the circumstances of the age agreeing, they made the world of letters a different world and the profession of letters a real profession, in possibility, indeed, a princely profession.

FROM their youth both Scott and Constable were Edinburgh men, and Edinburgh in those days was a capital that could rival London. It had as individual a character as any capital of Europe. Its university was famous for the learning of its professors. Up to 1800 essentially conservative, its legal and commercial houses had preserved something of an exclusive aristocracy. Henry Mackenzie had lingered long to be an honoured centre of a literary circle. It was a city of literary taste, and, when *The Pleasures of Hope* appeared, Campbell was soon noticed and was invited everywhere. The first panic years of the French Revolution passed, and Edinburgh emerged to outward appearance unchanged. Henry Dundas made of his secretaryship an autocracy, and Toryism still reigned supreme. But then the new generation in the new century began to make itself felt. Youth began its war against authority. The Whigs broke in upon the Tory ascendancy, and Jeffrey and Sydney Smith together with Constable launched the *Edinburgh Review*. And the launching of that journal was the greatest event that had happened in the profession of literature for at least half a century. In addition it ensured the reign of Edinburgh in glory for some twenty years. Its power and excellence were for seven years unrivalled, and for long it drew many of the best English critics into its own company of Scotch reviewers. In fact, for a time the lead in literature passed from London to Edinburgh.

AND it was only fitting that the new initiative should come from the North, for the North it was that had led the way towards that great blessing for the public, the abolition of claims to perpetual copyright and the coming of cheap reprints. Donaldson, the great protagonist in that cause, had also been an Edinburgh man. " Magnificent Donaldson," as young Boswell enthusiastically called him in 1761, made a fortune by cheap books, and when he left some of it to found a hospital he was by that but little more a benefactor to his fellows than he had been by running that very business which had made him rich. And in his day the bookselling trade of Edinburgh had prospered. A visitor to the city in 1774 found it the most profitable trade of the day. " If I am well informed," he said, " many thousand volumes are annually printed in this place and sold in London or elsewhere. The cheapness of labour here when compared with London, induces many Scotch booksellers who reside there to have their books printed in Edinburgh, and then sent to them : which they find better than printing at their own shops ; and for this purpose many of them have partners in this place." [1] And he notes that " a bookseller in this city, who is not only a polite man but a man of letters, is now printing a complete set of English classics in duodecimo, which, with the addition of a very handsome binding, amount only to eighteenpence a volume." [2] So that side of bookselling prospered, and al-

1 *Letters from Edinburgh*, 1776, B.M. 10370, aa. 25.
2 *Ibid.*

though the publishing of original works was very small, and in fact till the end of the century almost negligible, that was not without its compensations. It saved Edinburgh from having a Grub Street. Indeed, in Robertson's day it could be said that the trade of authorship was unknown in Scotland. So the honour of literature stood all the higher, and, when Scotland began to lead England in literature, the Scotch feeling that literature was something too fine and sacred to be produced merely for money gave a better tone to the profession without in the least diminishing the pecuniary rewards.[1]

BUT although Edinburgh led, London was not really left behind. The London trade was too well established. It had the experience of years and was ready to emerge from the stage of quiet consolidation. And it could meet a rising demand all the better because its publishers were accustomed to thinking and dealing in considerable sums. The new men in Scotland were not. Constable had to go to London to get some real acquaintance with publishing, and Adam Black, whose apprenticeship, " a deadly and disgusting servitude," began at the end of the century, has said that during it the only bookselling house that kept their accounts with any degree of accuracy was that of Bell and Bradfute.[2] Thus the new publishers, Constable and later the Ballantynes, were inclined to be rash because their enthusiasm had insufficient of the discretion of experience to check it, though Blackwood and Black were wiser and advanced more gradually.

---

[1] For life in Edinburgh, see Cockburn, *Memorials of his Time.*
[2] See Adam Black, *Memoirs.*

And naturally, as London must be the centre of the reading public, Constable and the Ballantynes and all who wished for big sales had need of London publishers in all their enterprises. For the *Edinburgh Review* itself a London agent was essential. And the London trade was quite ready to turn the genius of Scott into gold when the chance first came. Longman, when the second edition of the *Lay* was called for, responded with an offer of £500 for the copyright, and he added £100 later. It was true enterprise, for it was a price, as Scott said, " that made men's hair stand on end."

BUT then Constable stepped in at the very commencement of *Marmion*, and made the bold and generous offer of £1,050 for the poem that was only begun—an offer which, when it later became known, startled the whole literary world.[1] For some years the Wizard and the Czar of the North (to use the names of their later fame) were close together, despite not infrequent clashes, and they blazed unrivalled until Byron and Murray became a kind of opposed partnership. And then Murray, with little less enterprise than Constable but greater prudence, began quickly to rival, equal, and finally eclipse the boldly and carelessly insecure brilliance of the Edinburgh firm. But Constable had been the pioneer genius of publishing.

IN estimating the advance in the profession of letters it is always hard to decide what proportionate share in it the different parties had. Sometimes the public seem to push on the publishers, sometimes the publishers to draw on the public,

[1] Lockhart, *Life of Scott* (Edinburgh, 1902), iii. 4.

sometimes the authors to arouse the publishers and the public too. Here it seems perhaps more than anything to have been the personal magnetism of Scott and Constable, and Byron, and in a less degree Murray, drawing the public and other authors after them. Certainly the genius of Scott and Byron had a tremendous effect on the reading public. Their poetry appealed as poetry can never have done before. The passionate verse of Byron reached even to the working man and gave him a refuge in imagination from the hard life of post-war depression and industrial misery. The middle classes delighted in Scott and bought thousands of his poems and his novels, and even when Byron shocked them they could not help reading him.

WE have seen how the reading public grew steadily in the years before, when the average of contemporary literature was so mediocre, and it was only natural that people who wanted to read and had so far had little chance of the best to read, should besiege the bookshops and sit up all night to read the latest Waverley novel. The public was like a child enchanted with fairy tales joyfully found after a dreary acquaintance with prosaic moralizing. And the child was an Oliver Twist too. The wonderful thing would have been if the public had not grown. But it did. It became more acquainted with literature. It grew to want, and it came to receive good critical journalism. One new journal succeeded another. And, as far as the profession of authorship was concerned, there was constantly more for a writer to write and more people for him to write to. The opportunities and rewards of authorship multiplied. The national life became more literate in spite of the oppression of the long drawn-out struggle with Napoleon. That checked development, but it did not stifle it. The need of the poor and their demand for education became a pressing matter. The schools of the richer became more efficient. The universities put off their slumber. The presses of the publishers had to work their hardest. Publishing seemed bidding fair to stand out as the great business of the century.

(ii)

ALL these tendencies (into which we shall look in detail later) set the profession of letters well on its feet. It became an age of professional authorship, and in the ranks of the professionals were men of the first class. There were Southey, Leigh Hunt, Hazlitt, Coleridge, Gifford, Galt, and Washington Irving. Nor is it straining to include Scott after his first years, for the money which he earned he was compelled to earn by the necessity of ambition and later of debt, and he had in truth, despite the competency of his clerkship, no more freedom than the man whose compelling necessity was for money to live. And of the lesser men in that latter company there are plentiful records to show that the profession was then a very fair one for the man of good talent. There are the names of Gillies, and Laman Blanchard, and Croly, and (with reservations for his Shandonism) Maginn, to pick a few.

THE lives of Scott and Byron show at their highest the possibilities for very great genius.

135

Even for the *Minstrelsy* Scott obtained £500. The copyrights of his poetry rose to the great price of £4,000 for *The Lady of the Lake*. Byron's prices from Murray, though for long he would not take the money for himself, were little inferior. Starting with £600 for the first two cantos of *Childe Harold*, he averaged 500 guineas for such tales as *The Corsair* and *Mazeppa*, had £2,000 for the third canto of *Childe Harold*, £1,575 for the first two of *Don Juan*, with the *Ode to Venice*, and in 1821 received £2,710 for the rights of *Sardanapalus*, *The Two Foscari*, and *Cain*. He noted once in his diary " Mr. Murray has offered me one thousand guineas for the *Giaour* and *Bride of Abydos*. I won't. It is too much : though I am sorely tempted, merely for the say of it. No bad price for a fortnight's (a week each) what ? " [1] And it was assuredly not a bad price. In fact, both Scott and Byron had publisher and public almost at their beck and call, and the prices were not too much because the publishers, with the public behind them, were eager and able to pay them. And the say of it, as Byron calls it, was something to thrill people. But though they were unheard-of prices, they were prices which, proportionately less, publishers were willing to pay to lesser men. When we consider Milman's 500 guineas in 1822 for the poem *Belshazzar*, we see that Byron's prices were not exceptional.

It all shows what a profession literature was at that time for popular genius. Constable could not get enough out of Scott. Nor could others. Lockhart says of 1808 : " The eager struggling of the different booksellers to engage Scott at

1 Smiles, *A Publisher and his Friends*, i. 222.

this time, is a very amusing feature in the voluminous correspondence before me. Had he possessed treble the energy for which it was possible to give any man credit, he could never have encountered a tithe of the projects that the post brought day after day to him, announced with extravagant enthusiasm, and urged with all the arts of conciliation. I shall mention only one out of at least a dozen gigantic schemes which were thus proposed before he had well settled himself to his Swift . . . This was a General Edition of British Novelists—beginning with De Foe and reaching to the end of the last century—to be set forth with prefaces and notes by Scott."[1] For that Swift he was to have £1,500, and for an edition of Dryden he had recently had £756. Then by 1818, when the novels had been appearing for four years, his annual profits on them alone were not less than £10,000. And still they rose. In 1822, says Lockhart, " he must have reckoned on clearing £30,000 at least in the course of a couple of years by the novels written in such a period." [2] In addition Constable suggested prefaces to novelists and poets. He " would willingly have given him £6,000 more within a space of two years for [these] works of a less serious sort likely to be despatched at leisure hours, without at all interfering with the main manufacture." Nor was even that enough, but Constable thought " a little pinnace of the Halidon class might easily be rigged out once a quarter by way of diversion, and thus add another £4,000 per annum." [3] Lockhart can only call it almost mad exhilaration on Scott's part and extravagant excitement of mind on Con-

1 Lockhart, *Life of Scott*, p. 180.   2 *Ibid.*, p. 415.   3 *Ibid.*, p. 419.

stable's. Literature had proved for Scott the most splendidly profitable profession he could have chosen.

As early as 1799, when he was busy with the ballads, we find Scott urged to devote himself considerably to literature. A friend, Mr. Kerr of Abbotrule, then wrote to him : " With your strong sense and hourly ripening knowledge, that you must rise to the top of the tree in the Parliament House in due season, I hold as certain as that Murray died Lord Mansfield. But don't let many an Ovid, or rather many a Burns (which is better), be lost in you. I rather think men of business have produced as good poetry in their by-hours as the professed regulars ; and I don't see any sufficient reason why Lord President Scott should not be a famous poet (in the vacation time), when we have seen a President Montesquieu step so nobly beyond the trammels in the *Esprit des Loix*. I suspect Dryden would have been a happier man had he had your profession. The reasoning talents visible in his verses assure me that he would have ruled in Westminster Hall as easily as he did at Button's, and he might have found time enough besides for everything that one really honours his memory for." And Lockhart comments that " this friend appears to have entertained, in October 1799, the very opinion as to the *profession of literature* on which Scott acted through life." [1]

SCOTT himself put it thus : " I determined that literature should be my staff but not my crutch, and that the profits of my literary labour, however convenient otherwise, should not, if I could help

---

[1] Lockhart, *Life of Scott* pp. 94–5.

it, become necessary to my ordinary expenses. Upon such a post [as the Shrievalty or Clerkship of the Supreme Court for which he looked and which he obtained] an author might hope to retreat, without any perceptible alteration of circumstances, whenever the time should arrive that the public grew weary of his endeavours to please, or he himself should tire of the pen." [1] But though in theory he had the salary of his office on which to fall back, in practice the time soon came when he was as professional a man of letters as a man well could be. On the irregularity of *Quarterly* contributors he speaks most professionally of " the curse of gentleman writers " and the need of veterans, men who will keep their engagements. In reality he had two professions, and the legal had the less of his mind. For even in 1803 in conversation with Wordsworth " he spoke of his profession as if he had already given up all hope of rising by it ; and some allusion being made to its profits, observed that ' he was sure he could, if he chose, get more money than he should ever wish to have from the booksellers.' " [2] And once he had taken to the booksellers, he gave them an output greater than that of any man who devoted himself entirely to literature and had no other call upon his time.

CERTAINLY Scott at times depreciated literature as a profession. But then what author, or what man of any other profession, does not the same for his chosen career ? We find the tone in a letter to Crabbe in 1812, and the tone owes something to the kindly generosity with which Scott always went out to meet a friend's position. He says : " I

---

[1] Lockhart, *Life of Scott*, p. 136.   [2] *Ibid.*, p. 119.

have often thought it is the most fortunate thing for bards like you and me, to have an established profession and professional character to render us independent of those worthy gentlemen, the retailers, or, as some have called them, the midwives of literature, who are so much taken up with the abortions they bring into the world that they are scarcely able to bestow the proper care upon young and flourishing babes like ours. That, however, is only a mercantile way of looking at the matter ; but did any of my sons show poetic talent, of which, to my great satisfaction, there are no appearances, the first thing I should do would be to inculcate upon him the duty of cultivating some honourable profession, and qualify himself to play a more respectable part in society than the mere poet. And as the best corollary of my doctrine, I would make him get your tale of ' The Patron ' by heart from beginning to end." [1] And that is all very well as a kindly letter to a brother poet. But it certainly leaves most of the truth on one side. One smiles at the notion of Longman or Constable neglecting Scott's works for the abortions of others. And a writer in those days was hardly likely, and certainly had no reason to be a " mere poet." He would do as Scott himself, and nearly everyone else did, and write for the reviews, maybe for the *Encyclopædia Britannica*, and edit books, and be an all-round workman at literature. Every year made it easier to live by literature. Southey, refusing even to live in the centre but preferring the solitude of the Lakes, lived as regular and honoured a professional life as any

[1] Crabbe, *Life*, p. 57.

lawyer. Galt, when he left the world of business for the world of letters, wrote and earned with an undiminished regularity. " In 1822," according to Gillies, " the fortunes of literary men from high to low wore *couleur de rose.*" [1]

BUT although Scott, despite the resource of his legal income, was essentially a professional, he is not the best example of a great professional writer in the first quarter of the century because of his very magnificence. It seems almost false to rank his brilliance of genius in the common order of things, and the life of Southey is the more truly typical. He relied on nothing but his pen. In his own words his " whole estate was in his ink-stand." As Crabb Robinson noted in 1817, " literature is now Southey's trade : he is a manufacturer, and his workshop is his study. . . . His time is his wealth." And there he worked at literature as steadily as a man in a mercantile office at his ledgers. Hazlitt said of him in 1825 that " no man in our day (at least no man of genius) has led so uniformly and entirely the life of a scholar from boyhood to the present hour, devoting himself to learning with the enthusiasm of an early love, with the severity and constancy of a religious vow. . . . He passes from verse to prose, from history to poetry, from reading to writing, by a stop-watch." [2]

THE secret of Southey's success was his all-round knowledge and his ability to make use of it for the supply of the reviews. In them Southey, as many after him, found the solution of how to make

1 Gillies, *Memoirs of a Literary Veteran*, iii. 82.
2 Hazlitt, *Spirit of the Age* (1904), pp. 147–8.

literature a support. Poetry and history, sound
and thorough though his achievements in them
were, did not profit him. In 1814 he wrote of the
second volume of his history of Brazil, " I could
get more money from the *Quarterly* by one
month's employment than this volume will produce me," comforting himself that, " on the other
hand, this is for myself and posterity." In fact,
the *Quarterly*, to which from 1811 he was a regular
contributor, was his mainstay. Before that he had
contributed to other journals, but Murray paid ten
guineas a sheet where before he had had only four,
and soon he was getting a hundred guineas for
an article, and finding the only drawback Gifford's
" mutilations." And the money was not always
limited to the original article. Having already
received a hundred guineas for the article, he
received another £100 when by expansion he wrote
the *Life of Nelson*. So that henceforth he was
sure of a steady income, without writing anything
slipshod or in any way compromising his fine
sense of honour. " Writing for a livelihood," he
confessed in 1827, "a livelihood is all I have gained ;
for, having something better in view, and therefore never having courted popularity, nor written
for the mere sake of gain, it has not been possible
for me to lay by anything." But he had the
sufficiency for the day. And his success is
no unfair criterion by which to judge the
prospects of the many other writers who took
to the growing periodical press, and whose
earning power, if less because they had less talent,
might often be more because they were less
scrupulous. Not so easy a sufficiency was theirs,
but not a bad one if they were men who belonged

to the profession not by chance but by their real talents.[1]

SOUTHEY was in his way an all-round man of letters, but apart from his big works he kept mostly to the reviews, indeed, almost solely to the *Quarterly*. But the field of the profession was always widening, and the new aspirant tried his hand at everything, even poetry. We see Leigh Hunt rapidly advancing as a journalist in one paper after another, sometimes his own, sometimes with his brother, sometimes for other people. He deals in dramatic, and literary and political criticism. Like many another he tries the novel, and produces an historical tale, *Sir Ralph Esher*. He ran counter to everyone. " After having angered the stage, dissatisfied the Church, offended the State, not very well pleased the Whigs, and exasperated the Tories, I must needs " arouse personal hostility.[2] So he reviewed his earlier years, but in spite of it all he won through as an author by profession. When one thing fell off he turned to another. For example, in 1820 he translated the *Aminta* of Tasso, " to enable me," so he says, " to meet some demands, occasioned by the falling off in the receipts of the *Examiner*, now declining under the twofold vicissitude of triumphant ascendancy in the Tories, and the desertion of reform by the Whigs." [3] And he had another resource too, for " the *Indicator* assisted me still more, though it was but published in a corner, owing to my want of funds for advertising it, and my ignorance of the best mode of circulating such things." [4]

---

1 R. P. Gillies is a fair example of an average man of letters.
2 *Autobiography*, p. 211. He is referring to *The Feast of the Poets*.
3 Leigh Hunt, *Autobiography*, p. 273. 4 *Ibid.*

AND the indefatigable versatility of Leigh Hunt and Southey is henceforth the stock-in-trade of a professional author. Among the efficient journeymen of letters we find men like Roscoe (1791 to 1871) who, beginning to write in 1816 in local journals and magazines, continued to follow literature as a profession, and produced novels and tours and translations and editions of the novelists. There was Pinkerton, one of Longman's writers who wrote a General Geology and compiled and edited collections of Voyages and Travels. There was the prolific " Syntax " Combe with his numerous compilations from *The Description of Patagonia* in 1774 to the *History of Madeira* in 1821, with his biographical sketches totalling, before he had finished, more than two hundred, with his contributions to periodicals, and his poems that were letter-press to the drawings of Rowlandson. There was Egerton Brydges with his journalism and novels and volumes of compilations. There was Croly who left the Church, and turned to tragedy and comedy, and the novel, and was dramatic critic of the *Times*, and a reviewer who would set to on any book on any subject at a moment's notice. And there was Stebbing too, who in 1827 left his curacies in Norfolk and settled in London to work for the booksellers from morning to night till he became editor of the *Athenæum*. There were Theodore Hook, Maginn, and Gleig also of that later generation. The *Dictionary of National Biography* will yield many a name, and they all made literature their support and it did not fail them. For if they failed, it was not literature that failed them, but they who failed themselves. The embarrassed author was his own enemy. Combe was quite content to live a debtor in the bounds of the King's Bench, and Pinkerton should not have had his bevy of disreputable and riotous females at his doors. Nor was it the want of money that made the embarrassments of Hook, but the want of the knowledge of how to keep it, for he is said to have made even as much as £2,000 in a year from *John Bull*, and more from his novels and farces.[1]

THERE were all kinds of work to be done. Napier was a lawyer, who found a very profitable adjunct in the editorship of the *Encyclopædia Britannica*. For the sixth edition he made an agreement with Constable in 1813 by which he was to receive £300 between the making of the agreement and the sending to the press of the first part of the first volume and was to have £150 on the completion of each of eight half volumes, £500 on reprinting, and £200 for incidental expenses. For the Supplement to that edition Constable paid Scott £100 for each of his articles on the drama and chivalry. Doubtless many other writers found an opportunity of contributing. And when Napier edited, for Black, the seventh edition, which appeared from 1830 to 1842, the sum he distributed to the contributors was £13,887, while he himself received in all £8,755. And it was but one of the channels of profit for a writer with knowledge, for the publishers were anxious to make as much as they could of the great March of Mind that had set in throughout the country.

AND though the volume of popular literature was small compared with the flood rising in the middle

---

1 For authors in this paragraph, see *D.N.B.*

145

of the century, with proportionately fewer writers, the money its provision brought an author was as good, if not better. Gillies in 1850, admitting that " in 1822 we never dreamed of such goings on," adds reflectively that, " strange to say, even minor authors were paid and encouraged then." Gillies himself found translation a profitable line. In the early twenties he did eight volumes of translations and he records they " realized to me a considerable sum." A translation of *Faust* was one of Coleridge's projects and he agreed to an offer in 1814 of £100 from Murray, though thinking the terms " humiliatingly low." But that seems to have been his usual opinion of all offers. And it was to translation that many part-time authors looked for something to increase their other earnings. Crabb Robinson in 1805 found work at a guinea and a half a sheet producing a version of a political work against Napoleon. Then there were all the miscellaneous topical volumes for the man of letters to turn out, not badly paid. Lamb suggested one to Hazlitt in 1806, writing, " You might dish up a Fawcettiad in 3 months, and ask 60 or 80 pounds for it." [1] In fact, as Gillies said of 1822, the prospects of every kind of literary man were rosy. If the rose faded, as he says it did, in 1825, because the commercial panic of that year affected everyone engaged in literature, it did not fade for long. Gillies in 1828 had £200 from Colburn for a novel before he had written it. In 1829 Galt, who, while his rather facile popularity lasted, was very much the steady professional man of letters, was reckoning on £1,000 a year by his pen.

[1] P. P. Howe, *Life of Hazlitt*, p. 88.

And in the next decade but one journey-work was becoming for some too temptingly profitable. Borrow said of Allan Cunningham that he " took to bookmaking likewise—in a word, was too fond of Mammon." He might have said it of many. A GOOD example of a writer beginning in the post-panic years, good because it shows both the possibilities and the defects of professional writing, is given in the life of Laman Blanchard, as told by Lytton.[1] Having first tried acting for a week with a company of players at Margate, Blanchard quickly gave up all idea of the stage, disgusted by his brief experience of the beggary and drudgery of the country player's life, and found employment as reader in the office of Messrs. Bayliss of Fleet Street. His education had been very ordinary. Son of a painter and glazier in London he went to school at St. Olave's, Southwark. Too poor to accept a two years' scholarship for the university, he entered the office of a proctor in Doctors' Commons, but stayed there a very short time because his father wanted him at home to help him at his trade. Then followed the escapade on the provincial boards. But he had the necessary literary ability. He was not one of those of whom Christopher North complained, " uneducated, adventurers, who have been thrown upon literature only by having failed as attorneys, apothecaries, painters, school-masters, preachers, grocers——." And his office of reader gave him the opportunity to write. Messrs. Bayliss were then publishers of the *Monthly Magazine*, and to that he became a frequent contributor, and from both sources succeeded in gaining a tolerable competence.

1 See Bulwer Lytton, *Memoir of Laman Blanchard.*

147

Then, in 1826, he was appointed assistant secretary to the Zoological Society, and, says Lytton, " he held this post only three years, but these sufficed to establish him in his profession as a man of letters." He became sub-editor of the *Monthly Magazine*, then under the direction of Dr. Croly, and editor of the *Belle Assemblée*. Then he took to the partisan press and served on several different journals, and was for a time editor of the *Courier*. By the early thirties he was established. To quote Lytton, " his practice in periodical writing was now considerable ; his versatility was extreme. He was marked by publishers and editors as a useful contributor, and so his livelihood was secure."

FROM this career, as, in fact, from Southey's too, one thing is obvious. The main resource of the professional writer has already come to be journalism, and the great talent requisite versatility. That versatility might give its possessor further resources, particularly in the novel, but it was essential for the journalism alone. And versatility is not always a blessing. Its prime necessity was the defect of the course literature as a profession was inevitably taking. As it affected Blanchard, the charge is best made in the words of his biographer. " He certainly never fulfilled the great promise which his *Lyric Offerings* held forth. He never wrote up to the full mark of his powers ; the fountain never rose to the level of its source. But in our day the professional man of letters is compelled to draw too frequently, and by too small disbursements, on his capital, to allow large and profitable investments of the stock of mind and idea, with which he commences

148

his career. The number and variety of our periodicals have tended to results which benefit the pecuniary interests of the author, to the prejudice of his substantial fame. . . . There is a fatal facility in supplying the wants of the week by the rapid striking off a pleasant article, which interferes with the steady progress, even with the mature conception of an elaborate work." And Coleridge had felt the same need and his own want of that versatility and of the adaptability which is almost inseparable from it, twenty years before Blanchard started on the same career. In 1797, Coleridge said, " I retired to a cottage at Stowey, and provided for my scanty maintenance by writing verses for a London Morning Paper. I saw plainly, that literature was not a profession by which I could expect to live ; for I could not disguise from myself, that, whatever my talents might or might not be in other respects, yet they were not of the sort that could enable me to become a popular writer." [1]

PERHAPS the general charge against this defect of the profession of letters as a profession is made best by Leigh Hunt in his *Autobiography*. He puts the argument of the man who has the talent which justifies his writing and which, maybe, disqualifies him by nature from another profession, but which, by its originality and its superiority to mere profitable bookmaking, the condition of the profession denies him to profit by. " It is easy," pleads Hunt, " to say to a man —Write such and such a thing, and it is sure to sell. Watch the public taste, and act accordingly. Care not for original composition ; for inventions

---

[1] *Biographia Literaria*, p. 94.

or theories of your own ; for æsthetics which the many will be slow to apprehend. Stick to the works of others. Write only in magazines and reviews. Or if you write things of your own, compile. Tell anecdotes. Reproduce memoirs and topographies. Repeat, in as many words of your own as you can, other men's criticisms. Do anything but write to the few, and you may get rich. There is a great deal of truth in all this. But a man can only do what he can, or as others will let him. Suppose he has a conscience. . . . Suppose the editors and reviewers themselves will not encourage him to write on the subjects he understands best." [1] But every year was making it more inevitable for a professional writer to follow these maxims.

In fact, the betterment of the profession of letters was pecuniary rather than literary. It was the natural result of all the circumstances. Writers had to become journalists because journalism was what the growing public wanted, and writers by profession had to serve the public because the public was their only patron. When reading became widespread it was not the taste of good judges but the, in general too easily pleased, taste of Mr. Everyman that had to be met. And from the new class of .readers came the new class of writers. And between the two, literature produced for a living quite inevitably took a more popular turn, and the average professional writer became more superficial and dashed off articles instead of thinking out a solid work. Coleridge noted the tendency in 1817, though with rather too sweeping a severity. He found " that a command of some sort of language has become a widespread and mechanical accomplishment, so that men of no talent may use words to write what will convey some empty simulacrum of sense sufficient for idle and vacant minds to peruse with no effort." They produce what " spares the reader the trouble of thinking ; prevents vacancy, while it indulges indolence. . . . Of all trades, literature at present demands the least talent or information. . . . It is no less remarkable than true, with how little examination works of polite literature are commonly perused, not only by the mass of readers, but by men of first rate ability, till some accident or chance discussion have roused their attention and put them on their guard. And hence individuals below mediocrity not less in natural power than in acquired knowledge ; nay, bunglers who have failed in the lowest mechanic crafts, and whose presumption is in due proportion to their want of sense and sensibility ; men who, being first scribblers from idleness and ignorance, next become libellers from envy and malevolence— have been able to drive a successful trade in the employment of the booksellers, nay, have raised themselves to a temporary name and reputation with the public at large, by that most powerful of all adulation, the appeal to the bad and malignant passions of mankind." [1] And though Coleridge is patently exaggerating, there is a good measure of truth in his words. But, truth though there is, it is unnecessary to deduce that the new journalism was worse than the old. On the contrary, a comparison of the journalism, and indeed of the general literary

1 *Biographia Literaria*, p. 21.

production of 1820 with that of 1790, shows a decided average improvement.

BUT the tendency does point to one truth. Rogers perceived it. He said : " It is a prevalent error to suppose that a literary man can successfully carry on his pursuits without capital. On the contrary, he requires it quite as much as any mercantile man ; though perhaps not to the same extent." For if there was to be real substance in his work he must have the resources that would give him the leisure to accumulate his materials, and to digest them, and to lie at ease when his mind was overtired. " Seldom," wrote Coleridge, " have I written that in a day, the acquisition or investigation of which had not cost me the previous labour of a month." And in 1819 Campbell, after the experience of preparing his *Specimens of the British Poets*, confessed to the publisher : " I discovered in truth too late that it was a work which none but an author who possessed an independent fortune, or a collection of books such as Mr. Heber's, should have undertaken." In fact, earning a livelihood by authorship entailed limitations. It meant that the work that required long and sustained preparation was nearly always written by the man who had something other than his literature to rely on. Too often, if he achieved something more, it did not pay him. Southey's *Book of the Church*, the product of many months of work, brought Southey next to nothing.

BUT that one defect apart, the profession of letters in this period was a good profession for those who were fitted for it. It was still comparatively small. Gillies, writing in the middle of the century, remarks, " In those days how limited was the number of literary men, and now they are numberless ! There came more from the press in last November than during the whole year in 1809." And again he says that " in a literary as well as a commercial sense the strength of Ballantyne's publishing house depended on Scott alone," for good authors were by no means plentiful. That being so, it was not hard to get on, since the public demand was stronger than the supply, and high prices were paid even to third- and fourth-rate writers. And that gave the profession of authorship a strong power to attract men, so that inevitably the numbers began to creep towards the stage of being numberless. And for another thing, the new conditions of journalism made it easier for a man to get a footing in authorship than the conditions in which, periodicals being few, he might have to embark early on the publication of a book. Maginn, while still an obscure schoolmaster in Ireland, made his way into *Blackwood's Magazine* by his contributions hidden under the nom-de-guerre of Ralph Tuckett Scott. Quite accidentally, with no introduction, he established himself. AND the profession drew not only men, but women. Women writers, as we have seen, had already made a mark in literature. Now they advanced further. One of the most prominent names in the drama was that of Joanna Baillie. Mary Lamb assisted her brother with his books for children, or perhaps it would be truer to put it the other way round. She wrote for magazines. Crabb Robinson notes in December 1814 that " Miss Lamb has undergone great fatigue from writing an article about needlework for the new Ladies of Britain magazine." The sisters, Ann and Jane Taylor, were also among the best writers for children. In the novel there were Miss Edgeworth and Mrs. Inchbald and Hannah More and Miss Owenson. A Miss Benger about 1812 obtained quite considerable literary celebrity as a writer of biographical essays. Women were in fact in every field of literature, but they generally had one trait in common. " How strange it is," commented Crabb Robinson, " that while we men are modestly content to amuse by our writings, women must be didactic ! Miss Baillie writes plays to illustrate the passions, Miss Martineau teaches political economy by tales, Miss Marcet sets up for a general instructor, not only in her dialogues but in fairy stories, and Miss Edgeworth is a schoolmistress in her tales." [1] And though women did not make a very high proportion of the Review writers, they were not negligible on the Reviews either. On *Blackwood's* were Mrs. Hemans and Miss Caroline Bowles (Mrs. Southey). On *The Athenæum* in 1832 were Mrs. Fletcher and Mary Howitt. And Jerdan, the editor of the *Literary Gazette*, said that L. E. L. " did little less for the *Gazette* than I did myself." And L. E. L. was an incessant contributor to the Annuals and Albums which flourished in the late twenties. In fact, she earned large sums by her pen, and not least by her poetry. Her richly coloured, fluent and dramatic poems were best sellers, the *Improvisatrice*, for example, published in 1824, reaching its sixth edition the next year.

---

[1] C. Robinson, *Diary*, iii, 37

ALSO the place of women in the profession received the only other recognition it had not yet had, when women writers were nominated for Government pensions. In 1830 Lord Grey's ministry conferred a pension of £300 a year on Lady Morgan (Miss Owenson, the novelist) as an acknowledgment of her work in literature, or, as she preferred to think, as a deserved compensation for the abuse that Croker and other Tories had consistently paid her. That was the first pension of its kind a woman had received. Then Sir Robert Peel offered one to Mrs. Somerville, a writer who had " expounded La Place to the English scientific student." For women were by then interested in science too. Vicesimus Knox had found in 1820 that " a knowledge of Chemistry seems to have become a female accomplishment."

(iii)

A LARGE share of the credit for this improvement in the conditions of the profession of letters belongs to the booksellers. When the nineteenth century opened publishing was still very largely the monopoly of the big London houses. Despite the absence for some years of any marked genius among authors and despite the unsettling and depressing influence of the French war, they had been embarking on considerable fresh ventures. Holcroft's success with his publishers shows a spirit of quite generous enterprise on their part. The price of £500 for the copyright of the *Minstrelsy* in 1802 indicates vision in Longman. And young John Murray the Second was beginning to speculate. His father had died in 1793, and for four years afterwards he had been " shackled to a drone of a partner," but, being rid of him, he plunged and began to look out for good investments. In 1803, immediately after seeing it acted, he offered £300 for Colman's *John Bull*. And then Scott came brilliantly to the fore, and the success of the *Edinburgh Review* revealed much new talent.

ALL doubts about the profitableness of literature seemed to vanish from the minds of publishers. All became bold in their ventures, and the romantic spirit of the new literature seemed to be reflected in the daring enterprise of the booksellers. Everyone was anxious to secure the services of Scott. And then in the almost amazing productiveness of the following quarter of a century, with prominent writers on every side, and new aspirants constantly appearing, publishing flourished so much that it seemed likely to become the trade of the day and to overtop all other commercial enterprise. Constable, said Lord Cockburn, " almost convinced the world that Poetry, Romance, Philosophy and even Criticism were the first crafts and the most profitable in the world." Publishers, in fact, felt like men who had discovered a mine, whose richness, as they worked at it as fast as they could, seemed inexhaustible. Big prices as they gave for the copyrights, the results exceeded all expectations. Murray confessed to Scott in 1829 that his quarter share of *Marmion* " has been profitable to me fifty-fold beyond what either publisher or author could have anticipated." [1]   A writer in the

1 Lockhart, *Life of Scott* (Edinburgh, 1902), ix. 289.

News of Literature[1] in 1825 acknowledges that booksellers have become rich " because they have opened the mines of intellect to the people." And for an estimation of the profits of those days, let us note that Hunter, in seven years of partnership with Constable in the early middle years of Constable's publishing, drew from the business £21,000. And Croly, in 1829, said of the novels with which the enterprising Colburn had been flooding the market, that in the three previous years they had brought their owner £20,000 a year.

THE most dazzling figure in this world was the figure of Constable. When he began to make himself known in Edinburgh, there was no spirit at all in Scotch publishing. But there was talent in Edinburgh, and he began to draw that talent towards him by the generosity of his offers. Soon he had given £1,000 each for dissertations by Dugald Stewart and Playfair. In 1802 he was sharing a quarter of the *Minstrelsy*, and in the same year he came right to the forefront of publishing with the *Edinburgh Review*. He paid well, and his talented young men were not by any means confined to Jeffrey, and Sydney Smith, and Brougham. The untapped resources of Edinburgh became encouragingly clear. Then, after Longman had got the *Lay*, he stepped in, as we have seen, and secured *Marmion*.

BY then he had effectively broken into the monopoly of the London trade, and when he began to share in the Waverley novels, if the splendour of his success went rather to his head, it was largely because his vivid imagination kept showing him

1 T. Constable, *Archibald Constable*, iii, 479–82.

yet brighter prospects. In Scott's words " he had rendered his native country the mart of her own literature [because] he knew how to avail himself to an unhoped for extent of the various kinds of talent which his country produced." And he had got the lead of the whole trade. It was he who led the way to unheard-of prices. " Abandoning the old timid and grudging system, he stood out as the liberal patron and payer of all promising publications, and confounded not merely his rivals in trade but his very authors by his unheard-of prices. Ten, even twenty, guineas a sheet for a review, £2,000 or £3,000 for a single poem, and £1,000 each for two philosophical dissertations, drew authors [out of their] dens." [1] He was rather beside himself when he went striding up and down the room crying, " My God, I am all but author of the Waverley novels," [2] but, in fact, he was all but the author of the new conditions for writers. Scott, excusing himself to Lockhart after the smash in 1826, said, " It is easy, no doubt, for any friend to blame me for entering into connexion with commercial matters at all. But I wish to know what I could have done better—excluded from the Bar, and then from all profits for six years by my colleague's prolonged life. Literature was not in those days what poor Constable has made it." Scott, indeed, went so far as to say of Constable that " his life is of uncommon importance to literature."

THE possibilities of publishing were so great then that Constable was not the only publisher from

---

[1] Cockburn, *Memorials of his Time*, pp. 162–3.
[2] Lockhart, *Life of Scott*, p. 396.

the North to make himself equal with the big former monopolists of London. Blackwood, after apprenticeship with Bell and Bradfute, and experience at Mundell's branch in Glasgow and at Cuthill's in London, was set up for himself in Edinburgh in 1804. But he advanced much more slowly than Constable. Old books remained for long a prominent feature of his business, and he was content to be for a time Murray's agent for the *Quarterly*, and agent for Cadell and Davies, before he began about 1816 to come much into notice with his own books. But then with his *Maga* at once famous and notorious, and with shares in Waverley novels, he was soon in the first rank.

MEANWHILE, the Ballantynes, backed by Scott, went publishing away till the disposal of their surplus stocks became a nuisance. Their activity was immense, but their importance was nothing but their connexion with Scott. Yet their methods are interesting as showing the careless buoyancy which the contact with so much literary genius had given some of the trade. Murray was not one of them. He warned the Ballantynes that they were proceeding too fast on credit, " drawing bills for value not received." " How," he asked, " can you continue to destroy every speculation by entering upon new ones before the previous ones are properly completed ? " But speculation of every kind was much in the air, and the Ballantynes went on with their ventures by squandering Scott's money, and for some years they were maintained by the general condition of buoyancy and activity prevalent in the trade.

BUT when in due time Ballantynes crashed, and

Constable too, the firm of Black emerged to a high position, and so helped to keep up the high credit of Scotch publishing. And Blackie & Co. also, who did well in the ' number ' trade, had since 1809 been making steady progress with their own publications, while the brothers Chambers were rising from the very humblest beginnings to the position where, in 1832, they were able to launch one of the greatest ventures in popular publishing. And the commercial epic of Robert Chambers again shows the possibilities for a very determined young man to make his way through old books to first-class publishing. In 1818, only sixteen years old, he started his little second-hand bookshop, and, limiting the cost of his living to sixpence a day, he laid out all that was over in adding to his stock. He took up binding, and, rising at sunrise, would read *The Spectator* " to occupy idle time." Then he bought a " jangling, creeking, wheezing little press " for £3 and worked it by moonlight in his bedroom. In 1822 he published broadsides for the Royal procession of George IV in Edinburgh, and soon he managed to print and sell 750 copies of the *Songs of Burns* at a shilling each, and in ' numbers ' to book-hawkers. By 1823 he had saved £200 and with that he purchased a new shop in India Place. Then his steady progress continued, and the result was *Chambers's Journal* in 1832.

THE enterprise of Constable hardly needs any further illustration. He was always keeping his eyes open. But perhaps we may quote what was one of his boldest speculations, the purchase of the *Encyclopædia Britannica*. The last edition, the fifth, had been badly managed, but the sum

Constable had to pay for the copyright was between thirteen and fourteen thousand pounds, and there were many who prophesied his ruin. But he justified his foresight, and in nine years his profits were not less than £20,000. And the same willingness to take risks was not uncommon in the trade in those years. Murray's expenses in the publication of Campbell's *Specimens* were so large that he could hardly expect any profits on the first edition, but he was content to regard it as a speculative investment that would mature. And Murray sometimes burnt his fingers by his enterprise and generosity, as when he gave Crabbe £3,000 in 1819 for all his copyrights, and as when he launched his unfortunate newspaper *The Representative* that died in six months.

BUT this spirit of enterprise is probably best seen in Blackwood. He was always looking out for new writers with undiminished ardour. He seemed convinced that, if he would only look zealously enough, he might find another Scott, and once, when he got Galt, he thought he had found one. But he never stopped looking, until it became a joke about him that he asked everyone he met to contribute to *Maga*. Maginn, when in London, was given a roving commission to look out for likely contributors, and he was not the only recruiting sergeant. Nor did Blackwood's zeal end there, but he must also interest himself in the literary side, and revise his author's work. The earlier books of Galt he superintended through the press himself. And he wanted even to amend a Waverley novel, which roused Scott to the wrathful explosion to Ballantyne, " Tell him and his coadjutor that I belong to the Black Hussars of Literature, who neither give nor receive quarter. I'll be cursed but this is the most impudent proposal that ever was made." [1]   But if he made a *faux pas* with Scott, he did well by and with Scott's future son-in-law. With commendable foresight he lent or gave Lockhart, before he really settled down to literature, £300 to help him study in Germany, and in return received a translation of Schlegel's *Lecture on the History of Literature*. But nothing he ever did was greater than the creation of his magazine.

AND while this spirit was active in the legitimate members of the trade, it was of course strong too among the less legitimate.   They cut in with their piracies and trickery whenever they could.   And of the latter the Memoirs of Byron which Colburn issued in 1822 may serve as a typical example. Byron is told of it thus in a dialogue in the *Noctes Ambrosianæ* :   " a most audacious imposture : [Colburn] had heard the report of your having given your Life to Moore, and, accordingly, thinking he might make a good thing of it, he hires at once Dictionary Watkins, to set about Memoirs, which, to give old Gropius credit for industry, he touched up in a fortnight ;   and advertised it was, as *the* Memoirs of Lord B., particularly in the country papers . . . it imposed on many simple, chuckleheaded, open-mouthed people, as your autobiography." [2]   In that line, and in the more honourable lines, too, such as his novels, Colburn had as much enterprise as anyone.

NATURALLY ' the trade ' had several bad blunders

---

[1] Lockhart, *Life of Scott*, pp. 293-4.   [2] *Noctes Ambrosianæ*, No. iv.

to their discredit which showed anything but foresight. In every age of publishing one can
doubtless find them. But their enterprise was
their characteristic and their blunders were
accidental. To name a few of the blunders,
there was Cadell's summary rejection of *Pride
and Prejudice*, while Millers turned down *Childe
Harold*, and Murray was one of several who
refused *Rejected Addresses*. But a publisher can
hardly be expected to be any more infallible
than a literary critic, and the record of the
blunders of critics, who could number ? Publishers
at least had the best advice available. Murray,
for example, relied greatly on Gifford.

To give a fair statement of the relation of the
judgment of publishers to the prospects of authors,
we may quote a letter from Scott to Miss Seward
in 1807. He writes : " But who ever heard
of a bookseller pretending to understand the
commodity in which he dealt ? They are the
only tradesmen in the world who professedly,
and by choice, deal in what is called ' a pig in a
poke.' When you consider the abominable trash
which, by their sheer ignorance, is published
every year, you will readily excuse them for the
indemnification which they must necessarily
obtain at the expense of authors of some value.
In fact, though the account between an individual
bookseller and such a man as Southey may be
iniquitous enough, yet I apprehend, that upon
the whole the account between *the trade* and the
authors of Britain at large is pretty fairly balanced ;
and what these gentlemen gain at the expense
of one class of writers, is lavished, in many cases, in
bringing forward other works of little value. I do

not know but this, upon the whole, is favourable to the cause of literature. A bookseller publishes twenty books, in hopes of hitting upon one good speculation, as a person buys a parcel of shares in a lottery, in hopes of gaining a prize. Thus the road is open to all, and if the successful candidate is a little fleeced, in order to form petty prizes to console the losing adventurers, still the cause of literature is benefited, since none is excluded from the privilege of competition." [1] It is a sanely balanced view, and we have already seen, on the testimony of Gillies and others, that during this period the system worked well for all classes of writers. And we shall see the general satisfactoriness of conditions further confirmed when we come later to examine in detail the prospects in the fields of poetry, and the novel.

IN considering the policy which publishers pursue, it falsifies all if we do not remember to how many shifting influences they are subject. We need to remind ourselves that true literature is not the only, nor very often the most lucrative side of a publisher's business. The source from which he can make up his losses on unsuccessful volumes, is not so much the profits on good authors, as Scott suggests, but the profits on his household stuff. Murray had a rich and ceaseless spring of profit in Mrs. Rundell's *Domestic Cookery*. It sold on an average from five to ten thousand copies a year, and when it came to a dispute with Mrs. Rundell, Murray had to pay her £2,000 for the copyright. And in the twenties Murray writes to a correspondent in the

---

[1] Lockhart, *Life of Scott* (Edinburgh, 1902), iii. 17.

North, " You will perhaps smile to learn that with us next to the Scotch novels and Byron the best selling books are Dr. Kitchiner's." And Dr. Kitchiner's was eccentric stuff that had caught the passing fancy of the public. Nor can the fancy of the public, in its varying phases, be ignored by any publisher. It creates a division of publishing into a profession and a trade, of the same origin as the division in authorship. The supply of the better literary public makes it a profession, and the supply of what the early Victorians called ' the million ' often makes it degenerate into a trade. And in this connexion we may approve the saying of Isaac D'Israeli that " it is to be lamented for the cause of literature that even a bookseller may have too refined a taste for his trade ; it must always be to his interest to float on the current of public taste, whatever that may be ; should he have an ambition to *create* it, he will be anticipating a more cultivated curiosity by half a century ; thus the business of a bookseller rarely accords with the design of advancing our literature." [1] So, below those best publishers whose enterprise we have been noting, there are the many who keep almost entirely to short-dated investments, that is, in books that have an immediate sale, and decline to consider permanent works whose establishment is likely to be a matter of cumulative repute. But the better publishers maintain their good work, and balance it with the more popular. We see how it worked, in a letter of D'Israeli's to Murray in 1805 : " I had various conversations with Phillips. . . . He owns his *belles-lettres* books have given no great profits ; in my opinion he must

[1] I. D'Israeli, *Miscellanies of Literature*, 1840, p. 86.

165

have lost even by some. But he makes a fortune by juvenile and useful compilations."[1]

THE nature of agreements continued much the same as in the preceding twenty years. Many copyrights continued to be sold outright, especially those of novels, because it was very often the author's need to have a sum down. But the principle of half-profits steadily advanced in favour. About 1820 that was the basis upon which men like Hallam and Milman agreed. Murray advised it thus to one author who wanted a cash offer: "Under this system I have been very successful. For Mr. Croker's 'Stories from the History of England,' selling for 2s. 6d., if I had offered the small sum of twenty guineas he would have thought it liberal. However, I printed it to divide profits, and he has already received from me the moiety of £1,400."[2] And *Rejected Addresses* is another example to the point. The authors were willing to have parted with all their rights for £20. That was the offer which Murray refused to consider, and when John Miller, the dramatic publisher, agreed to half-profits their gain was considerable. By the third edition the profits were £1,000. For by 1812, if a book proved popular, there was quite a good-sized public who would buy it.

THAT action of Murray's in offering the better terms was typical of the publishers of his day. Taking them all round, they were worthy successors to the " liberal-minded men " of Johnson's experience. Everywhere there is testimony that they were fair and liberal. " Of the conduct

---

1 S. Smiles, *A Publisher and his Friends*, i. 49.
2 *Ibid.*, i. 340.

of Messrs. Longman he has attested that it was liberal beyond his expectation," said Lockhart of Scott.[1] The generosity of Constable's prices was a byword. We see Colburn paying £1,000 in 1817 for Lady Morgan's book on France, and giving large sums for novels, and like many another, additional sums when a publication ran unexpectedly well. And we see Blackwood, until he was justifiably tired of it, putting up with Hogg's recurrent demands for the sum of £50 which Hogg always thought Blackwood owed him but which Blackwood never did owe. And as for Murray, examples of his liberality might be nearly endless. Let there suffice the testimony of Washington Irving to " Murray, my publisher, conducting himself in all his dealings with that fair, open and liberal spirit which has obtained for him the well merited appellation of the Prince of the Booksellers," and of Gifford, when from illness he at last broke his connexion with the *Quarterly*, in his letter to Murray, saying " the only fault I ever taxed you with in pecuniary matters was with that of being *too liberal* to me."

THERE also continued the old intimacy and friendliness between author and publisher. Their relation was still a very happily personal one. Longman's soirées were a well-known feature of the publishing world. Crabb Robinson noted of them, in March 1812 : " Dined with Messrs. Longman & Co. at one of their literary parties. These parties were famous in their day. Longman himself is a quiet gentlemanly man. There were present Dr. Abraham Rees . . . ' Russia ' Tooke . . . Sharon Turner . . . Abernethy . . .

---

[1] Lockhart, *Life of Scott*, p. 160.

167

Dr. Holland." [1] And of the same period Leigh Hunt says : " Another set of acquaintances which I made at this time used to assemble at the hospitable table of Mr. Hunter the bookseller, in St. Paul's Churchyard. They were the survivors of the literary party that were accustomed to dine with his predecessor, Mr. Johnson," [2] and among them were Fuseli, Bonnycastle, Godwin and Kinnaird. And of that group Godwin himself became a publisher, and as publisher and author used to gather round him a good company. Crabb Robinson remarks, " I now and then saw interesting persons at his house ; indeed, I saw none but remarkable persons there."

MURRAY, as we should expect, was one of the most hospitable of them all. He drew to him the most distinguished writers, and not only his countrymen. It became the custom for prominent Americans who visited England to come to him with letters of introduction, and one American, Ticknor, recorded in May 1815 : " I dined with Murray, and had a genuine bookseller's dinner, such as Lintot used to give Pope, and Gay and Swift, and Dilly to Johnson and Goldsmith. Those present were two Mr. Duncans, Fellows of New College, Oxford ; D'Israeli . . . Gifford and Campbell." [3] And, in addition, Murray's drawing-room, which was in those days above the shop, became a kind of literary lounge where authors foregathered for gossip and discussion. In fact, between three and five each afternoon the assembly there partook of the nature " of a literary levée." NOR were the Scotch publishers backward in

---

[1] *Diary*, i. 377.   [2] Leigh Hunt, *Autobiography*, p. 188.
[3] Smiles, *A Publisher and his Friends*, i. 270–1.

imitating this excellent and healthy custom of keeping the closest possible personal connexion between the authors and themselves. Blackwood, in particular, set out in Prince's Street to rival over his shop the literary society which met in Murray's drawing-room, and there about 1820 might be met any day the old veteran Mackenzie, or Scott and his friend William Erskine, or Hogg, or the young men of the magazine, John Wilson and the Scorpion Lockhart ; while Ballantyne, says Scott of his own publications, " always gives a christening dinner, at which the Duke of Buccleuch and a great many of my friends are formally feasted." And in London we should not forget too the convivial gatherings at which Taylor and Hessey were wont to entertain in Waterloo Place their talented contributors to the *London Magazine.*

SUCH a custom, flourishing nobly in the conviviality of that age, could not help but bring about a sympathetic understanding between the two branches of the profession of literature. It cemented the common cause of author and publisher, and the mingling of author with author tended towards an *esprit de corps* in the profession. It gave the successful author acquaintance with men whom success sometimes deserted and whom he thereby had the chance to help ; and he often took the chance, and became, as we note later, a worthy patron. On the publisher's side, when the publisher began his dealing with an author, he would often support him through difficult times, and, as Murray did with Washington Irving, end by paying out of friendship and esteem more than the works justified commercially. And though the complaint was made, that, to quote Hogg, " it is a maxim with the trade to monopolize every author they once publish a book for, and that no man may take a share on any conditions," such jealousy was very natural on the part of the publisher and more likely than not to profit the author too.

UNDER these conditions the publishing trade from 1800 onwards progressively prospered. It passed through periods of difficulty. The taxation and uncertainty of the Continental war would now and again bring things near a crisis and cut down severely the demand for books. But the demand soon recovered and grew larger still. The crash even of 1826, when Constable, and the Ballantynes, and the London firm of Hurst and Robinson fell, put an end to rashness and imprudent progress on credits, but it was hardly more than a salutary reminder to the rest of the trade. Constable's vision of a reading populace was no chimera. With an object lesson in caution the trade went on to realize it.

(iv)

THE way the public was growing is shown most clearly in the progress of periodical literature, but there are many other indications. Above all, it is hard to over-estimate the influence such popular genius as that of Scott and Byron must have had on the growth of the habit of reading. They both had the rare quality, seen again later in Dickens, of going to the hearts of people high and low. They must have shown the charms of literature for the first time to many a one, and

led him and her to the book-shop and the circulating library. And those, in particular, who were
young in the days of that glory could hardly fail
to carry on with them an appreciation of the place
of literature in life. For Scott and Byron be-
witched the public mind with their poetic wizardry,
and well deserved their titles of the Wizard of the
North, and the Grand Napoleon of the Realms
of Rhyme. Indeed, according to all accounts,
they aroused without effort a furore of excitement
which in these days it is hard to realize. No
poetry had sold so quickly and extensively before.
By 1825 the *Lay* had reached its fourteenth
edition, and thirty-three thousand copies had been
placed on the market, and by the same year there
had been issued thirty-one thousand copies of
Marmion. Cadell spoke of the " intense anxiety "
with which *The Lady of the Lake* was expected.
None of Scott's works, he said, " excited a more
extraordinary sensation when it did appear. The
whole country rang with the praises of the poet."
And following the original issue in majestic quarto,
four octavo editions in a year brought it nearer the
pockets of the middle class, and its early sale soon
totalled some twenty thousand, while " some forty-
four thousand copies had been disposed of in this
country, and by the legitimate trade alone, before
[Scott] superintended the edition of 1830." When
Rokeby in 1813 sold only ten thousand copies in
three months, it was considered not as successful
as had been hoped. Even so Lockhart could
" well remember, being in those days a young
student at Oxford, how the booksellers' shops
there were beleaguered for the earliest copies, and
how he that had been so fortunate as to secure

one was followed to his chambers by a tribe of friends."

By then, too, Byron was dividing the attention of the public. The first cantos of *Childe Harold* sold to the extent of four and a half thousand copies in six months. They made him famous. Of *The Bride of Abydos* six thousand went in one month, and when *The Corsair* appeared early in 1814, Murray had to write, " I sold on the day of publication—a thing perfectly unprecedented—ten thousand copies. You have no notion of the sensation which the publication has occasioned." And in a few weeks Murray was saying, " You cannot meet a man in the street who has not read or heard read the *Corsair*." In fact, the public mind was tremendously excited and was revelling in the enchantments of the romantic and passionate poems. Mark Rutherford was not wrong when he showed his poor republican printer soothing himself with the rich emotion of Byron's verse. To meet the demand, cheap editions had soon to follow on the expensive first editions which the trade still produced. Murray, in 1818, prepared a uniform edition of Byron in three volumes saying, " These I shall print very handsomely, and to sell very cheap, so that every facility shall be given for their popularity." And when in 1827 there was still no uniform edition of Byron owing to difficulties about some of the copyrights, Murray simply had to act and buy up the outstanding rights for £3,885, because, so he wrote, " the public are absolutely indignant. . . . at least fifteen thousand copies have been brought here from France."

As for Scott's novels, after *Rob Roy* the usual

first issue consisted of ten thousand, for of *Rob Roy* itself the first edition of ten thousand was sold out in three weeks and a second of three thousand at once put in the press. And though, with *Ivanhoe*, the price was raised from eight to ten shillings for each of the three volumes, still twelve thousand of the original issue were sold. In spite of their coming so fast one after another, the demand seldom fell off more than slightly, while of the enthusiastic way in which they were received, we have a glimpse in Constable's record of the arrival in London of *The Fortunes of Nigel*. " So keenly," he wrote, " were the people devouring my friend *Jingling Geordie*, that I actually saw them reading it in the streets as they passed along. I assure you there is no exaggeration in this. . . . The smack Ocean, by which the new work was shipped, arrived at the wharf on Sunday ; the bales were got out by *one* on Monday morning, and before half-past ten o'clock 7,000 copies had been dispersed ! " [1] And when the novels came out in a collected edition in 1829 they continued to be bought with an eagerness which surprised both publisher and author. When eight volumes had been issued, the monthly sale had reached as high as 35,000.[2]

So Byron and Scott reigned till death, and in their deaths, no less than while they lived, was revealed the hold they had won over the imagination of the people. " One day," says Borrow, " I found myself about noon at the bottom of Oxford Street. . . . Happening to cast my eyes around, it suddenly occurred to me that something uncommon was expected ; people were standing in

---

[1] Lockhart, *Life of Scott*, p. 418.   [2] *Ibid.*, p. 575.

groups on the pavement—the upstair windows of the houses were thronged with faces, especially those of women, and many of the shops were partly, and not a few entirely, closed. . . . What could be the matter ? Just then I heard various voices cry ' There it comes ! ' and all heads were turned up Oxford Street, down which a hearse was slowly coming : . . . ' Whose body is in that hearse ? ' said I to a dapper-looking individual, seemingly a shopkeeper, who stood beside me on the pavement, looking at the procession. ' The mortal relics of Lord Byron.' . . . and then I turned my eyes upon the hearse proceeding slowly up the almost endless street. This man, this Byron, had for many years past been the demigod of England, and his verses the daily food of those who read, from the peer to the draper's assistant ; all were admirers, or rather worshippers, of Byron, and all doted on his verses." [1] So Borrow on Byron. And when Scott in his turn went, " almost every paper," says Lockhart, " that announced this event in Scotland, and many in England, had the signs of mourning usual on the demise of a King. With hardly an exception, the voice was that of universal, unmixed grief and veneration."

BUT there are plentiful signs of the growing popularity of reading apart from in the sales of Scott and Byron. Possibly the latter stimulated reading more than any other authors did, but other authors were beginning to get a very good share of this growing attention to literature. Between 1801 and 1816 Rogers's *Pleasures of Memory* went through eight more editions, totalling some

---

[1] *Lavengro* (World's Classics), pp. 253-4.

ten thousand copies, and in 1813, according to the *Quarterly Review*, " it is to be found in all libraries and in most parlour windows." Even such mediocre verse and prose as was gathered in the *Remains* of Kirke White edited by Southey went through ten editions between 1807 and 1823. For mediocre though it was, it had a wide class to whom it appealed by its evangelical piety, and the minds of evangelicals, and especially of Dissenters were, perhaps naturally, more eager and curious than others, and anxious for edification. At least Alaric Watts told Blackwood in 1821 that " all Dissenting works have many readers." [1] And when, further, we look for signs of an intelligent interest in the best literature among other than the older limited literary circles we see it in the courses of lectures by Coleridge on Dante and others, and the lectures of Campbell in Birmingham and Liverpool. When Crabb Robinson went to one of Coleridge's, he recorded that he was " gratified unexpectedly by finding a large and respectable audience generally of superior-looking persons, in physiognomy rather than dress." [2]

OF this comparatively new body of middle-class people who were better read than clothed, there is excellent testimony in the *Edinburgh Review* of 1812. The subject was Crabbe's recent volume of *Tales*, which, like the rest of his poems, the reviewer held that only the humbler classes could fully appreciate. " It was wise," he said, " and meritorious in Mr. Crabbe to occupy himself with such beings. In this country there are probably not less than *two hundred thousand*

---

[1] Oliphant, *William Blackwood and his Sons*, i. 499.   [2] *Diary*, ii. 85.

persons who read for amusement or instruction among *the middling classes* of society. In the higher classes there are not so many as *twenty thousand*. It is easy to see therefore which a poet should choose to please for his own glory and emolument, and which he should wish to delight and amend out of mere philanthropy. The fact too, we believe, is, that a great part of the larger body are to the full as well educated and as high-minded as the smaller ; and, though their taste may not be so correct and fastidious, we are persuaded that their sensibility is greater." [1]

THEY were, in fact, replacing the smaller public as the arbiters of taste. Publishers must as a general rule provide for the majority, and the taste of the middle-class majority was henceforth their guide. And yet, though the tastes of the new readers were different, they were not very different. Thus some readers shared the taste of the smaller literary public for belles-lettres, and their numbers grew, as Isaac D'Israeli found with the popularity of his *Calamities of Authors* and of the *Essay on the Literary Character* which, in his son's words, continued to " make belles-lettres charming to the multitude." And certainly the change by no means necessarily lowered the general standard of literature. Sir Richard Phillips " thinks belles-lettres are nonsense, and denies the existence of *taste* ; " but, says D'Israeli to Murray, " it exists ! I flatter myself you will profit under that divinity." And he was to a considerable extent right. The new public would have that kind of book, too, so long as it was presented popularly. In 1807 the *Monthly*

[1] Crabbe, *Life and Works*, p. 369.

Magazine was enjoying an extensive popular sale. It catered for the general reader, as he wanted it to. Then Longmans started an *Athenæum* monthly under Dr. Aikin, which was designed to rival it but to aim at a higher literary character. It failed because its sale was inadequate, for naturally a critical taste would not grow in a day. But literary taste did grow, especially in a demand for literary news. " Give us foreign literature, particularly German, and let them create news in all departments," wrote Murray to Blackwood in 1817 giving advice on *Maga*. And again in 1818 he urged Blackwood similarly, saying, " Sir Richard Phillips replied truly to D'Israeli who boasted of the *talent* he could muster, ' I don't care a farthing for talent.' Nothing is equal to the excellence of most of our papers abstractedly. The prominent feature of the magazine should be literary and scientific news, and most of all the latter, for which your editors seem to have little estimation, and they seem to be not the least aware that this is ten times more interesting to the public than any other class of literature at present. . . . Your editors want tact as to the public interest." [1]   And public interest was still literary, though less literary as science came more and more into the forefront of popularity, and less thorough as the old basis of classical learning grew rarer.

In fact, the change that came over the reading public as it grew, was in the main the result of the passing away of the old classical education. Mathias had felt that the classics were losing their place, and he had urged that they should be kept. But

---

[1] Smiles, *A Publisher and his Friends*, i. 480.

though they might be kept for the few, they could not hope to be adopted for the many. They were not what was wanted in the Academies, those continually increasing private schools which we have noticed before to have been coming to meet the new middle-class demand for an education which would more immediately fit lads for the expanding industrial world of the day. And the classics were losing ground in many of the old endowed grammar schools too. Everything tended towards an education that was less literary, and more secular and utilitarian. The ideal changes from one of thoroughness to one of extensiveness, where width of knowledge was accounted better than depth. And the change was helped on by the rise of competitive examination which, said T. L. Peacock, " takes for its *norma* ' It is better to learn many things ill than one thing well ' ; or rather, ' It is better to learn to gabble about everything than to understand anything.' " For the widening of the curriculum inevitably followed the demand for useful and scientific knowledge. However strongly the old schools stood by the old standard, they could only hold their posts secure for themselves and let the main tide of progress surge past them.

THE first quarter of the nineteenth century saw a very strong and important progress in teaching. Hundreds of thousands though there were in the big industrial cities of sweating-factories who could neither read nor write, the beginning of education for the poor had come. It was henceforth the object of an unremitting agitation. The Sunday Schools continued their good work of combined religious and secular instruction. An effort to provide universal education for those too poor to pay for it was made by Whitbread in his Parochial School Bill of 1807. The Bill was lost, but hope did not die. And meantime the new system associated with the names of Bell and Lancaster advanced in a spirit of rivalry. Bell had introduced the 'monitorial' method into London in 1798, and in 1801 Lancaster opened the Borough Road School. In 1808 the idea had gained such ground that the Royal Lancasterian Institution (later the British and Foreign Bible Society) was founded. But its aim in religious education was undenominational, and the Church of England was not long in entering the educational lists in opposition. In fact, the whole country was divided with bitterness over the question whether the poor should become merely Christians or additionally acquainted with the tenets of the Established Church. As the result Bell and his supporters brought to birth in 1811 the National Society to superintend the welfare of the poor of the Church. And between them the two Societies did much. But naturally, the population increasing as it was, what they could do was far from adequate. The people were crying out to be taught. The times were hard and the people restless. Wordsworth in 1817 feared " we are in danger of an insurrection of the Yahoos," and he was by no means alone. And so Parliament once again began to concern itself with the condition of the ' lower orders,' and in 1816 it had appointed a Select Committee to enquire into their education. But though the Committee in its report made several good recommendations on which Brougham based his Bill of 1820, nothing came of it. Brougham's Bill perished, and the years passed with no more than agitation and discussion until the roars of the Reform mobs again sounded hoarsely dangerous. BUT if the educational facilities of the poor remained inadequate, at least they were better and more plentiful than they had been before. And the education of the poor, and education in general, had a very valuable asset in Brougham. He was prominent among the founders of the first orphan school in London. He, with Dr. Birkbeck, did much to set going the Mechanics' Institutes throughout the country. He, with his propaganda and not least in the *Edinburgh Review*, kept the whole question of education well to the front. He, too, was one of the strongest supporters of the scheme for a University in London from which came the University College of 1826, to give at last such a rivalry to Oxford and Cambridge as the Academies had borne to the endowed schools, and to provide courses in Arts and Science from which Jews and nonconformists should not be shut out. Above all, he it was who realized that the public did not want schools only but literature also, and thereupon gave himself to the foundation of the Society for the Diffusion of Useful Knowledge. And all these efforts of his, coming to a head in the late twenties, were a prelude to the much quicker advance of popular instruction which came after the passage of the Reform Bill had cleared the way and released new energies.

IN fact, this period, though poor enough still in actual achievement, was rich in many progressive tendencies. The Universities and big endowed schools again drew students and rose in reputation and efficiency. The smaller endowed schools gained the sanction of Parliament to dispense with the restrictions of their charters and adapt themselves to new needs. The poor became anxious for education and were in some degree satisfied. And the education which the middle class as a whole received, was more up-to-date and wider. Thus along with the development of transport, and industry and manufacture, which we have already considered, went the development of educational methods and organization to produce a public, and in particular a reading public, such in its essential characteristics as we have to-day.

THE weak side of the new public was the superficiality of its reading, a natural enough product of the new facility. To a writer in the *Edinburgh Review* in 1829 the age seemed " mechanical in its intellectual and literary aspects." " The public nowadays," said he, " read a great deal but in so confused and immethodical a manner that they retain no impressions ; it is like an evanescent stamp upon wet sand." But although it has its truth, that is obviously the exaggeration common to one who criticizes his own day. Yet the same note had been sounded in the opening number of the *Athenæum* in 1828 where, in a comparison of the times with a century before, it was said : " Now, ten times the number of works are produced, but the labour of a few weeks is deemed sufficient for the history of one of the most extraordinary individuals. . . . It has been the fashion to impute this inundation of trifling books to the bad taste of the publishers, as if *they* were the persons that gave an impulse to the public mind. . . . A publisher is merely a merchant who deals in books. . . . If the wealthy and educated . . . will not pay the just price of works that cost an author years of study and research— if the limited sale of such productions leave, in general, a loss to both author and publisher— other and cheaper wares must be substituted, and the public be supplied with books got up in haste to suit the market." [1]

AGAIN the public then had its crazes for best-selling scandal. So we see the crowds standing ten deep at the doors of Stockdale the publisher on the morning when a new volume of the notorious Memoirs of Harriette Wilson appeared in 1825 ; and we need not be surprised that thirty editions were sold in a year. For those crazes are the weakness of the public in every age. And again there was the prolific trash that Hone sold and that he found sold very well—his parodies and catchpenny murderers' confessions and the cheap little political pamphlets with caricatures by Cruikshanks, the first of which, *The Political House that Jack Built*, was popular to the extent of a sale of a hundred thousand.

BUT such examples, except that they show that a great many people were reading something, do not give a true picture of public taste. The public, often though they bought trash and superficial though they tended to be, were in those days anxious more than anything for information. Their true taste and the trend of the age are best expressed in such words as these of Captain Basil Hall in a letter of January 1826 to Constable : " The thirst for information is so vehement that it

---

1 J. C. Francis, *John Francis*, i. 24.

cannot be quenched, and the more you feed it, the more you will have to feed it." It was the same thirst that at the same time led to the founding of the Society for the Diffusion of Useful Knowledge. And it is to the credit of the trade that they did feed it, and go on feeding it, and so take once more the opportunity of educating the people better than the professional educators were themselves doing or able to do. As Constable said to Mr. Leonard Horner in October 1824, " The present desire of knowledge among mechanics and manufacturers in every part of the island, which you have yourself so greatly promoted, has occasioned the publication of numerous works of a class hitherto unknown in this country, but all of them of a description inferior to what I hope may ere long be done." [1] And Constable projected, and but for his fall might have realized " an Encyclopædia or Dictionary entirely devoted to manufactures and mechanical arts," in producing which the main object would have been extensive circulation at a cheap rate. Such, indeed, was the effort to meet the demand that the market was soon very fairly full of cheap and informative books.

In this body of popular literature reprints of the older writers take a prominent place. Again it was the smaller publishers who broke in on the monopoly as Donaldson had done before. For despite the absence of legal rights the big publishers continued to sell their shares in lapsed copyright and to keep a monopoly by inflicting on the trade generally a kind of stringent etiquette. But in about 1819 Thomas Tegg made a big invasion, and though he naturally met with abuse,

[1] T. Constable, *Archibald Constable*, ii. 391.

was very successful. His editions might leave something to be desired for craftsmanship but they sold at half the price. And in this line in the early twenties too, there was Hone with his popular series of sixpenny reprints, while about 1830 there followed Pickering who also met with abuse but who also succeeded, and whose books were both cheap and good.

ALL these reprints were perfectly justifiable, but there must be added much real piracy in those years, though, as a rule, of works and by printers not worth the prosecuting. But the small fry of publishers kept their eyes open for works like *Wat Tyler*, of which Southey complained, " as there is no copyright, every one has printed it." *Queen Mab* suffered a like fate. *Knickerbocker's History of New York* suffered piracy in 1820, and then Murray had trouble over *Cain* and *Don Juan* being reprinted in cheap editions. Of the latter Byron is made to say in a *Noctes* conversation of 1822, " I was a good deal pained when I saw my books, in consequence of [Eldon's] decree, degraded to be published in sixpenny numbers by Benbow, with Lawrence's Lectures—Southey's Wat Tyler—Paine's Age of Reason—and the Chevalier de Faublas."[1] And though it was not very creditable to such men as Benbow, it is a sign of a public demand, and was in its way, together with the honest productions of Hone and Tegg, an educative work in so far as it encouraged the habit of reading.

IN directly educational productions there was much good and useful work brought out by William Pinnock. He set up in London in 1817,

---

1 *Noctes Ambrosianæ*, No. 4.

and for some years devoted himself to publishing histories and grammars and arithmetics and geographies and similar works. They were sold cheaply and they met a genuinely felt need ; and they brought a good income into the pockets of Pinnock. By his abridgement of Goldsmith's *History of England* he made £2,000 within a year, and he probably made between four and five thousand a year from his general output. But his books undoubtedly advanced the cause of popular education. And the older publishers were not inactive in the same line. Murray, for example, made a big schoolbook success of Mrs. Markham's *History of England*. And there were Croker's little histories. And there were the *Miscellanies* which the *Scotsman* of January 1827 declared to be " a prodigious engine for the diffusion of every species of useful and ornamental knowledge through the lower and middle classes of society." Nor should we omit to remember the ' number ' trade which continued to flourish, and to reach people in the small towns and villages whom the regular publishers and booksellers did not touch at all. Their scope is indicated in the following passage in a letter from Robinson to Constable : " Stevens published the *History of the Wars of the French Revolution* in two vols. quarto, and it died almost as soon as it appeared, and some years after it was made into waste paper. Baines of Leeds republished it . . . and circulated through the hawkers above twenty thousand copies in sixpenny Nos., but if my memory is correct Davies and Booth and other great hawkers only paid Baines twopence-halfpenny per No. . . . Davies and Booth were the greatest people in this line out of

185

London."[1]   And if we turn to the history of the house of Blackie, we learn something of the supply and demand for ' number ' works in Scotland. Of the second decade of the nineteenth century it is said that " in these days the visit of the travelling bookman often created quite a stir in country places.   In fact, so far from requiring to seek out the customers at their dwellings, the customers came, cash in hand, to the traveller's lodgings, eager to obtain the next number or part of the publication for which they had subscribed.   So eager were people to obtain the books that the traveller, having probably lost time on the earlier part of his journey, sometimes endeavoured, and that successfully, to redeem part of his loss by sending the town-crier to announce his arrival. Not only did existing subscribers flock to obtain their books and parts, but many people came to have their names entered as subscribers.   On one notable occasion it is reported that at least forty or fifty orders for large Family Bibles were taken in this manner in a single afternoon by Mr. Blackie himself."[2]   From which it is clear that ' number ' publishing was thoroughly worked, and must have done much to keep alive some intellectual activity in the rural districts.

AGAIN to supply and increase the wider reading public there were the second-hand book-shops and the remainder sellers.   The great name in the early years of the century was still Lackington's, but there was also Greenland, a very cheap and extensive second-hand bookseller in Finsbury. Their very large and cheap stocks attracted people

---

1 Constable, *Archibald Constable*, iii. 364.
2 W. G. Blackie, *Origin and progress of the Firm of Blackie & Son*, 1809-74, 1897, pp. 13-14.

who had not been readers before and who were not likely to go to the regular booksellers, for their pride's as well as their pocket's sake. For there were many people who began to share the desire for reading but who were too completely unacquainted with books to venture into a shop that did not cater for their peculiar needs. Theirs had been the experience of Lackington himself in the days of his friendship with Jones at Bristol. Lackington and Jones wanted to buy books, but they knew not what. In Lackington's words, " So ignorant were we on the subject, that neither of us knew what books were fit for our perusal, nor what to enquire for, as we had scarce ever heard or seen even any *title pages*, except a few of the religious sort, which at that time we had no relish for. So that we were at a loss how to increase our small stock of science. And here I cannot help thinking that had fortune thrown proper works in our way, we should have imbibed a just taste for literature, and soon made some tolerable progress." On his experience and its lesson he makes the comment : " As we could not tell what to enquire for, we were ashamed to go into the booksellers' shops ; and I assure you, my friend, that there are thousands now in England in the very same situation ; many, very many, have come to my shop, who have discovered an enquiring mind, but were totally at a loss what to ask for and who had no friend to direct them." [1] And Lackington did help to direct them. But though the poorer classes began more and more to want information, they continued to fight shy of the shops and to need drawing

[1] Lackington, *Memoirs*, p. 79.

187

in. So Chambers records : " Hundreds, I found, as Lackington had done before me, would buy books from a stall, who would not purchase them equally cheap in a shop." [1] But the second-hand shops did good work and the stalls as well.

THE remainder market, too, became bigger. It annoyed Constable to see how new remainders were going off so cheaply, and indeed the big publishers, as a body, rather tolerated than approved the system. But the system had come to stay—and the *Morning Chronicle* in November 1825 declared : " The demand of the body of the people has given quite a new complexion to the trade of late years. Formerly a book which did not sell in a year or two went as a matter of course to the trunk maker. Now the remainder of an edition after a certain time is disposed of at trade sales to a numerous class of booksellers on a small scale through whom it is distributed through every part of the metropolis and the country for the convenience of purchasers in humble life. This trade has sprung up within our own remembrance of the metropolis." [2] And, in fact, it had been largely Lackington's creation. But one of the biggest figures of the next generation in remainders as well as in cheap reprints was that of Tegg. He made a great bargain in the panic of 1826 by buying up the remainders of *Waverley* novels. Later, in 1834, he took over Murray's Family Library and made a popular success of that too.

No less important for the growth of the reading public was the increasing volume of literature for children. It was changed like the age, and

1 *Memoir of Robert Chambers*, 1872, p. 142.
2 Constable, *Archibald Constable*, iii. 478.

reflected the new spirit of information strongly. Already in 1802 Lamb wrote that " Mrs. Barbauld's stuff has banished all the old classics of the nursery ; and the shopman at Newbery's hardly deigned to reach them off an old exploded corner of a shelf, when Mary asked for them. Mrs. Barbauld's and Mrs. Trimmer's nonsense lay in piles about. Knowledge insignificant and vapid as Mrs. B.'s books convey, it seems, must come to a child in the *shape* of *knowledge*, and his empty noodle must be turned with conceit of his own powers." [1]   And for moral teaching there followed on the stuff of Mrs. Barbauld the *Original Poems for Infant Minds* of the Misses Taylor in 1804, and later their *Rhymes for the Nursery*, and their *Hymns*, all of which were widely popular and good enough of their kind.

BUT the old stories were gone before the breath of the " improved pedagogy," and Crabb Robinson finds in 1812 that " the Godwins very much admire Miss Flaxman's design for ' Robin Goodfellow ' but do not think they would sell.   Parents are now so set against all stories of ghosts that fifty copies of such designs would not sell in a year." [2]   Ghosts were replaced by information, so that no wonder Scott " detested and despised the whole generation of modern children's books, in which the attempt is made to convey accurate notions of scientific minutiæ : delighting cordially, on the other hand, in those of the preceding age, which, addressing themselves chiefly to the imagination, obtain through it, as he believed, the best chance of stirring our graver faculties also." [3]

1 E. V. Lucas, *Life of Lamb*, i. 283.   2 *Diary*, i. 379.
3 Lockhart, *Life of Scott*, p. 189.

This state of things roused Scott to producing *Tales of a Grandfather*, to be simple but not so simple as Croker's tales from history, and they had a " reception more rapturous than that of any of his works since Ivanhoe."

BUT such tales as Scott's were rare in their excellence, although they were of their own day, too, in ministering to the demand for knowledge. And knowledge, with a characteristic flavour not altogether successfully banished under the nom-de-guerre of Edward Baldwin, came from the pen and the publishing business of Godwin. There were his *Fables*, and his *Dictionary for Children* which defined revolution as " things returning to their first shape." But along with those were such good works as Lamb supplied, and such a series as that to which Lamb gave its first number in his *King and Queen of Hearts*, the Copper Plate Series issued at one shilling plain, and one shilling and sixpence coloured. And, while that series catered for the children of the better-to-do, Catnach about 1815 started a new line of children's books at a farthing for the poor. Pinnock, too, had special children's books among his educational publications, such as his series of eighty-three Catechisms at ninepence each, which met with extraordinary success and were collected as a *Juvenile Cyclopedia*. And, further, children had their magazines such as Darton and Harvey's *Minor's Pocket Book*, an annual in which Ann Taylor as a girl won a poetical prize and to which she afterwards became a regular contributor, and the *Youth's Magazine* which Jane Taylor served regularly from 1816 to 1822. And there would have been a very considerably bigger advance in literature for the young than there was if Constable's proposed Encyclopædia for Youth had proceeded. He approached Miss Edgeworth on the subject and offered payment at the rate of £1 a printed page, but the doings of 1826 put an end to it. Yet though this failed to come, juvenile literature had made good progress. And it remained for the most part the preserve of the increasingly numerous woman writer. In addition to such well-known names as those of Miss Edgeworth, and the Misses Taylor, there are many other names to which a good output of this kind is attached. There were Mrs. Dorset, Maria Hack, Mrs. Hofland, Mrs. Strickland, and most prolific of all Mary Elliott with some sixteen books to her credit in some twenty years.

FINALLY, we may note the increase in the use of advertising as a sign and a cause of the increase in the habit of reading. Advertising was not new. It had been the victim of a tax since 1712. But it had been comparatively negligible in the bookselling world, and probably the summaries of books in the *Critical* and *Monthly* Reviews (their reviews being no more than the baldest summaries) had been the best advertisement so far. But in Scott's day it was coming more into prominence. The same unintentional advertising that the reviews did was all the greater as the reviews multiplied and were quarterly and monthly and weekly too. And about 1821 when its sale was some three thousand the *Literary Gazette* was one of the best advertising mediums for books there was. It was a favourite source from which country papers quoted extracts, and once twenty provincial organs had been known to quote anecdotes from the same article. But commercial advertisement of books advanced as well, and publishers began to spend considerable sums on it. Constable was convinced of its uses. " Advertisements in the ordinary way in newspapers," he wrote to Robinson in 1825, " you may depend upon it, *always pay*. You may think otherwise, and be told otherwise ; but I say—advertise judiciously and you will never fail to reap the benefit." [1] Longman, in Wordsworth's opinion, advertised only too much and ate up all the author's profits. The poet complained that he got £9 8s. 2d. on the first edition of his book on the Lakes and was charged £27 2s. 3d. for the advertisements. Nor was Longman alone. Murray " advertises even more expensively than Longman, though that seems scarcely possible," said Wordsworth with somewhat despondent irritation. But the most go-ahead of publishers for advertising was Colburn. He was a prophet of the modern spirit and his advertisements were at once the scandal and the admiration of the literary world. Around 1830 he was spending, on an average, £9,000 a year on them.

AND as the reading public, from all these causes and in all these ways, continued to grow and to become more interested in science and more anxious to be informed, it also went on becoming more moral, as it had been doing during the half-century preceding. " I congratulate Young England," wrote Southey ironically, " upon the March of Modesty ! How delightful that it should thus keep pace with the March of Intellect ! . . . We have already a Family Shakespeare. . . .

1 Constable, *Archibald Constable*, iii. 341.

Mr. Murray cannot do less than provide the public with a Family Byron." [1]   And indeed, Murray did go so far as to agree to " a castigated edition of the Faërie Queene," but to the editor's annoyance he changed his mind before it was published, for the new public were not quite so squeamish as all that, or as Southey's irony would suggest. Yet they were squeamish enough.   How publishers feared their primness we may see from Lockhart's anecdote of the remonstrance made by James Ballantyne against the first draft of *St. Ronan's Well*.   He relates that " in the original conception, and in the book as actually written and printed, Miss Mowbray's mock marriage had not halted at the profaned ceremony of the church ; and the delicate printer shrank from the idea of obtruding on the fastidious public the possibility of any personal contamination having been incurred by a high-born damsel of the nineteenth century." [2]   So Ballantyne and Constable induced Scott to change it.   Thus far had the steady improvement of national taste gone in sixty odd years.

THE general tone of literature was now for the most part unexceptional, and the change is nowhere better illustrated than in the story Scott told of an old lady, a great-aunt of his.   " One day," he said, " she asked me when we happened to be alone together, whether I had ever seen Mrs. Behn's novels ?—I confessed the charge. Whether I could get her a sight of them ?—I said, with some hesitation, I believed I could ; but that I did not think she would like either the manners, or the language, which approached too near that of

[1] Southey, *The Doctor* (1856), p. 380.   [2] Lockhart, *Life of Scott*, p. 453.

Charles II's time to be quite proper reading. ' Nevertheles,' said the good old lady, ' I remember them being so much admired, and being so much interested in them myself, that I wish to look at them again.' To hear was to obey. So I sent Mrs. Aphra Behn, curiously sealed up, with ' private and confidential ' on the packet, to my gay old grand-aunt. The next time I saw her afterwards, she gave me back Aphra, properly wrapped up, with nearly these words : ' Take back your bonny Mrs. Behn ; and if you will take my advice, put her in the fire, for I found it impossible to get through the very first novel. But is it not," she said, " a very odd thing that I, an old woman of eighty and upwards, sitting alone, feel myself ashamed to read a book which, sixty years ago, I have heard read aloud for the amusement of large circles, consisting of the first and most creditable society in London ? ' " [1]

(v)

IN considering the growth of the reading public we have so far outlined only the broad progress up to 1825. In the quarter of the century preceding 1825 we have seen that public becoming appreciably bigger and in character more like that of to-day. Apart from the magic influences of Byron and Scott, it had been a natural development, an expansion that was part of the expansion of the national life. The condition in the industrial and commercial world had helped in making readers at once more numerous and more intellectually interested and various. Everything

[1] Lockhart, *Life of Scott*, p. 412.

tended to a wider but patchier knowledge, a taste less narrowly cultured but more generally diffused, a desire among all classes for news and information, and a very considerable levelling of classes in so far as publishers were concerned. The middle-class reader, because he was now the biggest purchaser of books, had come to have the biggest say in their production.

YET, even so, in 1825, many more readers though there were, the reading public was only a small proportion of the general public, and by no means a large proportion even of those whose education should have fitted them to be readers. But in 1825 there was born in the fertile brain of Constable the vital and vitalizing idea of literature for the people, of cheap books on a vast scale. It was a fit climax to a publishing career which had begun with unheard-of prices to authors. In a blaze of vision the poet-publisher saw a world of the immediate future in which on every side there would be cheap books and good books, and in which there would be no excuse for anyone not to read, and in which everyone would read. " A grand scheme of revolution in the whole art and traffic of publishing," Lockhart called it, and he draws a vivid picture of the scene at Abbotsford when Constable first expounded it to Scott one Saturday in May 1825.

NONE were present, he says, except Sir Walter, Ballantyne, Constable, and himself. " After dinner there was a little pause of expectation, and the brave schemer suddenly started *in medias res*, saying : ' Literary genius may, or may not, have done its best ; but the trade are in the cradle.' Scott eyed the florid bookseller's beaming countenance, and the solemn stare with which the equally portly printer was listening, and pushing round the bottles with a hearty chuckle, bade me ' Give our two *soncie babbies* a drap mother's milk.' Constable sucked in fresh inspiration, and proceeded to say that, wild as we might think him, certain new plans, of which we had all already heard some hints, had been suggested by, and were, in fact, mainly grounded upon, a sufficiently prosaic authority—namely, the annual schedule of assessed taxes, a copy of which interesting document he drew from his pocket, and substituted for his *D'Oyley*. It was copiously diversified, ' text and margent,' by figures and calculations in his own handwriting, which I for one might have regarded with less reverence, had I known at the time this ' great arithmetician's ' rooted aversion and contempt for all examination of his own balance-sheet. He had, however, taken vast pains to fill in the number of persons who might fairly be supposed to pay the taxes for each separate article of luxury, armorial bearings, hunters, racers, four-wheeled carriages, etc. etc. ; and having demonstrated that hundreds of thousands held, as necessary to their comfort and station, articles upon articles of which their forefathers never dreamt, said, that our self-love never deceived us more grossly than when we fancied our notions as to the matter of books had advanced in at all a corresponding proportion. ' On the contrary,' cried Constable, ' I am satisfied that the demand for Shakespeare's plays, contemptible as we hold it to have been, in the time of Elizabeth and James, was more creditable to the classes who really indulged in any sort of elegance then, than the sale of *Childe Harold* or *Waverley* is to this nineteenth century.' "

" SCOTT helped him on by interposing that at that moment he had a rich valley crowded with handsome houses under his view, and yet much doubted whether any laird within ten miles spent ten pounds per annum on the literature of the day. ' No,' said Constable, ' there is no market among them that's worth one's thinking about. They are contented with a review or a magazine, or at best with a paltry subscription to some circulating library forty miles off. But if I live for half a dozen years, I'll make it as impossible that there should not be a good library in every decent house in Britain as that the shepherd's ingle-nook should want the *saut poke*. Ay, and what's that ? ' he continued, warming and puffing ; ' why should the ingle-nook itself want a shelf for *the novels* ? '— ' I see your drift, my man,' says Sir Walter ;— ' you're for being like Billy Pitt in Gilray's print— you want to get into the salt-box yourself.' —' Yes,' he responded (using a favourite adjuration)—' I have hitherto been thinking only of the wax lights, but before I'm a twelvemonth older I shall have my hand upon the tallow.'—' Troth,' says Scott, ' you are indeed likely to be " The grand Napoleon of the realms of *print*." ' ' If you outlive me,' says Constable, with a regal smile, ' I bespeak that line for my tombstone, but, in the meantime, may I presume to ask you to be my right-hand man when I open my campaign of Marengo ? I have now settled my outline of operations—a three-shilling or half-crown volume every month, which must and shall sell, not by thousands or tens of thousands, but by hundreds of thousands—ay, by millions ! Twelve volumes in the year, a halfpenny of profit upon every copy of which will make me richer than the possession of all the copyrights of all the quartos that ever were, or will be, hot-pressed ! twelve volumes, so good that millions must wish to have them, and so cheap that every butcher's callant may have them, if he pleases to let me tax him sixpence a week ! ' "

" MANY a previous consultation, and many a solitary meditation, too, prompted Scott's answer. —' Your plan,' said he, ' cannot fail, provided the books be really good ; but you must not start until you have not only leading columns, but depth upon depth of reserve in thorough order. I am willing to do my part in this grand enterprise.' " [1] So the idea took fire in Constable's mind. Scott was to help with a life of Napoleon. All seemed promising. And though Lockhart could not forget how pride had its fall, and must write of its inception with the patronizing conceit of after-knowledge, promising it still seems to have been, as we look back. Indeed, it is hard for us, familiar though we are with popular literature, to read of that evening at Abbotsford without feeling, as sharers of a vision, something of the excited enthusiasm which Constable succeeded in communicating to Scott, until they were both saying that " the years to come were likely to be more prosperous than any they had as yet seen."

CONSTABLE went steadily on, with the conviction that everything was ripe for the scheme to succeed. He wrote in June to Robinson : " The demand in the higher and literary classes, or those who,

[1] Lockhart, *Life of Scott*, pp. 463–5.

not many years ago, were the only purchasers of books, and for whose taste alone publishers could speculate, I think you allow continues to be fully better than ever ; but there has been, and there exists at present, a desire of knowledge and a demand for books in the middle ranks and manufacturing classes of society altogether unprecedented, to supply which will occasion a demand to fully ten times the amount of any hitherto existing." [1] And again in November we find him writing to Scott to express his intention of raising the standard of the literature which ' the million ' was reading, for " the sale of cheap books in this country," he said, " is at present carried on to an extent altogether astonishing, but almost entirely in the hands of the most inferior class of traders." And so as one who conceived of publishing rather as a profession than a mere trade, he was determined to replace by good books the prevalent " sale of cheap books to corrupt men's minds and create mischief." To achieve that end many of his cheap books were to be republications of the best literature of the day.

HOWEVER, between the vision and the fulfilment came the disaster of 1826. But among many schemes that went awry, that of the *Miscellany* survived, and in January 1827 the first number appeared with a dedication to George IV. In spite of the still depressed condition of the trade it started well, and went on successfully to its completion in seventy-six volumes. And so popular literature on a large scale was after many years of gradual preparation at last in being.

NOR was Constable's *Miscellany* long without

---

[1] Constable, *Archibald Constable*, iii. 349.

imitation. Constable could write of " no fewer than three imitations—all originating from the plan of my work—but none of them, I think, constructed in the popular manner in which mine seems to have been." And in 1829 two more rivals came forward in the Family Library, and the Library of Entertaining Knowledge. They, too, were successful. The former was Murray's. He had been considering such a cheap, popular series at the same time as Constable, but had been slower, as was natural, since he was temperamentally slower than Constable. He intended to include in it histories, biographies, voyages, travels, and scientific works. And it extended to forty-seven volumes, after which the copyrights and remaining copies were acquired by Tegg. The latter was launched on the same day and was issued by Charles Knight for the Society for the Diffusion of Useful Knowledge. And between Murray and Knight the rivalry was a very friendly and hopeful one. " We have plenty of sea-room," wrote the latter, " and need never run foul of each other. My belief is that, in a very few years, scarcely any other description of books will be published, and in that case we that are first in the field may hope to win the race." [1]

Thus between 1827 and the passing of the Reform Bill cheap literature took on an important new aspect. It was indeed to be one of the chief educational forces of the future. What held it back then, and for some years, was the tax. For example there was Limbird's *Mirror of Literature* which, before Charles Knight and the Chambers brothers started, was a herald of cheap weekly

[1] Smiles, *A Publisher and his Friends*, ii. 296.

publications. It was a little sheet, sixteen pages of demy octavo, with one or at the most two woodcuts, and was sold for twopence. In the words of its contemporary *Athenæum* " it is just the humanizing volume that ought to delight the fire-side of every cottage in the kingdom : it is just the work the children would subscribe their halfpence for—and yet it is among the forbidden fruit ; it cannot pass by post without a tax of fourpence on every copy—its sale, therefore, is necessarily limited to the great towns—and we then wonder at the brutal ignorance of our agricultural population." [1] And what were constantly spoken of as the taxes on knowledge came in for general attack. In 1830 *The Examiner* was printing its price

> Paper and Print, 3*d.*)
> Taxes on Knowledge, 4*d.*) 7*d.*

And from about 1830 John Francis was in the forefront of the battle against them, until they were finally done away with. For they had to go, as year by year the need for universal education gained wider recognition.

But though this was only the beginning, and though the taxes checked advance in some directions, the reading public was by 1832 an extensive public. It was " an utterly enlightened age," " an investigating and reforming age " in the eyes of young Macaulay and many of his fellows ; and Macaulay even told Southey when he reviewed the latter's *Colloquies* in 1829 that it was " the most enlightened generation of the most enlightened people that ever existed." And,

[1] J. C. Francis, *John Francis and the Athenæum*, 1888, i. 40.

indeed, we can hardly pick up a collection of informative literature of that day without finding in the preface a reference to " the appetite of the present times for knowledge and scientific facts." We see Dilke in 1831 confident in the existence of a big cultured public. He had just bought the *Athenæum*. One of his first steps was to reduce its price from eightpence to fourpence, because he relied on a large sale and would not think he could not get it. " If the readers of the literary papers be so limited," he argued, " who were the thirty thousand purchasers of the early volumes of the Family Library, who were the fourteen thousand purchasers of the Lives of the Painters, a subject limited in its interest to the highest and most refined class of informed minds ? " [1] And he was rewarded by a sale six times that at the higher price.

" THE craving Dragon—the Public—like him in Bel's temple—must be fed." So Lamb had groaned, and the day had certainly come. The public was indeed a considerable one. We must not overestimate its extent. It is an English middle-class public which we are considering, and that public has always been prone to look on books as luxuries and on reading as idleness. But the reading public, if it was still far from a majority, was by 1832 a big and powerful body. Its promise was such that the *Scotsman* in 1827 gave vent to prophecy : " In a few years," it said, " we predict that every young man when his apprenticeship is done, will lay aside a shilling weekly for books—that a young couple taking up house will reckon thirty or forty volumes of Constable's

1 J. C. Francis, *John Francis and the Athenæum,* 1888, i. 44.

Miscellany as indispensable as a chest of drawers or an eight-day clock—and that the question ' Who is your bookseller ? ' will be as pertinent in every decent family as ' Who is your grocer ' or ' clothier ? ' " [1]   And though that prophecy was too hopeful, it is a good criterion by which to judge the growth and future of the reading public in the first quarter and in the second quarter respectively of last century.   Both were big.

(vi)

THOUGH the growth of the public and the enterprise of the publishers are to be seen in all fields, in none are they to be seen more clearly than in the development of journalism.   Journalism stands out henceforth as the great avenue to success in the profession of letters.   It was the opening which required neither capital nor influence to enter.   It lay ready for aspirants who were poor and humble as well as for those who had a position and an income, and for women as well as men.   And from the middle of the first decade of last century the opening became a bigger one with every year that passed.

JOURNALISM underwent in 1802, with the birth of the *Edinburgh Review*, the greatest change which had taken place in its history since Cave's *Gentleman's Magazine* had appeared in 1731. Before 1802 the higher possibilities of periodical literature had barely been conceived.   " Up to the year 1802," says Gillies, " what pitiful abortions were our so-styled reviews !   The object of their authors was to ' give an account of the

[1] Constable, *Archibald Constable*, iii. 484–5.

books ' ; and the notion that upon every occasion there should be a special drift to contend for, an opportunity caught and improved for benefiting the cause of literature, or politics, or morals, or science, by placing the subject in a new light, seemed never once to have entered into the calculations of our self-complacent editors. We had, it is true, our *English Review*, our *Monthly Review*, our *Critical Review*, our *British Critic* and other such trash." [1]   That is to say, there were magazines on the level of the Erasmus Darwins, and Hayleys, and their dull generation.   Then as the curtain of the new century went up on a fresh company of writers, young, romantic, full of life and rich in talent, it was apt, if not inevitable, that it went up on a new journalism too.

IF there had not been Scott to give fame to Edinburgh and to make it the literary rival of London, the *Edinburgh Review* would have done so.   It was in its policy as in its conception the Review of the young Whigs.   They revolted against the tyrannical dominance of the Tories in literature and life, and the writers and the publisher to give expression to their rebellion were at hand.   Among the writers [2] were Sydney Smith, largely its projector and its first editor, Francis Jeffrey, Brougham, Francis Horner, and for some time Scott ; and the publisher was young Constable, confidently ambitious, who had already shown his enterprise in undertaking his *Farmer's Magazine* two years earlier.   And this venture was no sooner begun than it was justified by success.   Its boldness and the undeniable cap-

---

1 R. P. Gillies, *Memoirs of a Literary Veteran*, i. 304.
2 For the *Edinburgh Review* see T. Constable, *Archibald Constable and his Literary Correspondents, passim.*

ability of its contributors at once rallied an appreciative public.

So the first influential, well-informed quarterly magazine with a definite spirit and policy, created a new standard for journalism. And although it issued from Edinburgh, it quickly made its way in London. In the beginning of 1807 the number sold there was 3,500, and soon after, when Murray became for a while the agent, about 5,000 out of the 7,000 printed in the north were sent south. In 1808 Scott wrote to Ellis that " of this work 9,000 copies are printed quarterly, and no genteel family *can* pretend to be without it, because, independent of its politics, it gives the only valuable literary criticism which can be met with." [1] Only a few months later Murray was complaining that its sale had " arisen to the enormous extent of *eleven thousand* ! " So its circulation soared, and, from the author's point of view, it out-topped all other publications by the scale of its payments. Southey, when he was asked to write for it, was much tempted, and only hesitated because, as he told Scott, his " moral feelings must not be compromised." Otherwise " the emolument to be derived from writing at ten guineas a sheet, Scotch measure, instead of seven pounds for the *Annual*, would be considerable." [2]

THEN the *Edinburgh*, having created a public, drew down on itself a rival. With the field to themselves, and, as Sydney Smith pointed out, the freedom which at that distance they could exercise towards the wits of the South, the

[1] Lockhart, *Life of Scott*, p. 197.
[2] Smiles, *A Publisher and his Friends*, i. 95.

reviewers were provocative in their independence. The younger Tories might have been with them at the start, but the stings of Jeffrey's colleagues gradually stung them into opposition. The gap that grew between the *Edinburgh* and Scott is a typical one. He wrote to Constable at the twenty-sixth number : "The *Edinburgh Review* had become such as to render it impossible for me to continue a contributor to it. *Now* it is such as I can no longer continue to receive or read it." And so the Tories began to consult with one another over the project of a Quarterly of their own. Even in Edinburgh itself there was plotting. Scott was one of those who gathered the con-spirators together. " Consider," wrote he sound-ing Ellis, " of the numbers who read [the *Edinburgh*], how many are likely to separate the literature from the politics—how many youths are there upon whose minds the flashy and bold character of the work is likely to make an indelible impression. Now, I think there is balm in Gilead for all this ; and that the cure lies in instituting such a Review in London as should be conducted totally independent of bookselling influence, on a plan as liberal as that of the Edinburgh, its literature as well supported, and its principles English and constitutional. Accord-ingly, I have been given to understand that Mr. William Gifford is willing to become the conductor of such a work, and I have written to him a very voluminous letter on the subject. Now, should this plan succeed, you must hang your birding-piece on its hooks, take down your old Anti-Jacobin armour, and ' remember your swashing blow.' In point of learning, you Englishmen have

206

ten times our scholarship ; and as for talent and genius, 'Are not Abana and Pharpar, rivers of Damascus, better than any of the rivers in Israel ? ' Have we not yourself and your cousin, the Roses, Malthus, Mathias, Gifford, Heber, and his brother ? Can I not procure you a score of blue-caps, who would rather write for us than for the Edinburgh Review if they got as much pay by it ? ' A good plot, good friends, and full of expectation—an excellent plot, very good friends ! ' " [1] And by February 1809 the plot was stripped of the secrecy in which its promoters had tried not very successfully to conceal it, and the first number of the *Quarterly Review* was brought to birth by Murray and Gifford.

THE *Quarterly* did not make the hit which the *Edinburgh* had made. It began well, but not brilliantly, and it was encumbered at the outset by the irregularity with which Gifford persisted in issuing it until the public grew used to its vagaries. But it became established. Its circulation reached 5,000, sank to 4,000 by its unpunctuality, and then rose steadily to 9,000 in 1816, and 10,000 in January 1817, while, in March 1817, Murray wrote, " Of the next number I am printing 12,000 ; the sale is not exceeded by the *Edinburgh Review*." [2] Its quality attained and continued as high as that of its rival. And in the rivalry, and in its progress, the growth of the reading public and the development of periodical writing are manifest.

HERE were two first-class journals with a wide circulation, and they could not help but educate

---

[1] Lockhart, *Life of Scott,* pp. 197–8.
[2] Smiles, *A Publisher and his Friends,* ii. 39. These volumes contain the story of the *Quarterly* and of Murray's treatment of his contributors.

readers and writers alike and make the journals that were below them better too, while at the same time they set up a new scale of payments for authors, and made periodical writing a more completely self-supporting profession. For, in the latter respect, they were both liberal. When the *Quarterly* began, it, too, paid ten guineas a sheet. Amateurs though many of the contributors might be, professional they had to be in the matter of payment. The unpaid contributor was banished. It still remained the fashion to believe that no gentleman wrote for money. It was a pleasant fiction. But Murray insisted on payment, and if it was refused the article was declined. And for the payments, we see Gifford starting with a salary of £200 as editor, and receiving £500 as an additional present in 1811 for his success, while Lockhart taking over the reins in 1825 began with £1,000 a year. Southey had a hundred guineas for his life of Nelson, and a hundred guineas became the usual product of one of his articles. The only drawback he could find lay in Gifford's editorial " mutilations." Otherwise, " I could get more money from the *Quarterly* by one month's employment than this volume [the second of his *History of Brazil*] will produce me." And the *Quarterly* continued his mainstay. His bigger works paid in comparison negligibly, so that he had to comfort himself that those he wrote " for myself and posterity." In fact, he told Coleridge, " The most profitable line of composition is reviewing. I have not received so much for the *History of the Brazils* in three volumes as for a single article in the *Quarterly*." THESE conditions naturally drew the better part of the profession into the ranks of the reviewers. Everyone could not expect Southey's hundred guineas, but a man like Isaac D'Israeli got £50 in 1820 for his article on Spence's *Anecdotes*. From 1814 Hazlitt was a contributor to the *Edinburgh*. Leigh Hunt was asked to contribute even to the *Quarterly*, which was a surprise to him, for, says he, " I was not aware of the little faith that was held in the politics of any beginner of the world." [1] And the reviews attracted a fine army of recruits both sought and unsought, which was no small thing for the health and progress of the whole profession. It became natural to enter the higher walks of the profession through their gates as Macaulay did. And as the years passed, the payments increased. The original ten guineas became sixteen, and then twenty, and even twenty-five.

Nor were the *Edinburgh* and the *Quarterly* the only quarterlies to appear, though they were the only ones to become established. There was the *Reflector* of 1810, of which Leigh Hunt wrote : " My brother projected a quarterly magazine of literature and politics . . . which I edited. Lamb, Dyer, Barnes, Mitchell . . . Scholefield (all Christ-Hospital men), together with Dr. Aikin and his family, wrote in it ; and it was rising in sale every quarter, when it stopped at the close of the fourth number for want of funds. Its termination was not owing to want of liberality in the payments. But the radical reformers in those days were not sufficiently rich or numerous to support such a publication." [2] And there was Charles Knight's irresponsible and irregular *Quarterly Magazine* of 1822 which only ran to seven numbers, but which

---

made a brave show and contained the early efforts of Macaulay and Praed, with contributions, too, from De Quincey and Derwent Coleridge.

NEITHER was the appearance of the *Edinburgh* and the *Quarterly* the only important advance in this period. Hardly less important were the additions to and the change in monthly periodicals. Excellent though the two great quarterlies were, they could not claim the excellence of lightness. Their quality imposed a limitation, and, as reviews, they were without the miscellaneous attractions of a magazine. Magazines there were, but they were survivors not too brightly adapting themselves to the demands of the new century. Something better was wanted than the *Gentleman's Magazine*, and the *Monthly Magazine* and the *Monthly Review*. The *Monthly Magazine* kept a good enough level, and pleased a wide public. It beat down again into silence the rivalry of Longman's *Athenæum*, published in 1807 at a shilling a month, and presuming " to have a higher literary quality." But it was up to someone to find what Longman saw dimly but which he and his editor, Aikin, failed to create. And the man to find out and supply what was wanted was Blackwood.

AGAIN in Edinburgh rose the spirit of enterprise, partly stirred by jealousy of ' crafty ' Constable. Constable had a small monthly, the *Scots Magazine*, but it did not require much to supersede that. Blackwood wished to counter the *Edinburgh* itself with a magazine " not so ponderous, more nimble, more frequent, more familiar." For that ordinary competence would not be enough. He had begun on those lines early in

1817 with a monthly magazine, edited by Pringle, and by Cleghorn of the *Farmer's Magazine*, but its sales were only two hundred and fifty, it never paid, and at the sixth number it died. Then convinced that he would only win success by something that would ' sting and startle,' he began *Maga* [1] with a rattling volley from the barrels of his brilliant young men. That first number was essentially an Edinburgh number, but then to capture Edinburgh was to build a reputation that was soon known in London. And in October 1817 Edinburgh was in a frenzy over the audacities of the Chaldæ MS. Lockhart, " the scorpion which delighteth to sting the faces of men," stung and startled with a vengeance. " Edinburgh rose to it like one man, delighted, amused, offended, furious." Christopher North said " it gave us both a lift and a shove." And Scott wrote to Laidlaw, " Blackwood is rather in a bad pickle just now—sent to Coventry by the Trade as the booksellers name themselves, and all about the parody of the two beasts. If Blackwood had good books to sell, he might set them all at defiance. His Magazine does well, and beats Constable." [2] In fact, actions for libel impended, but *Maga* was launched, and henceforth success was beyond doubt. In 1818 Murray bought half a share for £1,000, and of the seventh number 10,000 were quickly sold out. Lockhart and Wilson forced the pace. Maginn joined in. More responsible people like Coleridge contributed. And stormily but successfully *Maga* forged on. It sold well in London. In 1818 it paid contributors ten guineas

---

[1] For the full story of *Maga* see Mrs. Oliphant, *William Blackwood and his Sons*.
[2] Oliphant, *William Blackwood and his Sons*, i. 153.

a sheet, and in 1822 twenty guineas. One more string was added to the bow of the professional man of letters.

SOON Blackwood's had prominent fellows, like itself " more nimble and more familiar." In 1820 Taylor and Hessey, of Waterloo Place, brought out their *London Magazine* under Taylor's own editorship for the first four years, and they soon had a good band of writers round them. There were Coleridge, Lamb, Keats, Talfourd and Cary, and from 1824 Thomas Hood was the editor. Again the varied interest and the lighter treatment suited the public, and to judge of the importance of its existence to writers, it is enough to reflect that it made possible the creation of the Essays of Elia. Another of the monthlies was the *New Monthly*, which was started by Colburn to rival the *Monthly Magazine* of Phillips, and which from 1821 to 1830 was under the titular editorship of Thomas Campbell, the poet, with Cyrus Redding the journalist doing most of the work. It had a circulation of some 2,500, and, say the *Noctes Ambrosianæ*, " they lay out a cool hundred on advertisements every month." But Phillips, says Odoherty, does " capitally. He circulates between three and four thousand ; and his advertisements are very profitable." [1] For, indeed, the old magazines kept on their way.

IN addition new but more limited ones arose. Of such were *The Monthly Repository of Theology and General Literature* launched in 1806, *The Monthly Register* of 1802 to which Crabb Robinson contributed articles on German philosophy, and literature, and Ackerman's *Poetical Magazine* in

[1] *Noctes Ambrosianæ*, No. 1.

which from 1809 to 1811 appeared Combe's letter-press to Rowlandson's pictures. Again there was the *Monthly Mirror* in which about 1808 James Smith was a constant writer. So altogether the supply of magazine literature grew larger. In fact, its increase was one of the characteristics of the day. " Steamboats and magazines," said Christopher North, " are all the go at present. They've got a magazine at Brighton—another at Newcastle, for the colliers—another at Dundee—and, I believe, five or six about Paisley and Glasgow. You may choose which you like best—they're all works of genius—Hogg writes in them all." [1]

PUBLISHING enterprise, however, did not end in the production of the quarterlies and the additional monthlies. It extended to something even more solid than the former, and to something yet lighter and more nimble than the latter. On the one hand there was an attempt to produce substantial annuals on the lines of the *Annual Register* which had been founded in 1757 and with whose early numbers Burke had been associated. In 1803 Arthur Aikin was editing the *Annual Review*, which was " intended to comprise in one large volume an account of the entire English literature of each year." For assistants he had Southey and William Taylor of Norwich. It was another resource for journalists. Southey received four guineas a sheet, and Aikin and Taylor found in it an addition to the money they earned by their innumerable articles in other periodicals. It had some success, but the *Edinburgh Annual Register*, which the Ballantynes projected in 1810 as an opposition to

---

[1] *Noctes Ambrosianæ*, No. 1.

the politics and criticism of the *Edinburgh Review*, was not so successful. Southey and Scott contributed, but the scheme was too grandiose. " The public," says Lockhart, " were alarmed by the extent of the history, and the prospect of two volumes annually. This was, in short, a new periodical publication on a large scale." [1]

BUT, on the other hand, in the yet lighter periodical, enterprise was more successful. Indeed, in that field enterprise was so strong that failure no wise daunted, and attempt succeeded attempt, and rival dashed in pursuit of rival. None was more venturesome than Leigh Hunt. In 1808 he began *The Examiner* with his brother, and it ran until 1821 under his guidance. The brothers had dared to be outspoken and honest in dramatic criticism three years earlier in the *News*, and now in 1808 their independent writing in *The Examiner* opened a new era for the weekly paper. The weekly acquired from the journal of the Hunts such a personality and policy as the reviews had first gained from the example of Jeffrey and his friends. The themes of *The Examiner* were politics and literature, and the drama, its main objects " to assist in producing Reform in Parliament, liberality of opinion in general (especially freedom from superstition), and a fusion of literary taste into all subjects whatsoever." [2] And *The Examiner* was far from being Hunt's only venture. Of the others all were more or less short-lived, but all independent. *The Reflector, The Indicator, The Liberal, The Literary Examiner, The Companion, The Chat of the Week*, and *The Tatler* all show Leigh Hunt as a typical

[1] Lockhart, *Life of Scott*, p. 216.   [2] Leigh Hunt, *Autobiography*, p. 172.

periodical writer, not always weekly, sometimes quarterly, sometimes even daily. And, as a writer in weekly papers, he was but one of many, for the weekly literary journal had come to stay, and to fill a most important rôle in the formative education of the reading public, and to do not a little towards " breaking the ice between men's hearts," a phrase of Leigh Hunt's own.

THE weekly that soon led the van was Colburn's *Literary Gazette*, which began in 1817. Jerdan was a most efficient editor, and he had excellent contributors in writers like Procter and L. E. L. who hit no higher than the public taste. It was not long before it had a circulation of three thousand, and in 1820 it had an imitative competitor in the *Gazette of Fashion*. Steadily it rose in estimation, till in 1828 it met its most formidable rival in Buckingham's *Athenæum*. But for a while yet it was still not seriously rivalled. When the *Athenæum* appeared, *Maga* commented thus :

SHEPHERD. Nane o' a' the new weekly periodicals will ever cut out the Literary Gazette.

NORTH. Never, James. And simply for one reason—Mr. Jerdan is a gentleman, and is assisted by none but gentlemen.

SHEPHERD. And havein' taen the start he'll keep it—let the lave whup and spur as they like after his heels. But I like to see a gude race, so I houp nane o' them'll be distanced.

NORTH. 'Tis a pretty race. The Athenæum is well laid in upon his flank—and there goes the Sphynx and Atlas at a spanking rate—looking within the ropes like winners ; but the rider of the ould horse has him in hand, and letting him loose within a rod of the judges' stand, he will win the gold cup by two lengths at least—and I take him at even against the field for the Derby.[1]

So towards 1830 Jerdan still led in the pretty race of weekly journals. In 1828 the *Spectator*, also, had begun that career of steady success that is still far from ended to-day. The swelling list of them one may see in the *Times Handlist of Newspapers*. Buckingham was, like Leigh Hunt, one of the more venturesome and talented prospectors. He had begun his *Sphynx* before the *Athenæum*. It, too, was " a journal of politics, literature and news," and appeared twice a week— on Wednesday and Saturday evenings at the price of 7*d*. And he ran the *Verulam*, a weekly confined to scientific information alone, and priced 8*d*. But he was hardly the right man for the *Athenæum*. He was too unbusiness-like. Not even the help of Stirling and F. D. Maurice could make up for that failing. It was in 1830, when C. W. Dilke became both proprietor and editor, and raised the quality while lowering the price to 4*d*., that the *Athenæum* made real headway to the front against Jerdan, and against the *Examiner* which still ran successfully though Leigh Hunt had long broken his connexion with it.

THE rest of the weeklies and more frequent periodicals are for the most part comparatively insignificant, except in so far as they show the growth of the reading public and of professional literary opportunities. The former is again shown by the ability, even as the number of papers increased, for any one with strong enough in-

1 *Noctes Ambrosianæ*, No. 36.

dividuality to make a big mark : as the weekly *John Bull* did, founded in 1820 and edited wittily and assertively by Theodore Hook. Its " notices to correspondents " were read with delight, and, for its politics and criticism, it was, in the words of Christopher North, " a chariot armed with scythes." It made its mark instantly, and some £6,000 profits were said to have been divided at the end of the first year.[1] And, for the growth of literary opportunities, we see them and how they were taken advantage of, in the confession of Egerton Brydges : " I studied political economy with occasional bursts of industry, and communicated many articles to the daily or weekly journals." [2]

AND naturally the advance in journalism was no whit less in the sphere of the daily newspapers. At the opening of the century the circulation of even the best was small, so that a paper circulating between two and three thousand was considered unusually successful, but the tide was rising which swept on till at the end of the century a successful circulation was nearer a quarter of a million. In the early years, however, there were many papers and much activity. *The Times* and *Morning Post* were well established, and there were the *Morning Chronicle*, the *Morning Advertiser*, the *Morning Herald*, and the *Courier*, and the *Sunday Times* and the *Observer* in the front rank. Their quality improved, and they were more and more connected with the better writers of the day. Lamb wrote for the *Morning Chronicle*, Coleridge for the *Morning Post*, Campbell for the *Morning Chronicle*, Wordsworth for the *Courier*, and so on.

---

[1] *Noctes Ambrosianæ*, No. 1. [2] S. E. Brydges, *Autobiography*, i. 22.

MISCELLANEOUS work journalism frequently was, such as Lamb speaks of thus : " In those days [1801–1803] every Morning Paper, as an essential retainer to its establishment, kept an author, who was bound to furnish daily a quantum of witty paragraphs. Sixpence a joke—and it was thought pretty high too—was Dan Stuart's settled remuneration in these cases. The chat of the day, scandal, but, above all, *dress*, furnished the material. . . . O those headaches ! . . . No Egyptian taskmaster ever devised a slavery like to that, our slavery " [*i.e.* of coining half a dozen jests a day].[1] But miscellaneous drudgery though it might be, it was an addition to the resources of the profession. " We have seen Lamb," writes Mr. E. V. Lucas, " attempting to get work on the *Morning Post* and failing ; we have seen him on the *Albion* lampooning the Government, and at last putting an end to the paper, in August, 1801, by a too caustic epigram. Nowise daunted he made other efforts to add a journalist's pickings to his India House salary, and between 1801 and 1804, with long periods of inactivity, he occasionally succeeded." [2] OF course, there was better work also to be done. Landor, for example, consented at the pressing of Sir Robert Adair, the friend of Fox, to write now and again in the papers against the ministry. And work on *The Times* was an addition to income which writers often found valuable. In 1812 Crabb Robinson records that " Talfourd came with the request I would procure for him employment as a reporter for *The Times*, that he might be enabled to marry. This I did." Crabb Robinson himself had been a foreign correspondent for

1 E. V. Lucas, *Life of Lamb*, i. 266.   2 *Ibid.*, i. 261.

Walter in Germany and Spain. Barnes, who had obtained high honours at Cambridge and who, says Leigh Hunt, " might assuredly have made himself a name in wit and literature, had he cared much for anything beyond his glass of wine and his Fielding," was another of Walter's reporters, and " was afterwards identified with the sudden and striking increase in the *Times* Newspaper in fame and influence." [1] " The writer of the great leaders—the flash articles which made a noise—was Peter Fraser, then a Fellow of Corpus Christi, Cambridge, afterwards Rector of Kegworth, in Leicestershire. He used to sit in Walter's parlour and write his articles after dinner." [2] And another of Walter's men was William Combe, coming out each day from the King's Bench prison under the day rules to do his work.

SUCH few examples on *The Times* alone show what part the newspapers were playing in writing for a living ; while the offer of the editorship of *The Times* in 1817 to Southey shows how the status of newspaper work had risen. Then in 1814 there was an important advance in the means of production, and by the use of steam power Walter got *The Times* printed with greater speed and so with the possibility of wider circulation. Nor is it a small sign of the hopes that men entertained of newspaper enterprise that Murray ventured out in 1826 on the *Representative*. It was a failure from the start, perhaps, indeed, from before the start, because Murray tried to get as his editor Lockhart, and could not. But it was a failure

1 Leigh Hunt, *Autobiography,* p. 103. Barnes was editor of *The Times,* 1817–41.
2 Crabb Robinson, *Diary,* i. 292.

because the possibilities were mishandled, rather than because they did not exist.[1] They did exist, and the newspaper world of the twenties was well paid, and was already a bustling world. It called in more and more literary men as reporters, correspondents and sub-editors. Murray, in his desperate fight to keep his journal alive, called Dr. Maginn over from Paris to take charge of the lighter side of the paper at a salary of £700 a year and a house. Journalism was henceforth a very big branch of the profession of letters, and had, in consequence, plenty of amateurish hangers-on, "the glorious army of Parliamentary reporters," as North derisively called them, "who have been thrown upon literature only by having failed as attorneys, apothecaries, painters, school-masters, preachers, grocers——" But it is a sign of a profession established, when the incompetent flock round for the odd jobs.

As London journalism advanced, so did that of the provinces. Again the *Times Handlist of Newspapers* shows for each year after 1800 a steady issue of new periodicals all over the country. Many were born only to die, but their throng is a portent. The average number of new provincial periodicals each year was in the first decade of the century five, in the second decade eight, and in the third nineteen. And a fair percentage did go on appearing. In the first decade alone the *Kentish Herald*, the *Tyne Mercury*, the *Bristol Mercury*, and the *Nottingham Review* became securely established. Provincial papers were a training ground for the London press. Cyrus Redding, later Campbell's assistant on the *New Monthly*,

---

1 Smiles, *A Publisher and his Friends*, ii. 182-213.

was the son of a Baptist minister at Truro who began in 1806, at the age of twenty-one, a life's devotion to journalism. After starting in London he became in 1808 editor of the *Plymouth Chronicle*, and after some years' experience there he came back to London.[1] So, with many young men doing as he did, the connexion between the capital and the provinces strengthened. Charles Knight, the son of a Windsor printer, was another who went young to London, and, while on the staff of the *Globe*, he edited his father's *Eton and Windsor Express*. James Montgomery the " poet," when his verse had sunk beyond redemption, became editor of the *Sheffield Iris*, " a journal of liberal and enlightened views." And it was not the least of the merits of the provincial press that it came to serve as an advertising medium for books throughout the country.

THUS journalism advanced as a province for writers, and despite its burden of taxation and, indeed, ever fighting against that oppression, it tended to become increasingly the literature and the education of the lower classes. To show it briefly as a province for writers has been the purpose here. A more detailed treatment is not within the scope of this study, but two matters remain that deserve some consideration, the rise of the illustrated annual, and the influence of reviews on the sale of books.

THE illustrated annual [2] in the twenties, and for some twenty years, was the bane and blessing of its generation. To people of taste it was an offence. " The ornamental annuals, those greedy re-

---

[1] See Cyrus Redding, *Fifty Years' Recollections.*
[2] See *The Times Literary Supplement*, November 26, 1924, pp. 779-80.

ceptacles of trash, those bladders upon which the boys of poetry try to swim," groaned Wordsworth in 1830. But, no doubt, they pleased the sentimental, who would not willingly have read anything better, and it cannot be a crime to supply what people like merely because it is poorer than what they should like but do not. And, no doubt, they pleased the artists and writers who could not afford to be too scrupulous about what they produced. At any rate they were very popular as soon as they were invented. LEIGH HUNT relates how " it struck somebody who was acquainted with the literary annuals of Germany, and who reflected upon this winter flower-bed of the booksellers, these pocket-books, souvenirs, and Christmas presents, all in the lump—that he would combine the spirit of all of them, as far as labour, season and sizeability went ; and omitting the barren or blank part, and being entirely original, produce such a pocket-book as had not yet been seen. The magician in Boccaccio could not have done better. Hence arose the Forget-me-not, the Literary Souvenir, and the Keepsakes, which combine the original contribution of the German Annual with the splendid binding of the Christmas English present." The inventor was Rudolph Ackerman, an enterprising publisher who secured the right editor to know and follow the public taste.

THEN the imitators poured in. Sentiment ran riot to the satisfaction of the public and to the loathing of men like Scott and Lamb. Scott and Lamb and their fellows could not altogether withstand the importunities of persistent editors who craved their names as additional ornaments.

Scott consented so far as to give *The House of Aspen* and *My Aunt Margaret's Mirror* to Heath's Keepsake and got £500 for his hundred pages.[1] But their contributions were occasional and reluctant, and the main supply of literary matter, which was often no more than a commentary on or setting for the illustrations, was given over to minor writers.

FADED though their bright colours are to the eyes of posterity, the Annuals were a lure to the average public of that time. Moreover they were cheap. And if it is not enough for us to-day to esteem them merely for pleasing the ordinary reader and profiting the ordinary writer, we may find compensation in reflecting that in them at least was the first home of the short story.

As for the power of the reviews to influence the sale of books, the evidence is at best very conflicting. On the whole it would seem that the influence was, as often as not, not the influence which they intended to exert. In 1819 the appearance of *Don Juan* was hailed with a chorus of hostile criticism, but its effect was only to increase the public interest. In 1818 Blackwood wrote to Murray : " Coleridge . . . has attacked Shelley in an oblique and shabby manner. Does he know what that review has done ? I will tell you ; it has *sold* an edition of *The Revolt of Islam* which otherwise nobody would have thought of reading, and few who read can understand, I for one." [2] The attacks on Lady Morgan's book on France are said only to have stimulated the sales.

Lockhart remarks : " But Sir Walter regretted having meddled in any way with the toyshop of literature, and would never do so again, though repeatedly offered very large sums." *Life*, p. 564.

[2] Smiles, *A Publisher and his Friends*, i. 399.

When the *English Review* denounced James Montgomery's *Wanderer in Switzerland* as a "feeble outrage on the public," it made no difference to the popularity, which did not wane until the public appetite sickened of itself. So that on sales at any rate adverse criticism does not seem to have had very bad effects.

THAT in that age of too often blackguardly reviewing, the man himself might be hurt, though his book was, perhaps, not, is regrettably true. Lamb was one who suffered like that. He could not be called " a poor maniac " by the gentlemen of the *Quarterly* without feeling it. When Mrs. Aikin asked why Lamb did not write more, Crabb Robinson " mentioned as one cause the bad character given him by the reviewers." For mud and stones might frighten where they did not damage. It was an age when it could not often be said of a man as Campbell said of Scott, that " he reviews like a gentleman, a Christian and a scholar."

THE bark, in fact, of the reviews was worse than their bite, yet their praise does seem to have affected sales more than their blame. Crabbe's son tells how the *Edinburgh Review* led the way with warm eulogy of *The Parish Register*, and he adds : " I believe that within two days after the appearance of Mr. Jeffrey's . . . generous article, Mr. Hatchard sold off the whole of the first edition." [1] Henry Taylor, accounting for the dawn of Wordsworth's popularity, put it down to Wilson's articles in *Blackwood's*, and he says : " This opening was widened, I think, by two articles of mine in the *Quarterly Review*, one of

---

[1] Crabbe, *Life and Works*, p. 52.

which, I was told by the publisher at the time, had doubled the sale of his works." [1] Such instances go to show that the good word was stronger than the bad.

BUT, praise or blame apart, the reviews were invaluable for bringing a book or an author to the notice of a wide circle. We have seen how the country papers quoted freely from the *Literary Gazette*. And as a general tribute to the unpaid advertising influence of the reviews we may cite the opinion of Coleridge. " To anonymous critics," he wrote, " in reviews, magazines, and news-journals of various name and rank, and to satirists with or without a name in verse or prose, or in verse-text aided by prose-comment, I do seriously believe and profess, that I owe full two-thirds of whatever reputation and publicity I happen to possess. For when the name of an individual has occurred so frequently, in so many works, for so great a length of time, the readers of these works—(which with a shelf or two of beauties, elegant Extracts and Anas, form nine-tenths of the reading of the reading Public)—cannot but be familiar with the name, without distinctly remembering whether it was introduced for eulogy or for censure. And this becomes the more likely, if (as I believe) the habit of perusing periodical works may be properly added to Averroes' catalogue of Anti-Mnemonics, or weakeners of the memory. But where this has not been the case, yet the reader will be apt to suspect that there must be something more than usually strong and extensive in a reputation, that could either

---

[1] H. Taylor, *Autobiography*, i. 190.

require or stand so merciless and long-continued a cannonading." [1]

AND lastly, as a contemporary tribute that suggests what the periodical was doing for writers and public alike, giving expression and income to the one, and amusement and education to the other, we may quote again from the *Noctes Ambrosianæ* the following dialogue. It is a splendid tribute to the high quality and the abundance of journalism in 1829.

NORTH. Our current periodical literature teems with thought and feeling, James—with passion and imagination. There was Gifford, and there are Jeffrey, and Southey, and Campbell, and Moore, and Bowles, and Sir Walter, and Lockhart, and Lamb, and Wilson, and De Quincey, and the four Coleridges, S.T.C., John Hartley, and Derwent, and Croly, and Maginn, and Mackintosh, and Cunningham, and Kennedy, and Stebbing, and St. Ledger, and Knight, and Praed, and Lord Dudley and Ward, and Lord L. Gower, and Charles Grant, and Hobhouse, and Blunt, and Milman, and Carlyle, and Macaulay, and the two Moirs, and Jerdan, and Talfourd, and Bowring, and North, and Hogg, and Tickler, and twenty—forty —fifty—other crack contributors to the Reviews, Magazines, and Gazettes, who have said more tender, and true, and fine, and deep things in the way of criticism, than ever was said before since the reign of Cadmus, ten thousand times over,— not in long, dull, heavy, formal, prosy theories,— but flung off hand, out of the glowing mint—a coinage of the purest ore—and stamped with the

---

[1] *Biographia Literaria*, p. 26.

ineffaceable impress of genius. Who so elevated in intellectual rank as to be entitled to despise such a periodical literature ?

SHEPHERD. Nae leevin' man—nor yet dead ane.

NORTH. The whole surface of society, James, is thus irrigated by a thousand streams ; some deep—some shallow—

SHEPHERD. And the shallow are sufficient for the purpose o' irrigation. Water three inches deep, skilful and timeously conducted owre a flat o' fifty or a hunder acres, wull change arid sterility, on which half-a-score sheep would be starved in a month intil skeletons, intil a flush o' flowery herbage that will feed and fatten a haill score o' kye. You'll see a proof o' this when you come out to Mount Benger. But no to dwell on ae image—let me say that millions are thus pleased and instructed who otherwise would go dull and ignorant to their graves.

NORTH. Every month adds to the number of these admirable works ; and from the conflict of parties, political, poetical, and philosophical, emerges in all her brightness the form of Truth. Why, there, James lies *The Spectator*, a new weekly paper of some half-year's standing, or so, of the highest merit, and I wish I had some way of strenuously recommending it to the reading public. The editor, indeed, is Whiggish and a Pro-Catholic—but moderate, steady, and consistent in his politics. Let us have no turncoats. His *précis* of passing politics is always admirable ; his mercantile information—*that* I know on the authority of as good a judge as lives—is correct and comprehensive ; miscellaneous news are collected judiciously and amusingly from all quarters ;

the literary department is equal, on the whole, to that of any other weekly periodical, such as the *Literary Gazette*, (which, however, has the great advantage of being altogether literary and scientific, and stands, beyond dispute, at the head of its own class,) *Weekly Review*, *Athenæum*, *Sphynx*, *Atlas*, or others—I nowhere see better criticism on poetry—and nowhere nearly so good criticism on theatricals. Some critiques there have been, in that department, superior, in exquisite truth of tact, to any thing I remember—worthy of Elia himself, though not apparently from Elia ; and in accounts of foreign literature, especially French, and above all, of French politics, a subject on which I need to be enlightened, I have seen no periodical at all equal to the *Spectator*.[1]

(vii)

IN the time of Pope poetry had the pride of place both for profit and for pleasure. In the time of Johnson it still had, as surely it must always have, pride of place in the art of literature, but it was losing it to prosaic competitors in the profession of literature. In the dark days of Darwin and Hayley contemporary poetry was under a shadow even as an art. Now in the days of Scott and Byron journalism had usurped its pride of place for the profession, but poetry by its splendour and profusion again assumed pre-eminence as an art. And not only for Scott and Byron, but because of men like Campbell and Crabbe and Milman, who both wrote well and were paid well, it deserves to be noticed before

[1] *Noctes Ambrosianæ*, No. 42.

the novel, although it would have thrown our drawing of the profession of letters quite out of perspective to have discussed it before journalism. For that true professional man of letters, Robert Southey, to take but one example, would have been made to appear a poor mere scarecrow of his real self, had he first been shown as the poet and not as the reviewer.

SCOTT, by his first long poem, had redeemed poetry from the worse than mediocrity of the nineties, and from the minor satire of the *Anti-Jacobin* and Gifford. He had eclipsed the evangelical popularity of Cowper, and the select popularity of Rogers. He had won unheard-of prices for copyright. And so because of him and because of Byron after him, poetry for almost twenty years had a tolerable market once more. Before the *Lay* poets had begun to sing, but hardly to prosper. Campbell was a notable meteor, but *The Pleasures of Hope* brought him only £60. Moore, as ' moral-corrupting ' Thomas Little, sang too, but gained his society success more by his voice than his verse. Gifford translated *Juvenal*, and " rendered it a saleable and interesting book by the memoir of himself which he prefixed to it ; and indeed by that memoir brought himself into fame." Southey issued *Thalaba*, the first of his estimable but unesteemed poems, and the whole profits were £25. But then in 1805 the success of Scott made the hearts of the public and the publishers beat more generously. The success of the *Lay*, says Lockhart, " at once decided that literature should form the main business of Scott's life."

THE appreciation, however, of poetry that was

reborn through the old romance was an appreciation that remained erratic. Popular taste still
favoured the best of the older school, and when
Crabbe published *The Parish Register* in 1807, the
edition sold off very quickly, while *The Pleasures
of Memory* of " melodious Rogers " went steadily
on through fresh impressions. Trash like James
Montgomery's *Wanderer in Switzerland* (1806)
caught the public fancy for a time. And Southey
remained consistently neglected, with another £25
for *Madoc*, while Cary's *Dante* got so little known
that Coleridge was ignorant of it till by chance he
met Cary, and in 1810 Longmans refused to print
Count Julian even at Landor's expense. Even
when Scott's sales were soaring, the public would
still have nothing to do with Wordsworth's poems,
so that Crabb Robinson noted in 1812 : " Wordsworth is now convinced that he can never derive
emolument from them." The 500 copies of *The
Excursion* printed in 1814 were sufficient for six
years, and the second edition of 500 in 1820 was
not exhausted for seven years.

BUT, although the public would not buy some
poetry, it is evident that it became eager for
such as it could appreciate. In the same year
as Southey was saying of his edition of 500 of
Kehama, " I shall be surprised if they sell in
seven years," Scott received £4,000 for *The Lady
of the Lake*, and 25,000 copies of it were printed.
Those who did not read it, felt " the necessity
of having it for fashion's sake—a losing of caste
not to possess it." In 1812 Murray sold 4,500
of the first two cantos of *Childe Harold* in six
months. In fact, the public decidedly woke up
to poetry. Murray could offer 1,000 guineas

for the copyright of *The Siege of Corinth* and *Parisina*, and £2,000 for canto III of *Childe Harold*. Scott had 1,500 guineas for only half the copyright of *The Lord of the Isles*. In 1813 Hogg had from Goldie, a minor publisher, £245 for the *Queen's Wake*, " which, indeed," comments Mrs. Oliphant, " as the profits on a small book of poetry,—well known as a generally unsaleable article, and which was his first introduction to the world [1]—was comparatively a large sum, and would, we think, dazzle a provincial poet now [1895]; but the age was one which, in the flush of a poetic revival, read much poetry, and, what is perhaps of more importance, bought it." [2] Murray's hopeful esteem for poetry rose temporarily so high that in 1819 he gave Crabbe £3,000 for *Tales of the Hall* and the remaining copyright of his earlier works, and the elderly poet gleefully took the bills down to Trowbridge to show his son, for he had never before had anything but small sums.

THERE was, in fact, a boom in poetry of a certain kind. Murray paid Crabbe too generously, as it turned out, but his work sold steadily, and the great names of the popular school were those of Scott, Byron, Campbell and Moore. When *The Lord of the Isles* in 1815 only sold to the extent of 12,000 copies within a few months, it was considered a decided falling off from the sale of even *Rokeby*, and was markedly smaller than the enormous sales of Byron's poems. The enthusiasm felt in those years is shown by Lockhart's statement that when *Rokeby* came out, undergraduates at Oxford

[1] This is hardly accurate. He published his *Mountain Bard* in 1807, and had £90 on 1,000 copies.
[2] Oliphant, *Annals of a Publishing House* ; *William Blackwood and his Sons*, i. 320.

" had bets depending on the issue of the struggle, which they considered the elder favourite as making to keep his own ground against the fiery rivalry of Childe Harold."[1] And as Byron's poetry forged ahead, it justified Murray in giving 500 guineas for *Mazeppa* and 1,500 guineas for the first two cantos of *Don Juan* with the *Ode to Venice*. So, the price of poetry having risen from the very first appearance of Scott, we find a man like Campbell, in the intervals of editing his *Specimens of the British Poets*, writing poems to add to his income, and making quite a popular hit with such a poem as *Gertrude of Wyoming*. Milman, too, set himself to poetry in 1820, and for a few years was highly and indeed excessively paid for his rather monumentally grand poems like *The Fall of Jerusalem*. For that sacred tragedy Murray was confident enough to pay 500 guineas.

THEN, in the early twenties, came three poets whose appeal was more particularly to the ordinary reader, Bernard Barton, L.E.L., and Barry Cornwall. " There was a time " [1820-1840], says Barton's biographer, Mr. E. V. Lucas,[2] " when Bernard Barton was literally a Household Poet. . . . He had a multitudinous audience, composed of those readers who prefer that the teaching of poetry shall be explicit rather than implicit. We have seen how eager Bernard Barton was to write : hardly less eager was his public to read. His books were bought almost as rapidly as they were published, and as his poetic output was large his influence was extensively felt." For Barton's poetry was the simple and pleasing effusion of a

---

1 Lockhart, *Life of Scott*, p. 234.
2 E. V. Lucas, *Bernard Barton and his Friends*, p. 169.

warm and poetical heart, easily able to be appreciated by the ordinary English reader who is by nature more susceptible to what the *Monthly Review* of 1824 called " the happy delineation of the domestic affections, and all the warmer but calmer feelings of the heart," than to the sublimer creations of genius and art.

FOR the same reason, the poetry of L.E.L. succeeded. Her reputation is reflected in the *Noctes Ambrosianæ.* Tickler asks : " Is not L.E.L. a child of genius, as well as of the *Literary Gazette* ; and does she not throw over her most impassioned strains of love and rapture a delicate and gentle spirit, from the recesses of her own pure and holy woman's heart ? " ; to which North replies, " She does." [1]

As for Barry Cornwall, North called him " one of my pet poets—quite a love," affirming " he is so free from everything like affectation." [2] And he was " quite a love " of the public too, and with L.E.L., and Mrs. Hemans, he was the kind of poet who pleased the public in the illustrated Annuals. " Is there not often," asked Tickler of Mrs. Hemans's poetry, " a rich glow of imagery in her compositions, fine feelings and fancies, and an unconstrained and even triumphant flow of versification which murmurs poetry ? " [3] To that the voice of the majority of her contemporaries would gladly have cried ' Yes.' For this group of poets had extended the popularity of poetry more widely in some directions than even Scott and Byron. They were the poets of the average devotee of the circulating library.

REVIEWING the poetry that was popular, it is not

---

[1] *Noctes Ambrosianæ,* No. 21.   [2] *Ibid.,* No. 19.   [3] *Ibid.,* No. 21.

difficult to understand the unpopularity of its opposite. Leigh Hunt was a small enough figure as a poet, but names, to posterity, far greater than his were then smaller still. Lockhart in 1817 threatened to turn his satire from Hunt to the " younger and less important members, the Shelleys, and Keatses, and the Webbes." Shelley, according to Egerton Brydges, was " ridiculed while alive, and represented in most of the literary journals as a bye-word of absurdity, charlatanism, and incomprehensibility." [1] There was no money at all in such poetry as theirs, and we have seen that there was for years none in Wordsworth's either. Wordsworth's popularity did not begin until about 1825. Then Hazlitt wrote : " the tide has turned much in his favour of late years. He has a large body of determined partisans." [2] But his popularity, when it came, was never more than a select one.

GOOD poetry, then, where it was " understanded of the common people," had a boom, and was for a time commercially worth the writing. But its days of prosperity were soon numbered. Poetry became a drug. " The success of Scott's, and especially of Byron's Poems, called into existence about this time a vast array of would-be poets, male and female, and from all ranks and professions. Some wrote for fame, some for money ; but all were agreed on one point, namely that if Mr. Murray would undertake the publication of the poems the authors' fame was secured : ' that the works would excite the admiration of the world,' or that ' the author would become inde-

---

1 S. E. Brydges, *Autobiography*, i. 322.
2 Hazlitt, *Spirit of the Age* (1904), p. 164.

pendent and celebrated throughout Great Britain.' " [1] Miss Jane Porter was one writer, whom the ambition of poetry roused, and she sent to Murray *Lord Ronald, by a Border Minstrel*, but she withdrew when Murray told her that he had " *waded through seven hundred rejected poems in the course of a year.*" That was in 1817. In March 1821 Wordsworth wrote to Crabb Robinson, " As to poetry, I am sick of it ; it overruns the country in all the shapes of the Plagues of Egypt." [2] In fact, as Moore said to Scott, " hardly a Magazine is now published, that does not contain verses which some thirty years ago would have made a reputation." And Scott, playfully flourishing his stick, answered : " We have, like Bobadil, taught them to beat us with our own weapons." [3] But a good level though much new poetry attained, there was too much of it. Poetry is an article for which the appetite of the English public is soon sated. And by the early thirties when Taylor came forward with *Philip van Artevelde* and Tennyson appeared, the commercial boom in poetry was over.

(viii)

MEANWHILE the professional man of letters found another field for his labours gradually improving. The novel hardly needed the genius of Scott to bring it into prominence as a literary form. The human desire for a tale could be relied upon to do that, with the help of the circulating library. And the general intellectual

[1] Smiles, *A Publisher and his Friends*, i. 341.
[2] Crabb Robinson, *Diary*, ii. 203.
[3] Lockhart, *Life of Scott*, p. 481.

trend of the age, with its scientific interests, and its thirst for information, and its penny magazines, and its mechanics' institutes, and its whole ' march of mind,' favoured prose against poetry. Murray in 1818 even thought it worth while to ask Byron, in the midst of his poetic output, " Do you never think of prose ? " And North in his wild way said : " Since the extinction of English poetry, there has been a wide extension of the legitimate province of prose. People who have got any genius find that they may traverse it as they will, on foot, on horseback, and in chariot." Nor was there in any form a wider extension than in the novel, nor more varied ways of traversing it.

AGAIN, as the reading public went on growing bigger, it was impossible for the theatres, even had their attractions been greater, to compete with the novel. The theatres were out-distanced, if not superseded, and the change found expression and comment in the dialogue of the *Noctes*. The discussion is over what branch of literature Odoherty shall for the moment apply himself to, the novel, the essay, the drama or a " great quarto disquisition, on ' The Decline and Fall of Genius.' " The dialogue continues,

EDITOR. I would advise to let alone the drama. I do not think it at present a good field for the exertion of genius.

ODOHERTY. For what reason, honey ?

EDITOR. I think the good novels, which are published, come in place of new dramas. Besides, they are better fitted for the present state of public taste. The public are merely capable of strong sensations, but of nothing which requires knowledge, taste, or judgment. A certain ideal dignity of style, and regularity of arrangement, must be required for a drama, before it can deserve the name of a composition. But what sense have the common herd of barbarians of composition, or order, or anything else of that kind ?

ODOHERTY. But there is also the more loose and popular drama, which is only a novel without the narrative parts.

EDITOR. Yes, the acting is the chief difference. But I think the novel has the advantage in being without the acting, for its power over the feelings is more undisturbed and entire, and the imagination of the reader blends the whole into a harmony which is not found on the stage. I think those who read novels need not go to the theatre, for they are in general beforehand with the whole progress of the story.

ODOHERTY. This is true to a certain extent. But novels can never carry away from the theatre those things which are peculiarly its own ; that is to say, the powers of expression in the acting, the eloquence of declamation, music, buffoonery, the splendour of painted decorations, etc.

EDITOR. You are perfectly right. Novels may carry away sympathy, plot, invention, distress, catastrophe, and every thing—(Vide Blair).

ODOHERTY. Do you mean Dr. Blair, or Adam Blair ?

EDITOR. The latter. I say the novels may carry away all these things, but the theatre must still be strong in its power of affecting the senses. This is its peculiar dominion. Yet our populace do not much seek after what strikes and pleases the senses ; for the elegances of sight and hearing

237

require a sort of abstract taste which they do not seem to have. Any thing which is not an appeal through sympathy to some of their vulgar personal feelings, appears to them uninteresting and unmeaning.[1]

And in that, North, though he speaks a little wildly, speaks more than a little shrewdly.

IN 1800 the popularity of the novel both with readers and with writers was well on the rise. It had been stimulated by the work of men like Godwin and Holcroft, and romancers like Mrs. Radcliffe. Then Miss Owenson,[2] excited by reports of Fanny Burney's genius, began to work her thin but glittering vein, and brought out steadily a supply of bright tinsel romances that had a very considerable ephemeral vogue. First she staged her tales in her own native Ireland, and for the *Wild Irish Girl* of 1806 she had 300 guineas from Johnson, and it went through seven editions in two years. Those tales made her known, but, being Irish, they roused party feeling, and she gave them up. Then came in 1809 her *Woman, or Ida of Athens*, in four volumes, again a contemporary success, whose readers included Jane Austen. *The Missionary*, an Indian tale, followed. A guest of the Marquis of Abercorn, Miss Owenson read her manuscript aloud to a company among whom were Lord Aberdeen, the Princess of Wales, Lord Palmerston, and Lord Castlereagh, and the last " was so fascinated that he offered to accompany her to town, and having sent for Mr. Stockdale of Pall Mall, the work was absolutely disposed of to

---

1 *Noctes Ambrosianæ*, No. 1.
2 See W. J. Fitzpatrick, *Lady Morgan : her career, literary and personal*.

that publisher for £400 in the study of Lord Castlereagh." Her success continued and her prices rose. She had £550 for *O'Donnell*, £1,200 for *Florence McCarthy* containing a caricature of Croker, a hard critic of her in the *Quarterly*, and Egerton Brydges says that to her and Miss Edgeworth prices as high as £1,500, and £2,000, were at times paid. For Miss Edgeworth, in her better way, was also a steady writer, and from 1806 had been an able practitioner of the art of the fashionable novel. Such was the public demand for novels adequate to their more or less ephemeral taste.

IN 1800, too, we have a glimpse in Horace Smith of a young man aspiring to authorship and trying the novel, and no doubt he was but one of many young men to do the same. He was twenty-one and a clerk in a City counting-house when in that year he took the field as a domestic novelist with a Family Story which " dealt with the felicities of domestic life in a highly moral and improving manner after the fashion of the day." It was sufficiently successful to encourage the same publishers to bring out the next year his second novel *The Runaway, a novel with a purpose, or the Seat of Benevolence.* And very soon followed *Trevanion, or Matrimonial Errors*, on the mischief of secret marriages. They were all the kind of novel that is the staple of the circulating library, and from these books of Smith's it would seem that there were enough readers for publishers to be willing to publish them, and to give, perhaps a small, but at least an encouraging return to the author.

THEN through the first decade the Horror romance continued to flourish. The school of ' Monk '

Lewis still held readers by its spectres and spells, and people were eager for such works as *The Mysterious Hand, or Subterranean Horrors* and *The Demon of Sicily*, so that when the youthfully immature Shelley, with the itch of writing upon him, dashed off *Zastrozzi*, he found a publisher in Paternoster Row who gave him £40 for it. Then he hopefully went on with *St. Irvyne*, saying, " it is a thing which almost *mechanically* sells to circulating libraries." And though his confidence in the future of *St. Irvyne* was a mistaken one, that kind of horror and romance certainly did sell mechanically. *St. Irvyne* probably failed because the mixture of his magic potions had been different by a subtle difference from the standard mixture acceptable to that class of reader.

EVEN a writer with a quite eclectic appeal, like Miss Austen, was not neglected by the growing public of novel readers. *Northanger Abbey*, indeed, as we all know, lay in the publisher's drawer, unrisked, though he had paid a paltry £10 for it. But in 1811 *Sense and Sensibility*, a novel never likely to attract the many, and published anonymously, gradually attracted attention, and soon gave £150 profits. By that and *Pride and Prejudice*, and *Emma*, the profits up to her death were approaching £700.

NOVELISTS became numerous. The older novelists were edited and reprinted, as by Mrs. Barbauld in 1810 in fifty volumes, and cheap reprints, too, came out. And then in 1814 appeared *Waverley*. At once it stood out from the ruck of novels. But it did not stand out to contemporaries so prominently as it stands out to us. For the moment it was another, although surely it was generally recognized as a better, best-seller, and Constable asked in November 1814, " Had we ever more popular works than Alison, Sinclair, and Waverley ? " Scott had wisely declined Constable's offer of £700 for the copyright, and published on a basis of half-profits. *Waverley* caught on with the public, and by its staying power, if not by its initial success, showed its superiority over the *Alisons* and *Sinclairs*. It had sold 1,000 copies in five weeks. By the end of 1814 4,000 more had been printed. In 1815 1,000 followed, in 1816 1,500, in 1817 2,000, and so on. And all the time novel succeeded novel from Sir Walter's galloping pen. He did not have almost to create a public for the novel as he did for poetry. But his genius had an equally wonderful effect in waking up fresh readers to the delight of the prose romance, and in considerably multiplying the number of readers already existing. *Guy Mannering*'s first impression of 2,000 was sold in two days, and in 1816 Murray wrote to Blackwood about *Tales of My Landlord* : " You may go on printing as many and as fast as you can ; for we certainly need not stop until we come to the end of our, unfortunately, limited 6,000. . . . My copies are more than gone and if you have any to spare pray send them up instantly." [1] Still the enthusiasm of their reception increased, and in 1817 *Rob Roy*'s first 10,000 went in three weeks. Nor did the huge sales of each succeeding new novel stop those that had come before from going on selling. And by new novels alone Scott, according to Lockhart, " must have reckoned on clearing £30,000 at least in the course of a couple of years."

[1] Smiles, *A Publisher and his Friends*, i. 469.

IN the wake of Scott the novelists crowded in, as the poets had done before them. The better writers found the profits good. In 1817 Godwin made a success of *Mandeville*, and profits of some £1,100 are said to have been divided on the first edition. In 1819 Hope's *Anastasius*, partly owing to the belief in Byron's authorship, was widely read, and passed through many large editions. Blackwood, ever on the look-out for another Scott, thought, around 1822, that he had discovered one in Galt, and Galt did make a splendid running for a few years, till he had, with his persistent industry, worked out all that was in him. Of his *Annals of the Parish* 500 copies were sold in London in three or four days, and the almost immediate sale in Edinburgh was 400. " In short," said Blackwood, " I have seldom published a more popular or valuable book." And when, in the *Noctes*, Odoherty is made to say, " Why, no novels sell now except the Author of Waverley's," the Editor's reply is : " Write a good one and I'll warrant you 'twill sell. There's Adam Blair has taken like a shot ; and Sir Andrew Wylie is almost out of print already."

INDEED, it would seem that a novel need not be any too good a one either for it to be profitable to the author, and presumably to the publisher. Gillies says : " As a prose writer, the good Ettrick Shepherd certainly held but a very low rank ; but he has recorded that about this date [1822] he received £600 for two novels of three volumes each, which, according to his own avowal, were written and printed in desperate haste for the mere purpose of gain, and without any intrinsic

242

merits whatever."[1] Good work like Miss Ferrier's, with the friendship of Scott, brought that lady £1,000 from Blackwood for *Inheritance* in 1824, and, despite that novel's indifferent success, £1,700 from Cadell in 1831 for *Destiny*.

BUT the publisher who made a speciality of novels was Colburn. He was an enterprising man, proprietor of the *New Monthly*, and for a time part proprietor of the *Literary Gazette* and of the *Athenæum* successively, and he made a commotion in the profession by the audacity of his energetic advertising. From about 1825 he began to give himself up systematically to the production of novels, particularly fashionable novels. More and more novels issued from his press, and bigger and bigger grew the puffs with which he launched and maintained them. And he was for years supreme in the field he had chosen. Writers drew naturally to him, for the zeal with which he made his output of novels grow was an open invitation to the man who could write and who wanted money. Colburn was generous, too. "Sir," said Christopher North, "if I were a novelist, I am by no means sure that I should have any objections to deal with Mr. Colburn, for I hear the man's a civil man, and an economical, and an exact, and a thriving "—North quarrelled chiefly with his puffs. Horace Smith published with him *Brambletye House*, the historical novel of the Restoration, which, according to Leigh Hunt, " ran a hard race with the novel of *Woodstock* "[2] in 1826. Colburn gave £500 for it, and when it succeeded unexpectedly well, added £100, so that

1 R. P. Gillies, *Memories of a Literary Veteran,* iii. 85.
2 Leigh Hunt, *Autobiography,* p. 188.

Smith was encouraged to go on writing historical novels. In 1828 Colburn paid Gleig £750 for his three-volume novel *Chelsea Pensioners*, and those prices he could well afford, for Croly, in offering his weird romance of *Salathiel* to Blackwood in 1827 for £500 for the first edition, asserted that by publications of the kind of *Salathiel* Colburn had made some £20,000 a year for the three previous years.[1] And in fact Colburn did much for the novel writer. If he had a fault, it was in the encouragement he gave to facile writing. We see indications of it in his paying Gillies £200 in 1829 for a novel, *Basil Barrington*, before it was written.

So the novel came to take the prominent position in the libraries and book-shops, and in ordinary reading, that it has held ever since. Critics began to denounce its prolificity. Sure sign of its high status, it became fashionable to write a novel. " I am glad," noted Lady Charlotte Bury in her diary of 1818, " that people of *ton* have taken to writing novels ; it is an excellent amusement for them, and also for the public." Southey lamented, " Is there any season in which some sprigs of nobility and fashion do not bring forth hot-house flowers of this kind ? . . . What are the Annuals but schools for Novelists, male and female ? " And, of course, there was the main supply of the undistinguished novels, often so pleasantly and so capably written, which are the output of a high proportion of the profession of letters, and of whose existence there is no more delightful reminder than such a passage as this from Thackeray: The lady " owns that in youth she was very much

[1] Oliphant, *William Blackwood*, i. 481

in love with Valancourt. Valancourt, and who was he ? cry the young people. Valancourt, my dears, was the hero of one of the most famous romances which ever was published in this country. The beauty and elegance of Valancourt made your young grandmammas' gentle hearts to beat with respectful sympathy. He and his glory have passed away. Ah, woe is me that the glory of novels should ever decay ; that dust should gather round them on the shelves ; that the annual cheques from Messieurs the publishers should dwindle . . . Alas, our novels are but for a season ; " [1] and yet they were not for quite so short a season as they had been earlier, for, as Rogers noted, " Now-a-days, as soon as a novel has had its run and is beginning to be forgotten, out comes an edition of it as a ' standard novel ' ! " [2]

(ix)

ALTOGETHER the profession of letters was in this period a profession by which a man could earn a satisfactory living, if he was a man who had any right by talent to be of the profession. Provided he was a good, all-round writer he could find in journalism and the novel in particular, and in histories, and books of travel and of information as well, an adequate income   And the fetters on his independence as a writer were of the lightest ; if indeed they were not negligible.   Since Johnson's day, the ordinary writer had had no need for the help of patronage.   He set to work at literature just as confidently as a barrister at pleading, and

1 Thackeray, *A Peal of Bells* (*Roundabout Papers*).
2 G. H. Powell, *Table Talk of Samuel Rogers*, p. 108.

with, perhaps, less fear of lean early years. He neither expected nor desired to be patronized. He might not be like Blake, and turn pale at the very offer of money, but he wanted and was able to stand upon his own legs.

THERE had been something of the fairy god-mother about the patrons of the golden age of patronage, when Queen Anne was on the throne, and Harley and St. John in her counsels. At least by 1820 there seemed to have been, when a man read of the gifts to poets of banknotes, closed in gilt pebble snuff-boxes. But that kind of patronage was not likely to come again, except in a dream. Those who acted the patron in the early nineteenth century were like the well-meaning people who did more harm than good to a Clare or a Bloomfield, and made a short-lived show of a poet farm-hand, even interrupting his work in the fields to look at him. One of those patrons was Capell Lofft of whom Byron wrote to Barton in 1812 : " I am not sorry to hear that you are not tempted by the vicinity of Capell Lofft, Esq ; though if he had done for you what he has for the Bloomfields, I should never have laughed at his rage for patronizing." [1]

MOREOVER, with the profession as it was, to come within reach of a patron at all was to confess to some degree of failure. It might be the most honourable of failures like Wordsworth's ; or it might be because the writer felt his talents too high for ordinary journey-work, and was not averse to patronage that would let him write only what he wanted to write, and Crabbe had been a man like that ; or it might be and often was, because the

[1] E. V. Lucas, *Bernard Barton*, p. 163.

man ought to have chosen another profession, and
to have kept literature as a hobby.

THAT is the broad truth. Patronage was dead,
and what we have to speak of in this section is little
more than its ghost. Influential friendship would
be a better name for most of it. The prospects
of help a writer might entertain from official
circles had already, as we have seen, almost disappeared. Burke's legislation and Pitt's premier-
ship had been effective stiflers. When Addington
came in, Combe lost his pension. Campbell
was extraordinarily fortunate to get his. Moore
was in 1803 appointed Admiralty Registrar at
Bermuda, and after a short visit transferred the
duties to a deputy, but he had made a society
success and had the influence of the Prince of
Wales. Examples of any official patronage are
few enough, and when a writer did get a government place, his writing had little to do with his
gaining it. Leigh Hunt had a clerkship in the
War Office in 1808, which, says he, " was given
me by Mr. Addington, then prime minister, afterwards Lord Sidmouth, who knew my father." [1]
And after a while he felt he could not keep that,
considering the politics of the *Examiner* which he
was then editing. Moreover, people were beginning to attack sinecures. Even Scott's Clerkship
of the Court of Session came under fire, and it was
said " that if a Clerk of Session had any real
business to do, it could not be done well by a man
who found time for more literary enterprises than
any other author of the age undertook."

WHEN attacks so mean as that could arise, sinecures
were sure to be suppressed, although, indeed, there

[1] Leigh Hunt, *Autobiography*, p. 175.

were not many to suppress. Laman Blanchard had served the Whigs well enough in the *Courier* to justify an appeal for a small appointment, but it was made in vain. " The fact really is," says Lytton telling Blanchard's story, " that governments, at present, have little among their subordinate patronage, to bestow upon those whose abilities are not devoted to a profession. The man of letters is like a stray joint in a boy's puzzle ; he fits into no place. Let the partisan but have taken orders—let him but have eaten a sufficient number of dinners at the inns of Court—and livings, and chapels, and stalls and assistant-barristerships, and commissionerships, and colonial appointments can reward his services and prevent his starving. But for an author there is nothing but his pen, till that and life are worn to the stump : and then, with a good fortune, perhaps on his death-bed he receives a pension and equals, it may be, for a few months, the income of a retired butler ! " [1]

NOR was there so very much for the man of letters, even had he taken orders. As it is written of Sydney Smith, " There cannot be a more striking proof of the slenderness of the provision made for the reward or encouragement of intellectual eminence in this country than the fact that Sydney Smith with his fulness of reputation and with his politcial friends in power, felt compelled to accept the small living of Foston-le-Clay in Yorkshire, which was with some difficulty obtained through the exertions of Lord and Lady Holland, from the Whig Chan-

---

[1] L. Blanchard, *Sketches from Life, with a memoir of the author by Sir E. Bulwer Lytton* 1846, i. xxiii–iv.

248

cellor, Lord Erskine." And Wordsworth remarked to Rogers, " It is a disgrace to the age
that Cary has no preferment ", for though Cary
was denied on the ground of his occasional mental
trouble, that was a poor ground for denial.[1]
YET all along the better writers who had the
interests of the profession at heart did not want
patronage except for very special cases. In
particular they disliked the miserable philanthropy
of the Literary Fund. Scott often thought too
well of things, and he praised it to Crabbe in 1809
as " that admirable institution for the relief of
distressed authors," but Southey was the truer
professional writer, and to Murray he suggested,
in 1812, an article in the *Quarterly*, saying, " I
should like to say something upon the absurd pur-
poses of the Literary Fund, with its despicable
ostentation of patronage, and to build a sort of
National Academy in the air, in the hope that
Canning might one day lay its foundation in a
more solid manner." [2] But no Academy arose
that pleased Canning. Instead there was founded
the Royal Society of Literature, and Canning
refused to join the Committee, for, said he, " I am
really of opinion with Dr. Johnson, that the
multitudinous personage, called the Public, is
after all the best patron of literature and learned
men."
BUT, despite Canning, there were some creditable
pensions awarded round 1824. They were given
to literary men through the Royal Society of
Literature by George IV, although they ter-
minated at his death. The greatest pensioner was

---

[1] Clayden, *Rogers and his Contemporaries*, ii. 171–4.
[2] Smiles, *A Publisher and his Friends*, i. 237.

Coleridge, and no doubt his £100 a year was very acceptable. Yet it was only a little burst of patronage. Would-be patrons, in fact, did not receive much encouragement. " Southey," noted Crabb Robinson, " read me a curious correspondence between himself and Brougham, soon after the latter became Chancellor.[1] Brougham . . . begged Southey to give him his opinion on the sort of patronage which, usefully and safely, might be given by the government to literature. Southey's answer was very good—cutting, with all the forms of courtesy." [2]

THE social recognition, however, of literature by people of wealth and rank continued. Society welcomed into its circle many a writer who pleased it, and who was glad to be the object of that kind of recognition. Biographers are fond of remarking on it. We read of " the avidity with which Miss Owenson's society was courted," and that, about 1813, Miss Edgeworth was " courted by all persons of distinction in London with an avidity almost without example." We have seen Miss Owenson as a guest of the Marquess of Abercorn. Then there was Thomas Moore, introduced by Lord Moira into the circle even of the Prince of Wales, and charming all by his remarkable musical gifts. A brilliant new writer was almost sure to be lionized ; the authors of *Rejected Addresses*, for example, were at once taken up by the best people. The Dowager Countess of Cork was but one of several great ladies in being " anxious to have the Smith brothers at her soirées." And when Keats dined with the brothers he found, " they know all the fashionables."

[1] i.e. about 1830.   [2] Crabb Robinson, *Diary*, iii. 29.

SCOTT, inevitably, was the lion of several seasons, and in Lockhart's account we can read between the lines just how much all this society reception was worth. " Scott," he says, " more correctly than any other man I ever knew, appreciated the value of that apparently enthusiastic *engouement* which the world of London shews to the fashionable wonder of the year," and he tells how Scott said of " this ephemeral *réputation du salon*," " It may be a pleasant gale to sail with, but it never yet led to a port that I should like to anchor in." [1] And in no man's life is the futility of this lionization more clearly evident than in that of Clare, the poor farm worker who was gifted with a limited, but natural lyric muse. " Persons of taste and generosity in the upper classes took him by the hand." Lord Exeter, hearing his wages were only £30 a year, sent for him to give another £15. Others joined his Lordship, and then, after having disturbed his life, the popularity died away again while his real poetic merit went on increasing.

IN that world where high society and men of letters mingled, the greatest figure for almost the first half of the century was that of Samuel Rogers, the melodious poet and retired banker. With the help of his reputation as a poet, and of his considerable wealth, he steadily made for himself the name of a great connoisseur and a liberal host. Under May 1804, in the pages of Dr. Burney's diary, we read : " [Rogers] is a good poet, has a refined taste in all the arts, has a select library of the best editions of the best authors in all languages, has very fine pictures, very fine drawings, and the finest collection I ever

[1] Lockhart, *Life of Scott*, p. 201.

saw of Etruscan vases ; and, moreover, he gives the best dinners to the best company of men of talents and genius I know ; the best served, and with the best wines, liqueurs, etc. . . . His books of prints of the greatest engravers from the greatest masters in history, architecture and antiquities are of the first class. His house in St. James's Place, looking into the Green Park, is deliciously situated and furnished with great taste." [1] In August 1810 he received a note, no doubt not a unique one : " I am commanded by H.R.H. the Princess of Wales to say she will call for you in St. James's Place to-morrow evening at eight o'clock to take you to the play." And all the time the friendship of Lord Holland was his, and it was no small a power. In Macaulay's words, Rogers was ' the oracle of Holland House.' No wonder then that he was a prominent figure. " He was," says his biographer, " the one man, and his house was the one house, that every stranger from the Continent, or from the United States, or from the English shires, desired to see," [2] and, " it is scarcely too much to say that he kept open house for men of letters, and many distinguished writers of the time owed to him their introduction to London Society." [3] Crabbe was one. " Mr. Rogers introduced me," he said of 1817, " to almost every man he is acquainted with ; and in this number were comprehended all I was previously very anxious to obtain knowledge of." To Crabbe it was an intoxicating experience.

THE position which Rogers had made was a position from which a man could do a very great

1 Clayden, *The Early Life of Rogers*, p. 449.
2 Clayden, *Rogers and his Contemporaries*, i. p. vi.
3 *Ibid.*, i. 13.

deal of good, especially to writers. And Rogers did not neglect his chances. Where he was satisfied that merit existed, he could do much to make it known, and his wealth gave him an opportunity of helping by a timely loan or present. Unobtrusively, and often unsuspected, for he hid much kindness beneath the satirical mask of a cynic, he did give help time and again. Moore, talking to Lord John Russell in 1831 about a loan, said, " Rogers does more of such things than the world has any notion of," and Lord John replied, " Not only more than the world has any notion of, but more than anyone else could have done. Being himself an author, he was able to guess the difficulties of men of letters, and to assist them not only with his ready purse, but with his powerful influence and his judicious advice." To run over but briefly some instances where he gave assistance there was the Distributorship of Stamps which he very seasonably obtained for Wordsworth by a hint to Lord Lonsdale ; there was the £100 he paid to free the dying Sheridan from bailiffs ; there was his setting up Thomas Miller as a bookseller to enable him to print his own writings ; there was a loan to Campbell of £500. Also we read how Rogers objected to Moore's making himself a slave to the booksellers, saying, " There is my £500 ready for you." There was Cary's pension, too. And there was what he induced other people to give. " What a noble-minded person Lord Lonsdale was ! " Rogers said. " I have received from him, in this room, hundreds of pounds for the relief of literary men." [1]

BUT some of the best and most characteristic

1 G. H. Powell, *Table Talk of Samuel Rogers*, p. 162.

services of Rogers were in the way of bargaining with publishers, a way which is really the only way in which an author can accept help without feeling that he is unbecomingly dependent on another. Dr. Johnson had used to help authors similarly, and Pope, too, before him, and many other great authors later, but hardly anyone can have done so much as Rogers. He was the recipient of request after request. " I am still," wrote Coleridge in 1815, " most desirous to undertake the translation either of Cervantes or of Boccaccio's Works, the Don Quixote and Decameron excepted, and want no other encouragement than a settled promise from some responsible publisher, such as Mr. Cadell, that he will purchase the manuscript when it is ready for the press. . . . Should you find an opportunity to speak to Mr. Cadell, I should be only so far solicitous about the terms as that they should not be *humiliatingly* low in proportion to the labour and effort." [1] Wordsworth, too, wrote in 1822, saying : " Some time ago you expressed . . . a wish that my sister would publish her recollections of her Scotch tour, and you interested yourself so far in the scheme as kindly to offer to assist in disposing of it to a publisher for her advantage. We know that your skill and experience in these matters are great." [2] And when Wordsworth was preparing *The Excursion* in 1814 he had sought Rogers's help, and he sought it later too. Nor did Rogers ever refuse help, either to a man like Wordsworth, or to a lesser man like Crowe, Professor of Poetry at Oxford, who also " had

[1] Clayden, *Rogers and his Contemporaries*, pp. 192–3.
[2] *Ibid.*, i. 344.

ready aid and counsel in his transactions with publishers," or to lesser men still.

So in Rogers we see a very influential man helping men of letters. And he was not alone. Of Rogers's own class there was Shelley, who was always ready with his purse. Though he himself had only £1,000 a year, he gave T. L. Peacock £100 a year for some seven years, until Peacock was in a position to do without it ; and he gave Leigh Hunt a present of £1,400 to free him from debt. Indeed, says Hunt, " his last sixpence was ever at my service, had I chosen to share it." And Scott, too, did not forget his less fortunate fellows. He got up a subscription for a new edition of the *Queen's Wake* for Hogg, " our poor friend . . . who really requires to have public attention drawn to him now and then." He once gave Maturin a gift of £50, and in all ways, we may be sure, he was never sparing in his " little unremembered acts of kindness and of love." In fact, Lockhart says, " there was perhaps nothing (except the one great blunder) that had a worse effect on the course of his pecuniary fortunes than the readiness with which he exerted his influence with the book-sellers on behalf of inferior writers." Southey, too, did what he could. Thus author helped author, and that help is one of the pleasantest things to see in all the profession of letters.

BUT there were many all over the country who, though they had not the same riches of income and of influence, had equal riches in generosity of heart. Cyrus Redding testified that there were " always plentiful instances of kindly patronage of clever youths." And Southey, in telling the story of Kirke White, said : " It has been too much the custom to complain that genius is neglected, and to blame the public, when the public is not at fault. They who are thus lamented as victims of genius, have been in almost every instance the victims of their own vices. . . . In this age and in this country whoever deserves encouragement is sooner or later sure to receive it. Of this Henry's history is honourable proof." For young Kirke White in Nottingham around 1800 found several people who were willing to maintain him while he studied and who delighted to encourage his talent for poetry. And there had been in Exeter people who helped Gifford similarly to be a student and a poet.

EVERYWHERE there were kindly individuals who gladly gave a helping hand to struggling talent. One Allsop sent £100 to Coleridge as a present in admiration of his genius. And a typical man of goodwill was Dr. Robert Anderson of Edinburgh, " who acted as editor-general to all incipient poets." Gillies celebrated him, saying : " What a pompous dictator about trifles was good old Dr. Anderson to whom, *malgré cela*, the late Thomas Campbell, it may be said, owed his great reputation, for without the doctor's help the author of the *Pleasures of Hope* would probably never have struggled into public notice at all." Crabb Robinson introduced Hazlitt to a publisher, and Lady Mackintosh introduced him to the *Edinburgh Review* as a contributor.[1] And if one were to search into the lives of the literary men of that age, not a few would be found to have known the favours of an Allsop or an Anderson or a Crabb Robinson, to show, as Southey said, that

[1] Crabb Robinson, *Diary*, i. 461.

there were benefactors enough to make the plea absurd that a man was starved through his very talents.

BUT though we dwell rightly on the roll of benefactors, we must not forget that those whom we name as patrons, or their like, played but a very small part in the profession of letters. The public is always the first power, and the publishers the second. If we must talk of patrons, let us remember that Johnson called the bookseller the best patron. And the publishers of 1820 were quite as alive to their responsibilities as had been those of 1770. Patrons, strictly speaking, publishers can never be, for unless they wish to be bankrupts, they must first of all be business men. But patrons they often deserve to be called because of their admitted liberality. We have seen how Gifford, as the result of his dealings with Murray while he was editor of the *Quarterly,* said to Murray : " The only fault I ever taxed you with in pecuniary matters, was with that of being *too liberal* to me." Murray's liberality in fact is written large in all his dealings. When Washington Irving's works began to fall off with the public, Murray, because he thought so highly of them himself, concealed their decline from Irving and continued to accept and to pay so high for his books as to leave himself with losses instead of profits. When Crabbe died, and his son wrote a Life, Murray gave the whole profit on the first edition of 5,000 to the son. And with such generosity he well earned his nickname of Emperor of the West. Nor was Murray the only generous publisher. Blackwood, too, took a genuine interest in his authors. Lockhart he supplied with the means of continental travel to round off his education.

THE social life, also, which publishers provided with their dinners and their drawing-rooms was a helpful thing and a friendly. And for the general relation of author and publisher let the words of Leigh Hunt stand for it. In 1823 he was stranded in Italy without the money for his passage home. " Suffice to say," he tells, " that the author's customary patron—the bookseller—enabled me to make homewards." Even let the words of the egregious James Montgomery to Constable in 1806 sum up the position of the man of letters, for though his poetry was not genuine, these words ring true : " I trust I shall never degrade myself by stooping so low as to solicit the patronage of any persons, however rich or great, except noble-minded booksellers, and enlightened and candid readers, of whatever rank the latter may be."[1]

1 Constable, *Archibald Constable*, ii. 169.

EPILOGUE

THE PROSPECT IN 1832

The depression before the Reform Bill. Literature for the people. The multitude of readers : Cobbett's comment. The multitude of writers : Carlyle's comment.

NOTE.—The references in the footnotes throughout the volume are to the editions given in the Bibliography.

THE opening of the fourth decade of the century is the opening of a fresh chapter in the history of the profession of letters. In particular it is the opening of a fresh chapter in the history of the reading public. It is the time of passing, too, from one generation of writers to another. Byron is already dead. Scott, Crabbe, Hazlitt, Lamb and Coleridge are gone before 1834 is out. The new men are getting into stride. Macaulay, Carlyle, Benjamin Disraeli, Lytton, Henry Taylor, G. P. R. James, and the great, popular Dickens step in succession into the limelight.

ABOUT 1830 there was a pause. The troubled tide of life surged into the world of letters. For the time nothing mattered but the struggle for reform in Parliament. The passion of resistance and the passion of enthusiasm met like two great waves, and above their impact the ship of State trembled through all its timbers. The company at the Ambrose Tavern lustily drank to the *Immortal Memory of the British Constitution*, but their hearts were anxious for the State, fearing " the spring that brings back her summer will be a bloody one." [1]

1831 passes with riots and growing frenzy lest the people after all be cheated. In October there is a riot at Bristol, " it is to be feared very bloody—" notes Crabb Robinson, " a proof that

[1] *Noctes Ambrosianæ*, No. 45.

the mob are ready to shed blood for the Bill." [1] In December Dorothy Wordsworth writes " of the turbulence of our great towns and cities," and her " poor brother is often heart-sick and almost desponding—and no wonder." Brother and sister alike are sick with the fear of sudden and devastating change. To the sister " one visible blessing seems already to be coming upon us through the alarm of the cholera." " Every rich man," she writes, " is now obliged to look into the bye-lanes and corners inhabited by the poor, and many crying abuses are (even in our little town of Ambleside) about to be remedied." [2]

As the agitation for reform waxed stronger, the circulation even of the stable *Quarterly* fell away. Nothing would do but Reform. Propaganda had been tried. " Lord Brougham," wrote Murray to Blackwood in December 1830, " is writing and circulating all sorts of trash to quiet the people ; proving to them that they get much more by machinery than without it." But the inevitable was not to be put off. On June 7th 1832 the Royal assent was given to the Reform Bill. The tumult slackened. Though unrest remained, the obsession was lifted, and the writing and the selling of books once more resumed its normal course.

BUT a noticeable pause there had been in the trade of literature. " I learned in Scotland," said Wordsworth in 1831, " that the bookselling trade was in a deplorable state, and that nothing was saleable but newspapers on the Revolutionary side." " Indeed," wrote Washington Irving in February 1832, " the book trade is in such a

---

[1] Crabb Robinson, *Diary*, ii. 518.　　　　[2] *Ibid.*, ii. 523.

deplorable state that I hardly know where to turn to ; some are disabled, and all disheartened. There is scarce any demand for new works, such is the distraction of the public mind with reform, cholera, and Continental revolutions." [1] And Mrs. Shelley wrote thus to Murray about Godwin in May of the same year : " You are but too well aware of the evil days on which literature is fallen, and how difficult it is for a man, however gifted, whose existence depends on his pen, to make one engagement succeed another with sufficient speed to answer the calls of his situation. Nearly all our literati have found but one resource in this—which is the ample scope afforded by periodicals. A kind of literary pride has prevented my father from mingling in these ; and, never having published anything anonymously, he feels disinclined to enter on a, to him, new career." [2]

THERE Mrs. Shelley tells us that journalism, as we have already seen, was the mainstay of the professional man of letters. And its ample scope has never ceased to become ampler. Journalism has advanced by leaps and bounds. The world even of 1850 was an enormous advance on the world of 1830. The entries of new periodicals of all kinds in London and the suburbs for these twenty-five years number in the *Times Handlist of Newspapers* not less than fourteen hundred ; and for Wales and the provinces not less than six hundred. And among the best of them stand out *Fraser's Magazine* founded in 1830, *Punch* founded in 1841, Chambers's *Edinburgh Journal* founded in 1832, the *Illustrated London News* founded in 1843, and the *Daily News* founded in 1846. And it

---

[1] Smiles, *A Publisher and his Friends*, ii. 261.   [2] *Ibid.*, ii. 328.

seems another bound forward when we meet Dickens's *Household Words* in 1850.

ONCE the pause was over, the profession of letters as a whole went steadily forward, and not journalism only. The chief change was an accentuation of the prosaic and informative tendency of the years that had gone before. Poetry was on the shelf again. Murray refused to take it, for he was now become solid rather than enterprising, and had given up novels too. Of 1834 Henry Taylor, at a loss with *Philip van Artevelde*, wrote : " At that time the Publishers would have nothing to say to poets, regarding them as an unprofitable people. My manuscript seems to have been in search of a publisher months." And then Moxon took Taylor's poem, for Moxon was one of the new men of enterprise, and he did much to make popular the recent poets in his new series of republications.

BUT what especially makes this period a new period, is the progress in literature for the people. Murray's *Family Library* and Constable's *Miscellany* had led the way with good cheap books for middle-class readers. But Constable's idea of " books for the million " came nearer realization in 1832 with the appearance in January of Chambers's *Edinburgh Journal*. The Chambers brothers knew what they were about. As separate young publishers they had worked with almost amazing industry, building up their business with unremitting attention, and leaving no stone unturned to understand it. And they both knew something by experience of what the public wanted. Robert Chambers had contributed to Constable's series a popular *History of the Rebellion of* '45, and had edited the *Edinburgh*

Advertiser. William Chambers had economically walked about Scotland in his leisure in order to impart some originality to his exhaustive *Gazetteer* ; then they collaborated in the *Journal*, and they were both men who brought the worthiest aims to their publishing enterprise. The *Journal* was to instruct and amuse. It proclaimed that " the grand leading principle is to take advantage of the universal appetite for instruction which at present exists." And it was hoped that every schoolboy and every labourer would find it to his taste.

IN none of this was the *Journal* actually new. The year before there had been Mudie's *Cornucopia* at three halfpence. And for some ten years before that there had been a whole flock of cheap little serials of an informative quality, but too irregular, and short-lived, and sometimes of no more than one number. They had made a slight impression in the towns, but the march of mind was still slow in the country districts, and it was Chambers's *Edinburgh Journal* that really achieved the first conquering raid into illiterate territory. It, too, was only three halfpence, and after twelve numbers the weekly impression was 31,000, and after twenty numbers the weekly impression for Edinburgh and London together was 50,000, reaching 60,000 in 1835, and a few years later 80,000, and it made its way even into the hills of Galloway, where the shepherds were said to read it constantly.

BUT the Chambers brothers were no sooner under way than in March 1832 the *Society for the Diffusion of Useful Knowledge* took some of the wind out of their sails with their *Penny Magazine* published under an agreement with Charles Knight. The

Society had good contributors for their good purpose—among others were Allan Cunningham, Thomas Pringle, and George Long, reliable all-round men, and the whole roll of their contributors held some two hundred names—and at the close of the year the sales of the *Penny Magazine* outstripped those of the *Journal*. In weekly and monthly parts the *Penny Magazine* sold some 200,000 copies, which might be taken as representing some million readers. The *Penny Magazine* was not the first of the Society's publications. To rival Constable's *Miscellany* they had already been issuing some histories and biographies in a *Library of Useful Knowledge*, and also with Charles Knight's help they had brought out a *Library of Entertaining Knowledge*. But these books had been too dull to be a great success, and that dullness was the flaw in their otherwise good *Penny Cyclopædia* with which they followed up the success of the *Penny Magazine*. It appeared in 1833, and soon reached a sale of 75,000 copies, but then it dropped steadily until the sale was only 20,000. For the work was too scholarly, and the books were rather text-books for students than volumes capable of a popular appeal, and it was a popular rather than a technical audience that wanted them, and indeed that existed. And moreover there was the keen rivalry of Chambers's *Information for the People*, which also came out in 1833, and of which altogether some 170,000 sets were sold. In fact, the *Society* had to raise the price of the *Penny Cyclopædia* to fourpence, and it was stopped in 1845, after a heavy loss had been incurred, due partly, no doubt, as Chambers said, to the fact that " a society cannot as a rule compete with private enterprise." And the enterprise of Chambers was steady and well-informed. Besides, in 1835 came Chambers's *Educational Course*, a series of books for schools, to get hints for which William Chambers even made a visit to Holland.

So literature for the public progressed. And it might have been more successful still but for the "taxes on knowledge." They were a great burden. The amount paid to the revenue on the *Penny Cyclopædia* alone totalled by the end £16,500. But John Francis and others waged a constant warfare against them. The newspaper tax was reduced in 1837, and was abolished in 1855, and the tax on paper was finally done away with in 1861. Then publishers were really unshackled in their efforts to satisfy the popular demand. A man like John Cassell could go on unchecked in the zealous circulation of popular education, which he had already begun when the pressure of taxation was still there. And what that pressure was one may see fairly set forth in a pamphlet of 1852 by J. Chapman, on *The Commerce of Literature, or Cheap books and how to get them*.

BUT the pressure of taxation did not prevent a great deal of progress from being made. For the demand was there, and was growing all the time. The passing of the Reform Bill had meant a great step forward in the growth of the reading public. Men at Westminster quickly saw that, having created many new electors, their first duty was to do something to see that these electors had a chance to be educated as citizens. And so some advance was made towards a conception of National education, and in 1833 the first State grants for schools were made. There was to follow the creation of the Board of Education and the Act of 1870.

MEANTIME, from the thirties, an equally great power was at work to change the mind as well as the face of England. The unification which the better roads and the quicker coaches had been bringing about, was hastened by the growing network of railways. They effectively broke down the last barriers between town and country and they must share, with the national schools, the credit and the responsibility for the level uniform mediocrity of education which has since then become general.

THE schools and the railways between them did much for the reading public. How much the railways did it may be hard to estimate, but when we consider the almost endless volume of bookstall literature, we can hardly doubt that what they have done has been considerable. Cheap bookstall literature was plentiful before the middle of last century, and one of its most popular purveyors was G. W. M. Reynolds with his penny fiction.[1] His tales were as prolific as they were popular. " They formed the literature of the servants' quarter, the sempstresses' workroom, and the mechanics' shop, and if they did no great good they did no great harm, and unquestionably relieved a world which was somewhat drab at its best. The circulation must have run into millions." [2] Even Thackeray looked at them, for, in a lecture in New York in 1852 on Charity and Humour, he mentioned Reynolds's *Mysteries of London*, saying, " Years ago I treated myself to sixpennyworth

[1] See *The Times Literary Supplement,* January 24, 1924. Notes on Sales, G. W .M. Reynolds and Penny Fiction.
[2] *Ibid.*

of this performance at a railway station. . . .
A couple of years after I took sixpennyworth more
of the same delectable history. . . ." And though
Thackeray mocked, no doubt Reynolds meant a
lot to the working people.

THUS 1832 is a convenient boundary at which
to stop this survey. After 1832 it is a changed
world. The ' doctrinaire ' for one has changed
it—the doctrinaire of whom Cobbett wrote in the
Register : " Above all things he is distinguished for
his disregard and contempt for provender for the
belly and the back ; except for his *own* belly and
his *own* back, which he is very willing to furnish
out of the labour of those whom he dooms to live
upon water porridge and potatoes, being, however,
always ready to supply them with ample *food for
their minds* out of his inexhaustible storehouse of
' Useful Knowledge ' and of ' Penny Magazines.'
It is a curious fact that, within these four or five
years, no less then four corn mills in the neighbour-
hood of Uxbridge, and several in the neigh-
bourhood of Maidstone, have been turned into
papermills ! One would think that the poor souls
had actually taken to eating the books."

IT is a changed world, too, in the swollen multitude
of its writers as well as of its readers. Writers
multiplied until Ruskin groaned out : " Just think
what a horrible condition of life it is that any man
of common vulgar wit who knows English grammar, can get, for a couple of sheets of chatter in
a magazine, two-thirds of what Milton got altogether for *Paradise Lost*."

IN the age of Victoria the profession of letters and
the world of readers are a surging complexity.
Let the words of Carlyle suffice for a glimpse :

" ALL apprenticeship except to mere handicraft
having fallen obsolete, and the ' educated man '
being with us emphatically and exclusively the
man that can speak well with tongue or pen, and
astonish men by the quantities of speech he has
heard (' tremendous *reader*,' ' walking encyclopædia,' and such like)—the Art of Speech is
probably definable in that case as the short
summary of all the Black Arts put together. . . .
" IF the young aspirant is not rich enough for
Parliament, and is deterred by the basilisks or
otherwise from entering on Law or Church, and
cannot altogether reduce his human intellect to the
beaverish condition, or satisfy himself with the
prospect of making money—what becomes of him
in such case, which is naturally the case of very
many, and ever of more ? In such case there
remains but one outlet for him, and notably
enough that too is a talking one : the outlet of
Literature, of trying to write Books. Since, owing
to preliminary basilisks, want of cash, or superiority to cash, he cannot mount aloft by eloquent
talking, let him try it by dexterous and eloquent
writing . . . To the British subject who fancies
genius may be lodged in him, this liberty remains ;
and truly it is, if well computed, almost the only
one he has.
" A CROWDED portal this of Literature, accordingly ! The haven of expatriated spiritualisms,
and alas also of expatriated vanities and prurient
imbecilities : here do the windy aspirations, foiled
activities, foolish ambitions, and frustrate human
energies reduced to the vocable condition, fly
as to the one refuge left ; and the Republic of
Letters increases in population at a faster rate

than even the Republic of America. The strangest regiment in her Majesty's service, this of the Soldiers of Literature. . . . The immortal gods are there (quite irrecognisable under these disguises), and also the lowest broken valets ;—an extremely miscellaneous regiment. In fact, the regiment, superficially viewed, looks like an immeasurable motley flood of discharged play-actors, funambulists, false prophets, drunken ballad-singers ; and marches not as a regiment, but as a boundless canaille,—without drill, uniform, captaincy or billet ; with large *over*-proportion of drummers ; you would say, a regiment gone wholly to the drum, with hardly a good musket to be seen in it—more a canaille than a regiment. Canaille of all the loud-sounding levities and general winnowings of Chaos, marching through the world in a most ominous manner."[1] BUT the vehemence of Carlyle was wasted on the inevitable. As everything had led up to 1832, and one cannot see that it could have been otherwise, so the more febrile development of the years that followed seems alike the development of destiny.

[1] Carlyle, *Latter Day Pamphlets* (1898), pp. 183, 190–1.

BIBLIOGRAPHY OF BOOKS USED [1]

THE DICTIONARY OF NATIONAL BIOGRAPHY

J. W. ADAMSON. *A Short History of Education.* 1919.

The Adventurer. 1751–3.

JANE AUSTEN. G. E. Mitton, *Jane Austen and her Times.* 1905.

—— *Sense and Sensibility.*

B. BARTON. E. V. Lucas, *Bernard Barton and his Friends.* 1893.

H. BELLOC. *The Cruise of the " Nona."* 1925.

A. BELJAME. *Le Public et les hommes de lettres en Angleterre au 18e siècle.* 1883.

W. BESANT. *The Pen and the Book.* 1898.

BLACK. *Memoirs of Adam Black.* Ed. A. Nicholson. 1885.

W. G. BLACKIE. *Origin and Progress of the Firm of Blackie and Son.* 1809–74. 1897.

BLACKWOOD. Mrs. Oliphant and Mrs. Porter. *William Blackwood and his Sons.* 3 vols. 1897.

LAMAN BLANCHARD. *Sketches from Life.* With a memoir of the author by Sir E. Bulwer Lytton. 1846.

G. BORROW. *Lavengro* (World's Classics).

J. BRITTON AND T. REES. *Reminiscences of Literary London.* 1896.

S. EGERTON BRYDGES. *The Autobiography, Times, Opinions and Contemporaries of Sir E. B.* 1834.

T. CAMPBELL. W. Beattie, *Life and Letters of Thomas Campbell.* 3 vols. 1849.

W. CHAMBERS. *Memoirs of Robert Chambers with Autobiographic Reminiscences of William Chambers.* 1872.

J. CHAPMAN. *The Commerce of Literature.* 1852.

COCKBURN, LORD. *Memorials of his Time.* 1908.

S. T. COLERIDGE. *Biographia Literaria* (Everyman Library).

—— *Letters.* Ed. E. H. Coleridge. 2 vols. 1895.

—— *Table Talk.* Ed. T. Ashe. 1884.

T. CONSTABLE. *Archibald Constable and his Literary Correspondents.* 3 vols. 1873.

G. CRABBE. *Life and Works.* Ed. by his son. 1860.

---

1 All references in the footnotes are to the editions given here. Other books to which reference has been made will be found in the notes throughout.

Diary of a Visit to England in 1775. Ed. S. Raymond. 1854.

I. D'ISRAELI. *Miscellanies of Literature.* 1840.

—— *Works.* Ed. with Memoir by B. Disraeli. 7 vols. 1858–9.

J. C. FRANCIS. *John Francis, Publisher of the Athenæum.* 2 vols. 1888.

W. GIFFORD. *Autobiography.* 1827.

R. P. GILLIES. *Memoirs of a Literary Veteran.* 3 vols. 1851.

HALÉVY. *Histoire du Peuple Anglais au XIXe Siècle.*

J. L. AND B. HAMMOND. *The Rise of Modern Industry.* 1925.

W. HAYLEY. *Memoirs.* 1823.

HAZLITT. *Spirit of the Age* (World's Classics).

—— P. P. Howe, *Life of Hazlitt.* 1922.

HOLCROFT. W. Hazlitt, *Memoirs of Thomas Holcroft* (World's Classics). 1926.

W. HONE. F. W. Hackwood, *Hone, His Life and Times.* 1912.

LEIGH HUNT. *Autobiography.* 1860.

S. JOHNSON. Boswell, *Life of Johnson.* Ed. G. B. Hill. 6 vols. 1887.

—— *Lives of the Poets.* Ed. G. B. Hill. 3 vols. 1905.

—— *Journey to the Western Isles of Scotland.* Ed. R. W. Chapman. 1924.

—— *Johnsonian Miscellanies.* Ed. G. B. Hill. 1897.

W. P. KER. *Collected Essays.* 1925.

J. LACKINGTON. *Memoirs.* 1803.

C. LAMB. E. V. Lucas, *Life of Charles Lamb.* 2 vols. 1905.

—— E. V. Lucas, *Charles Lamb and the Lloyds.* 1898.

Letters from Edinburgh (B.M. 10370, aa. 25). 1776.

L. E. L(ANDON). L. Blanchard, *Life and Literary Remains of L. E. L.* 2 vols. 1841.

T. J. MATHIAS. *The Pursuits of Literature.* 16th Edn. 1812.

F. A. MUMBY. *The Romance of Bookselling.* With a Bibliography by W. H. Peet. 1910.

HANNAH MORE. A. M. B. Meakin. *Hannah More.* 1911

LADY MORGAN. W. J. Fitzpatrick, *Lady Morgan : her Career, Literary and Personal.* 1860.

JOHN MURRAY. S. Smiles, *A Publisher and his Friends.* 2 vols. 1891.

H. J. NICOLL. *Great Movements and those who achieved them.* 1881.
  (For Cheap Literature and the Repeal of the Fiscal Restrictions on Literature).

DE QUINCEY. *The English Mail-Coach* (Works, Vol. XIII). 1897.

CYRUS REDDING. *Fifty Years' Recollections, Literary and Personal.* 3 vols. 1858.

—— *Literary Reminiscences and Memoirs of Thomas Campbell.* 2 vols. 1860.

J. W. ROBBERDS. *A Memoir of the Life and Writings of the late William Taylor of Norwich.* 2 vols. 1843.

W. ROBERTSON. Stewart, *Life of Robertson.* 1801.

H. CRABB ROBINSON. *Diary.* Ed. T. Sadler. 3 vols. 1869.

S. ROGERS. P. W. Clayden. *The Early Life of Samuel Rogers.* 1887.

—— P. W. Clayden, *Rogers and his Contemporaries.* 2 vols. 1889.

—— G. H. Powell, *Table Talk of Samuel Rogers.* 1903.

" MARK RUTHERFORD " (W. H. White). *The Revolution in Tanner's Lane.* 1887.

W. SCOTT. J. G. Lockhart, *Life of Scott.* Edinburgh. 1902.

—— J. G. Lockhart, *Life of Scott* (Everyman Library).[1]

SHERIDAN. *The Rivals.*

ADAM SMITH. *The Wealth of Nations.* 1776.

SYDNEY SMITH. Lady S. Holland. *A Memoir of the Rev. Sydney Smith.* 2 vols. 1855.

R. SOUTHEY. *The Doctor.* 1856.

—— *Life and Works of Cowper.* 16 vols. 1835.

H. TAYLOR. *Autobiography,* 1800–1875. 2 vols. 1885.

W. M. THACKERAY. *Roundabout Papers* (The Oxford Thackeray). n.d. ? 1908.

---

1 References in the notes are to this edition unless otherwise indicated.

BIBLIOGRAPHY

The Times Handlist of Newspapers. 1620–1920. 1920.

The Times Literary Supplement. January 24, 1924 (Notes on Sales). November 26, 1924. pp. 779–780.

C. H. TIMPERLEY. *A Dictionary of Printers and Printing.* 1839.

H. D. TRAILL. *Social England.* 6 vols. 1893–7.

G. M. TREVELYAN. *British History in the Nineteenth Century,* 1782–1901. 1922.

KIRKE WHITE. *The Life and Remains of Henry Kirke White.* (Dove's English Classics.) n.d.

—— *Works of Henry Kirke White.* Edit. R. Southey. 1852.

JOHN WILSON. *Noctes Ambrosianæ.*

W. WEST. *Fifty Years' Recollections of an old Bookseller.* 1850.

The World. 1753–1756.

INDEX

INDEX

Holland, Lord, 126, 127, 248, 252
Hone, publisher, 182, 184
Hood, Thomas, 212
Hook, Theodore, 144, 145, 217
Hume, David, 21, 22, 28, 76, 106
Hunt, Leigh, 45, 52, 57, 58, 86,
    93, 104, 135, 143, 144, 149, 168,
    209, 214, 215, 216, 222, 234,
    247, 255, 258
Hurst and Robinson, 170

Inchbald, Mrs., 154
Industrial Revolution, 40–44
Irving, Washington, 135, 167, 169,
    184, 257, 260
Ivanhoe, 173

Jeffrey, Lord, 130, 206, 224, 226
Jerdan, William, 154, 215, 216, 226
Johnson, Samuel, 18, 19, 20, 21,
    22, 25, 26, 57, 65, 67, 68, 85,
    90. 92, 99, 101, 106, 115, 123,
    127, 249, 254
Journalism, 20, 24, 99–105, 150–
    154, 203–228, 261

Keats, John, 212, 234, 250
Kenrick, William, 28
Ker, W. P., 46
Kitchiner, Dr., 165
Knight, Charles, 200, 209, 221, 263

Lackington, James, 22, 23, 28, 29,
    30, 31, 33, 41, 50, 52, 56, 61,
    62, 63, 67, 69, 82, 83, 106, 108,
    109, 186, 187
Lady of the Lake, 136, 171, 230
Lady's Pocket Magazine, 59
Lamb, Charles, 11, 45, 146, 189,
    190, 209, 212, 217, 218, 224, 226,
    228, 259
Lamb, Mary, 153
Landon, L. E., 154, 215, 232,
    233
Landor, W. S., 128, 218, 230
Lane, publisher, 98, 113
Lay of the Last Minstrel, 133, 171
Life of Nelson, 142, 208
Literary Fund, 124, 249
Literary Gazette, 154, 191, 215,
    225, 228, 243

Literary Societies, 70
Lloyd, Robert, 23
Lockhart, J. G., 136, 162, 169,
    171, 193, 195, 211, 219, 226, 231,
    232, 242
Lofft, Capell, 246
London Magazine, 212
Longmans, 129, 133, 140, 155,
    167, 177, 192, 230
Lonsdale, Lord, 253
Lyrical Ballads, 92

Macaulay, Mrs., 68
Macaulay, T. B., 35, 201, 209, 210,
    226, 259
Macaulay, Zachary, 95
Mackenzie, Henry, 130, 169
Magazines, 101–105, 203–213, 235
Maginn, William, 144, 153, 211,
    220, 226
Mail-coach, 37–40, 99
Marmion, 133, 156
Martineau, Miss, 154
Mathias, T. J., 69, 72, 73, 77, 78,
    79, 96, 97, 112, 120, 121, 207
Maturin, Charles, 255
Merry, Robert, 88
Methodism, 33, 44, 76
Miller, J., 166
Miller, T., 253
Milman, H. H., 136, 166, 226, 228,
    232
Minstrelsy of the Scottish Border, 136
Mitford, Miss, 94
Moira, Lord, 250
Moira, Lady, 124
Monk, The, 97, 239
Montagu, Mrs., 68
Montgomery, James, 221, 224, 230,
    258
Monthly Magazine, 101, 210, 212
Moore, Thomas, 226, 229, 235,
    247, 250, 253
More, Hannah, 50, 61, 69, 78,
    79 note, 81, 82, 85, 154
Morley, Lord, 14
Morning Post, 24, 99, 217
Moxon, E., 262
Mudie's *Cornucopia,* 263
Mundell, bookseller, 125
Murphy, Arthur, 85, 122
Murray, John, I., 101, 105, 156

277